Black Empowerment With an Attitude!

You Got A Problem With That?

James Clingman

"Once more–with feeling"

Copyright © 2007, 2017 by James Clingman
Cincinnati, Ohio
All rights reserved

Published and Distributed by:
HAIK Publishing
113 Saddlehorn
Easley, SC 29642
513 315 9866

Interior and Cover Design by TWA Solutions.com

All rights reserved. No part of this publication shall be reproduced, stored in a retrieval system, or transmitted in any form or by any means, electronic, mechanical, photocopy, recording, or otherwise, without the prior written permission of the copyright owner.

Dedication

This, my fourth book on economic empowerment, is dedicated to those who had (and have) the fortitude, the boldness, and the "Attitude" necessary to stand up, speak up, and then lead the way to true freedom for Black people. They were (and are) not concerned about what others thought about their Blackness and their willingness to promote Black empowerment. They were (and are) determined, dedicated, focused, and strong. Theirs are the shoulders on which we stand today.

Muhammad Ali	Maria Stewart
Mary McLeod Bethune	Sojourner Truth
Frederick Douglass	David Walker
William Wells Brown	Maggie Lena Walker
Martin Delany	Harold Washington
Joe Dudley	Ida B. Wells
T. Thomas Fortune	Fannie Barrier Williams
S. B. Fuller	Coleman Young
A.G. Gaston	
Edward Gardner	
Marcus Garvey	
Fred Gray, Esq.	
Maynard Jackson	
Walter P. Lomax, Jr. M.D.	
Jackie Robinson	

Learn more about these icons, teach your children about them, and then add more names to this list.

The time has come for the Blackman to forget and cast behind him his hero worship and adoration of other races, and to start out immediately to create and emulate heroes of his own. We must canonize our own martyrs and elevate to positions of fame and honor Black men and women who have made their distinct contributions to our racial history.

Africa has produced countless numbers of men and women, in war and in peace, whose lustre and bravery outshines that of any other people. Then why not see good and perfection in ourselves? We must inspire a literature and promulgate a doctrine of our own without any apologies to the powers that be. The right is the Blackman's and Africa's.

Let contrary sentiments and cross opinions go to the winds. We are entitled to our own opinions and not obligated to or bound by the opinions of others.

Let no one inoculate you with evil doctrines to suit their conveniences. There's no humanity before that which starts with yourself, 'Charity Begins at Home.' First to thyself be true and thou canst not then be false to any man.

[God] first made us what we are and then out of our own creative genius we make ourselves what we want to be.

— *Marcus Garvey*

"Be angry, but do not sin…"
Ephesians 4:26

Acknowledgements

Too many Brothers and Sisters to name

You reside throughout the United States, from coast to coast and corner to corner. You reside in Africa, Europe, the Caribbean, Brazil, and Australia. You have shared yourselves with me through your letters, telephone calls, and e-mails.

You have encouraged me, chastised me, corrected me, yet loved me in spite of my imperfections. You have come to my aid in my hour of need. You have confided in me, and you have had the confidence in me to present me to your friends and associates. You have trusted me enough to participate in my charitable endeavors, without ever having met me in person.

You have invited me to speak at your functions and events. You have even opened your pulpits to me to "preach" to and address your congregations. You have "inoculated" me with your vaccine of love and deep concern for our people. And you have sacrificed with me to offer whatever you could contribute to the empowerment of Black people.

It's not so much <u>who</u> you are, as it is <u>what</u> you <u>do</u>.

May God lavishly bless all of you and keep you safe.

Contents

Introduction 11

Good Stuff 17

Aren't you proud to be Black? *19*
A Tribute to Consciousness and Commitment *22*
Children of Black Wall Street—The Real "Survivors" *25*
AKA's and Omega's Providing Economic Leadership *30*
There is an "I" in "We," but it's silent *33*
Wanna be free? Come go with me *36*

Puzzling Stuff 39

Masochistic Black Folks *41*
Puzzled people *44*
Free at last! Finally! For real this time! *47*
Black Leadership—Serving us or serving us up? *50*
The Tsunami after the Tsunami *53*
Profit and Loss Statements *56*
Have you made your Covenant yet? *59*
Trying to run away from Blackness *62*
The Chinese Connection *65*
Amos Wilson was right: "We are, indeed, out of our minds" ... *68*
Who and what are we fighting? *71*
Civil Rights versus Civil Wrongs *75*
Elitist Hip-Hopcrisy *78*

O.K. Martin, you can go back to sleep now *81*
America's Melting Pot: Blacks are the only ones melting *84*

Economics Stuff 87

Are we serious about economic empowerment? *90*
Black sales force not benefiting Black people *93*
The Black Hair Care Tragicomedy *96*
The African American Trade Deficit *100*
Let's Boycott Boycotting *103*
The Fate of the Black Union *106*
Muestrame El Dinero *109*
Animal Farm—The Black Version *112*
Gas Prices—Complain, Restrain, and Sustain *115*
Spreading the pain of high gas prices *118*
We Demand; They Supply *121*
Black Economic Insurance Policies *124*

Dumb Stuff 127

Chasing the Illusion of Equality *129*
Dumbing Down Black America *133*
Buffoonery, Exploitation, and Taboo *136*
Media Bias versus Media By Us *139*
Rewarding Friends and Punishing Enemies *142*
Black on Black Economic Violence *145*

A Letter to White Americans 148

Dear White Americans, Especially the Men *150*

Church Stuff..164

Integration: Why did the churches get a pass?...................167
Integration: Why did the churches get a pass?...................170
(Parts One and Two)
The Power of the Collective and the Collection..................173
God don't bless no mess, does He?.....................................176
"What does it profit a man…"..179

Minority Stuff..183

Ban the M-Word 185
Minority Rules 188
Who Speaks for Black People? 191

Politics Stuff...194

Are we getting the leadership we deserve? 198
Executive Privilege and Privileged Executives....................201
Bush Leaguers and Minor Leaguers...................................204
Let's get rid of Congress!...207
A Right Cross and a Left Hook..210
The Bushites—Sleaze with Ease 213
Iran—"Déjà vu all over again"..216
Please, Don't Vote!..219
Government—All Checks with no Balance 222
Republican Debate—A Reagan Séance.............................225
Vote for me and I'll set you free!..228
A New Iraq or a New Orleans?..231
"At the bottom of politics lies economics" 234

Black Empowerment with Attitude!

Prison Stuff **237**

Let's Boycott Prisons!...*239*
Stupid Black men (And Women)................................*242*
Do we really care about our children?.......................*245*
Prisons and Blacks: Occupancy High;
Opportunities for Development Low...........................*248*
Georgia on my Mind...*251*

The Right Stuff **254**

Don't Live in the Past; Learn from it..........................*257*
Taking Action...*260*
Organized and United Resources for Self-Sufficiency......*263*
A Case for Dieting and Plastic Surgery.......................*266*
Civil Rights Symbolism and Economic Substance.......*267*
"The Eagle Flies on Friday"..*272*
Common Sense Leads to Common Cents......................*275*
It's tax filing time. What should we do?......................*278*
Tiny men growing into big babies................................*281*
Listen up! "Turn off Channel Zero".............................*284*
A Reconsideration of Black History Month.................*287*
Should Black People Leave America?..........................*290*
The Key to our Consciousness......................................*293*
Buying Black—It just feels good..................................*296*
The Million Dollar Club..*299*
10-11: Another date we must never forget..................*302*
An Open Letter to Black America,
written by Bob Law and Jim Clingman......................*305*
Are you ready to Bring Back Black?............................*308*
New Year—New Strategy...*311*
The Culmination of Freedom......................................*314*

Epilogue 317

Being About the Father's Business 321

More *Stuff* You Should Know 322

INTRODUCTION

Having been accused of being angry and displaying anger in response to the condition of Black people and in response to how we are mistreated in this land that our fathers and mothers helped build, I must admit that I <u>am</u> angry. My anger is similar to the anger parents feel when their child darts into the street or does something dumb and ends up getting hurt. That kind of anger comes from deep love and concern; it also comes from fear for the safety and well-being of a loved one. When it comes to Black empowerment and the lack thereof, coupled with discrimination, injustice, and inequity that are doled out on a daily basis to Black people by the establishment, rather than anger, I call it "righteous indignation," but you can call it anger if you want.

It is my right, my obligation, and my responsibility to be righteously indignant in the face of exploitation, abuse, condescension, and general mistreatment of anyone, but most especially Black people. So I offer no apology for my righteous indignation or for my willingness to "do the right thing, for the right reasons, all of the time," as President of Cincinnati State Community and Technical College, Dr. Ron Wright, preaches and practices. The "right thing" in this case is for me to use whatever gift I have been blessed with to correct the situation, not to hurt someone else but to empower our people.

Thus, I embark upon another journey with the writing of this book, hopeful that we will do as Marcus Garvey admonished us, confident that we will realize the dream of MLK rather than continue in our dream-state, and praying that we will put on the Godly principles of that "New-Self," we read about in Ephesians 4:24, and espoused by Dr. Tony Roach, of the Minda Street Church of Christ in Abilene, Texas, in his <u>God's</u>

Love Bank Curriculum. We must adopt a New Self-Love and a New Self-Image in order to change our situation in this world.

Am I Indignant? Yes. Am I Saddened? Of course. Am I Concerned? You better believe it. Am I Angry? Most definitely! So this book, *once more with feeling*, will obviously be reflective of our need to empower ourselves, but it will also call for a special kind of "attitude" in doing so. Be prepared for a harsh reality check in some of these essays. There are no intentional esoteric passages included here, just plain talk. As I have said before, "I don't write to impress; I write to express." Thus you will find this to be a book that is easy to read and easy to understand.

Having included "special" articles in my previous books, namely, *The Parable of the Talents*, *Eavesdropping on the Elders*, and in response to the *Letter to Black Americans*, also called *Kudos to Black Americans*, I added a special piece to this book as well; it's titled, *Letter to White Americans*. It hits pretty hard, but don't get scared; it is a historically accurate recollection of the last century that describes what white folks, mainly white men, have wrought on Black people.

So, if you think the last book, Black-O-Knowledge, *Stuff we need to know*, was a bit on the "suggestive" side, as the saying goes, "Fasten your seatbelts; you ain't seen nothin' yet." There is a lot more "stuff" in this book that we need to know as well.

The "Attitude" with which this book is written can be characterized as my last desperate wake-up call to our people. It begs, screams, and cries out for progress on our part, by our own means. It admonishes, rebukes, and scolds us for our less than expected stewardship of the resources with which we have been blessed. And it reveres, respects, and loves us as a people, a proud people, a strong resilient people, and a people with the capacity to do great things collectively and cooperatively.

Black Empowerment must be accompanied by an "Attitude" if we are going to build an economic future for our children, if we are serious about obtaining an economic foothold in our neighborhoods with the goal of turning them into real communities, and if we are determined to move from being consumers, for the most part, to producers, wholesalers, retailers, and distributors.

We need "Attitude" when it comes to standing against injustice, both social and economic injustice, and doing what must be done to stop it. We need "Attitude" when it comes to allaying our fear of speaking out, no matter who the perpetrator may be. We need "Attitude"!

If you cannot see what is going on in this country when it comes to Black people and how we are both viewed and treated by the "establishment," you are blind. Additionally, if you see it and refuse to confront it, refuse to speak against it, and refuse to "get involved"—on behalf of your own freedom, you are no better than those who in past times kowtowed to the whims of the "massa," to the detriment of their own brothers and sisters. You are no better than those who told "massa" that Nat Turner was planning a revolt.

Can't you see that Black folks are no more than an inconvenient afterthought to those who control this society? Look at Rwanda; look at Sudan; look at television, especially B.E.T., MTV, VH1, et al; look at the prison industrial complex; look at politics; look at immigration; look at New Orleans, before and after Katrina; look at education; look at politics; look at economics. Look at all of these and more, and tell me if you see Black people in any kind of prioritized position in the country we helped create, the country we fought for, the country for which our people died.

Consider the "minority" trick-bag for a moment and tell me that our people have not been "bamboozled," as Malcolm said. The folks that ran this country in the 1960's looked out and saw the horrific acts perpetrated against Black people and finally said, "Enough. This is too much even for us to accept; at least we have to pretend we care enough to intercede in this civil injustice toward Black people."

They passed a few affirmative action laws and then went about business as usual after that. Soon thereafter, the laws placed in force for the rights of Black people became laws for "minorities" and even some of our so-called Black leaders bought-in to the minority game. Look at us now; we have to fight over meager percentages of business with every other so-called "minority," despite being the ones who made the sacrifices and took the *beat-downs* in the first place.

Why have we fallen so low? Why have we acquiesced to *volunteer slavery*? Why do we finance our own oppression by buying everything everybody makes rather than making something of our own and buying that? How have we come to be the doormat of the world? And why do we accept it all? We are doing our best disappearing act, and if we fail to turn things around, well…

When the Queen of England was here in May 2007, she attended several events, and folks were waiting to see if she would apologize for the Trans-Atlantic Slave Trade presided over by her country. Of course, she did not, which didn't bother me, but it sure did upset some of our people. What I would have preferred would have been for her to break off a few of those billions her country made on the backs of enslaved people.

She went to the "White" House, for a "White" tie dinner, attended by, as far as I could see on television, 99.9% "White" folks. The only Black person I saw in camera-shot was one of our elders serving her what looked to be a glass of wine, and pulling out George Bush's chair for him. The butler was the only Black person I saw! Maybe Condi was somewhere curtsying or Clarence Thomas was somewhere bowing for the Queen, but I didn't see them. The only Black person I saw was serving tables.

An afterthought, that's all we are; and if anything is going to be done about it, guess who will have to do it. After our "official" arrival in this land, in 1619, up until now, we have been overlooked, mistreated, denied access, used and abused, enslaved, auctioned off, whipped, branded, raped, lynched or otherwise murdered, unjustly incarcerated, corralled in urban centers and then destroyed by urban renewal, shot 27 times, 41 times, and 50 times by police officers, hosed down, bitten by dogs, beat down for trying to walk across a bridge, cheated by banks and insurance companies, used in wars, used as guinea pigs for medical experiments, denied the right to vote even after the 15th Amendment, excluded from economic development projects, paid less than white folks for doing the same jobs, denied employment and promotions, discriminated against at every turn, gerrymandered, firebombed, maced, tasered, choked, prodded in the rectum with a broomstick in the hands of police officers, abandoned to drown in the polluted and alligator infested water left in Katrina's wake, and then, to add insult to injury, or just to really let us know how much of an afterthought we truly are, nearly two years after Hurricane Katrina, Black people in New Orleans are still homeless, still jobless, and still suffering.

Yeah, I'm angry, and you should be too. As a matter of fact everyone in this country should be angry at how millions of people have been mistreated for nearly 400 years. But this is not about everyone else; it's about us—Black people. It's about a simple question: "What are we going to do now?"

I say we first get some understanding of what our future predicament holds if we allow this kind of treatment to continue. Then we commit to working together, like other groups are doing across this nation, to empower ourselves with the resources we have. And, if you are not already angry, get angry; get angry enough to get to work, everyday, contributing to our children's future and the empowerment of our nation within this nation.

We don't need another year, another presidential election, another corrupt administration, another decade, much less another 400 years, to make us realize that we are on our own. We have work to do and we must do it with an attitude.

As you read this book, let your "Attitude" be stimulated, let it grow to the point of action, and let it be inspired by the fact that Black people have already accomplished great things in this country, and we can do the same again. We have "been there and done that" when it comes to business development, job creation, fighting against injustice—and winning; we have been victorious by cooperating with one another, looking out for one another, and pooling our resources to assist our people.

So, if you don't have one already, get an "Attitude" and let's achieve Black Empowerment.

**It takes courage to have an attitude;
So here are our marching orders:**

"Be strong and courageous, because you will lead these people to the land I swore to their forefathers to give them. Be strong and very courageous…do not turn to the right or to the left, that you may be successful wherever you go. Have I not commanded you? Be strong and courageous. Do not be terrified; do not be discouraged, for the Lord your God will be with you wherever you go." **Joshua 1:6-7**

The Good Stuff

"Be as proud of your race today as your fathers were in days of yore. We have a beautiful history, and we shall create another in the future that will astonish the world." —**Marcus Garvey**

Black people were conditioned to believe that we were inferior, not good enough, second-class, less-than, incapable, incompetent, and all the other negative adjectives used to describe us. We were even made to believe that the word "Black" was something odious, abhorrent, loathsome, ominous, dangerous, and threatening. So much so that even today some of our brothers and sisters continue to suffer from the vestiges of that psychological imprisonment. That's a shame, which is why it is vital that we, at every turn, speak truth to those negatives, that we tell our own stories, and that we affirm our own greatness and goodness. He who defines you controls you. We must define ourselves.

There is so much "good stuff" we could write about Black people; it could very well be an entire book in itself. (Hmmm) We have accomplished so much in this world, not just since we arrived here in America, but thousands of years prior to that. Of course, most of us already know that, but do we really celebrate it in our daily lives? Do we teach and reiterate it to our children? Are we so proud of it that we live lives that are reflective of that good stuff?

Being the first to inhabit the earth, the first to record its history, the first to set up educational systems, the first to calculate, the first to explore, the first to calibrate, the first to navigate, the first to build, and the first to worship, there is no way we should ever be ashamed of who we are. There is no way we should ever be afraid to shout from the mountaintops, proclaiming the greatness of our ancestors, our great-grandparents, and our parents.

In this country, having survived the mistreatment they suffered daily—for hundreds of years—our relatives are our beacons, our paragons of strength, and their strong shoulders still hold us up today.

Be proud, and reflect on the greatness and the goodness of your people as you read the following essays. And please share them with your children.

Aren't you proud to be Black?
June '06

YOU KNOW, SOMETIMES IT PAYS TO take a little time to reflect on just who we are. From time to time we should think about our relatives, and our people in general, and reflect on the contributions they have made to this world and, most especially, to this country. We should take time out to give ourselves credit for being, as Dr. Ed Robinson, Author, Journey of the Songhai People, calls us, "The fittest of the fittest of the fittest" Black people on the face of the earth. Don't you think we deserve kudos for not only surviving but thriving in this land we call America? I do. So, let's begin.

If you had the privilege of knowing your grandparents and great-grand parents, you were probably witness to some of their amazing talents and abilities. You also had access to their knowledge and wisdom, although many of us didn't learn from it. We saw our relatives build houses without architectural drawings, cure diseases without doctors and prescriptions, stop bleeding with cobwebs, raise enough food for their families and two or three others, cure meat in a smokehouse, dig wells, and draw poison out of cut with a piece of fatback.

Our relatives could make a meal out of what we thought was nothing; they could sew up the holes in our socks, patch our jeans, and put cardboard in our shoes to make them last just a little while longer. They could deliver babies, as my great-grandmother did in the birth of my brother and me. They helped one another with whatever they had, and it was dinner time at all the neighbors' houses anytime we wanted to stop by.

Remember the hambone, checkers, buttermilk and cornbread, homemade ice cream you had to churn, a pot of beans and some cornbread all week long, and that nasty, greasy, slimy, castor oil? How about having to take cod liver oil every morning, and cold oil and sugar, goose grease, rock candy and whiskey, and that stinking little bag some of us had to wear around our necks when we were sick? Our relatives knew their stuff, didn't they?

The music they made was unbelievable. Their voices and their mastery of musical instruments, even without the benefit of formal training, was something to behold. Our folks were some piano-playin', guitar-pluckin', drum-beatin', horn-blowin', string strumin', high-steppin', sangin' brothers and sisters—and they still are. Doesn't that make you proud?

And then there were the economic cooperatives and benevolent societies they established to help take care of burials and other critical issues. Our people knew they had to pool their resources, and they knew they had to take care of themselves. That's how they could to do so many things with their hands. As I look back at my parents, grandparents, aunts, and uncles, I am amazed at what they did during what were pretty rough times.

They established their own business enclaves all over this country, places like Greenwood in Tulsa, Oklahoma, and the Hayti District in Durham, North Carolina. They amassed wealth beyond imagination and, comparatively speaking, far beyond what most of us have today. Prohibited from participating in the general marketplace and without the government subsidies handed out to white owned corporations, Black people started businesses and eventually created A.G. Gaston Enterprises, S.B. Fuller Company, Madame C.J. Walker's Hair Products, Johnson Publishing Company, and Motown Records. What strength and determination they had.

Aren't you proud of who you are, where you came from, and what your relatives did to make sure you had food on the table, clothes on your back, and a roof over your head? We should celebrate our Blackness and always cherish our culture. As Dr. Claud Anderson teaches, we should be proud to be Black because God made us first, in His likeness and image; and He placed us in a perfect place, on land that contained every vital mineral and natural resource necessary for growth and prosperity. He gave us enough wisdom to share with the world and bring others out of the darkness into the light of knowledge. We are His special people.

So with all of that going for us, why wouldn't we be proud of who we are? A lack of pride and love for ourselves would be an affront to God; it would be like slapping Him in His face and saying, "I don't like what You did. Yes, you made me first, you made me special, you gave me wisdom, you gave me the richest land on earth, and you made me the strongest among men but, God, you also made me Black, and I don't want to be Black. It's too hard being Black; it's too stressful being Black, God. And if you want to know the real truth, God, I am ashamed of being Black." *"...shall what is formed say to him who formed it, 'Why did you make me like this'?"* Romans 9:20

Can you imagine some of our people thinking that way? I know we have been through a lot in this country and the struggle continues, as they say, but truth can never be destroyed; hold on to it. We are still here, still standing after all the blood, sweat, and tears of our people. Black people have persevered, and we will continue to do so.

Take a moment to give some credit to your people, those who survived so you could be here today, "the fittest of the fittest." Give honor to those who have passed on and be proud of what they did. Be proud of whom you are and the legacy you are obligated to uphold. Understand that you too must pass on a legacy, and that will only happen if you love yourself and your people, if you value your history, and if you take pride in the greatness of Black people.

Continue to be strong in the same manner in which our forebears were strong. They endured, they persisted, they fought, and they won. We must do no less.

A Tribute to Consciousness and Commitment
Jan. '06

It's not the critic who counts, not the one who points out how the strong man stumbled or how the doer of deeds might have done them better. The credit belongs to the man who is actually in the arena; whose face is marred with the sweat and dust and blood; who strives valiantly; who errs and comes up short again and again; who knows the great enthusiasms, the great devotions, and spends himself in a worthy cause and who at best knows the triumph of high achievement and who at worst, if he fails, at least fails while daring greatly so that his place shall never be with those cold and timid souls who know neither victory nor defeat.

— Theodore Roosevelt

I CHOSE TO DEDICATE MY FIRST article in 2006 to those whose level of consciousness and commitment keeps them fighting for true freedom. Because of my very personal understanding of what it takes of you and what it takes out of you, having been involved in collective Black economic empowerment for many years, I feel the need to acknowledge and thank you.

During the past decade I have met and worked with many whom I consider not only consciously committed to economically uplifting our people, but also just plain-old smart, and highly qualified to lead us— not by talking but by doing. I have seen them go through everything from being ostracized, ridiculed, and left financially bereft, to suffering heart attacks, the ravages of cancer, and even assassination. Yes, some are gone, but there are others still here, still fighting, not on a stage, not for notoriety or acclaim, but because they are consciously committed to economic empowerment for our people.

In my travels across this country I have become friends with so many who are unafraid to stand up and be Black, so many who, by their example, show us not only what to do but how to do it. I have met entrepreneurs who have taken their economic destiny into their own hands and left the "new plantations," broken the shackles of psychological enslavement, and continue to do whatever they can to help others.

I am so proud to know so many and to be loved by so many of the same mind and the same heart as I have for our collective economic empowerment. So, this is for you—all of you; for you have kept me going; you have kept my fires burning; and you have provided those "booster shots" I have needed along the way. I want so much to name all of you, but that would be futile.

While others may continue to get the adulation, the visibility, the material rewards, and all the other trappings of only talking about our problems but never offering anything to solve them, while some of them may even get their rewards by going against their own people, know that it's you who will bring us through the tough spots and take us where we need to go. You will always make the sacrifices; you will always do what is necessary rather than what is expedient. You will always stand up, speak up, and put up, and never give up, because freedom is in your DNA. You are the remnant of David Walker and Harriet Tubman, strong and unyielding despite threats and hardships.

You are the ones who will stand in the gap for our children and love them unconditionally, giving your time and resources to raise them up rather than put them down. You are the ones who will fight for the rights of your people; you are the ones who will educate our youth. You are the ones who will look the establishment in its eyes and say "Oh, no you don't. I am not going to sit silently while you mistreat Black people, or anyone else for that matter, but especially Black people. I will call you out every time I see it, and I will work to change it."

You are the ones who will accept no less than what is right and equitable. You are the ones who will never accept the proverbial 30 pieces of silver, never allow yourself to be used as a token, a pass-through, a mouthpiece, or a lap dog. You are the ones who will always make footprints rather than butt prints, because you will always be busy working on initiatives that lead us to economic freedom.

This is a tribute to you, the warriors out there, not the critics and criticizers, not the theoreticians and pontificators filled with pompous rhetoric and shallow deliberation, and surely not those "cold and timid souls who know neither victory nor defeat."

I will end with another quote; one that I feel is even more apropos. It is from Frederick Douglass' tribute to Harriet Tubman:

The difference between us is very marked. Most of what I have done and suffered in the service of our cause has been in public, and I have received much encouragement at every step of the way. You on the other hand have labored in a private way. I have wrought in the day—you in the night. I have had the applause of the crowd and the satisfaction that comes of being approved by the multitude, while the most that you have done has been witnessed by the few trembling, scarred, foot-sore bondmen and women, whom you have led out of the house of bondage… The midnight sky and silent stars have been the witness of your devotion to freedom and of your heroism…

I thank YOU, my brothers and sisters, for your conscious commitment to true freedom for our people.

Children of Black Wall Street—The Real "Survivors"
Mar. '07

MY FINAL SPEAKING EVENT IN BLACK History Month 2007 was by far the most rewarding and inspiring; it strengthened my resolve to continue to fight for what is right and to stand against what is wrong. Having had the absolute pleasure of being in the company of six survivors of the riot in the Greenwood section of Tulsa, Oklahoma in 1921, I received yet another "booster shot" necessary to keep me from being infected with complacency and apathy. My consciousness was lifted once again; my spirit was buoyed, springing to new heights; my soul was touched by the ruminations of those elders; and I was energized by their zest for life, their spryness, and their pride.

The Northeast Church of Christ in Oklahoma City and its Northeast College Students Network designed and executed a week-long series of educational, inspirational, and informative commemorations and celebrations in honor of the "Indomitable Spirit" of the Survivors of one of this nation's dirty little secrets: The Tulsa Race War, in which hundreds of Blacks were murdered and their prosperous community was burned to the ground.

Allow me to offer kudos to the Northeast Church of Christ congregation and also say that Oklahoma City should be proud to have such a progressive, caring, spirit-led group of people in its midst. While I could use the remainder of this article just listing the folks who made it all possible, knowing they are not looking for individual recognition, I will instead discuss the Survivors and their story of tragedy and triumph.

The tragedy of the Black Wall Street massacre, replete with firebombings, shootings, and burning bodies, usually dominates conversations about what took place in Tulsa on May 31, 1921. The aftermath of Black survivors being rounded up, placed in makeshift concentration camps, and having to wait for a white person to come and "claim" them, to the mass graves, abandoned mines, and the river in which Black bodies were discarded, to the families torn apart and left with absolutely nothing, are the primary aspects of most discussions of Black Wall Street. But there is "the rest of the story:" The triumph of Black Wall Street.

We celebrated the triumph, the victory of resurgence, the "Renaissance," as Dr. Kevin McPherson noted during our panel discussion, the strength and resiliency of Black people who, against all odds and in spite of the worst that could happen to them, came back to rebuild Greenwood. They did such a great job of literally rising from the ashes left by the fires of a hateful, jealous, and envious white mob, so much so that four years later, in 1925, the National Negro Business Association held its convention in Greenwood.

Although small children then, most of the survivors living today can remember their parents and grandparents telling them what when on back then, how they escaped, the relatives they lost, and the resulting abject poverty that ensued after the riot.

Eddie Faye Gates, author, former teacher, and community activist has done yeoman's work interviewing the survivors and chronicling their recollections of the "Riot on Greenwood," as her book on the subject is titled. She attended and participated in the celebration in Oklahoma City and shared poignant recollections of her meetings with the survivors. She laments, "There are only 82 still alive." Bless her for capturing their stories in her book and having them placed in the Greenwood Cultural Center for all to see. Gates is also working with noted Harvard Law Professor, Charles Ogletree and others to obtain reparations for the survivors.

The six Tulsa Race Riot Survivors I had the honor to meet and spend three days with are: Mr. John Melvin Alexander, my "Navy buddy," with whom I shared breakfast and lunch; Mrs. Hazel Jones, just as feisty as she wants to be; Thelma Knight, whose son and daughter had to move fast to keep up with her; Mr. Julius Warren Scott, the "youngest" survivor, as he puts it; Mr. James Steward, the quiet one, but a sharp dresser; and my man, Mr. Wess Young, who proudly wore a gold medallion around his neck signifying his role as "Survivor; he was always fired up.

Maybe I will have the privilege of meeting more of the "Children of Black Wall Street," especially the oldest one, who is 105 years old, and the one who plays in a jazz band in France; Sister Gates said he is 89 years old and still doing his thing. Whether I do or not, I will always remember the times I shared with the six survivors, their liveliness, their humility, and their Indomitable Spirit.

I ask you to ponder the words of the President of Tulsa Chamber of Commerce, immediately following the riot: "The deplorable event is the greatest wound Tulsa's civic pride has ever received. Leading businessmen are in hourly conference and a movement is now being organized… to formulate a plan of reparation." Sound familiar? Eighty-six years later and the Children of Black Wall Street are still fighting for their reparations. How can this country, and those who supposedly run it, not be so ashamed of the Tulsa Race Riot that they would not immediately grant reparations for the lives lost and the millions of dollars in property destroyed back then?

We celebrated the triumph, and it's not over yet. The fight continues in International Court, since our own courts would not do the right thing. Even better, we still have the "real" Survivors amongst us, their laughter, their spirit, and their strength which will, in turn, strengthen us in our resolve to stand up and speak out against injustice.

I thank all of you for that once-in-a-lifetime experience. I am so proud to have been selected to share in your celebration of the Survivors of Black Wall Street-and the "Children" they left behind.

(For that special occasion, I wrote the following poem, which I read to the survivors during my speech at their reception.)

James Clingman

Against All Odds-You're Still Here

You heard the screams and cries that day
That dreadful day in May
And now after 86 years have passed
The memory still won't go away

As children back then you surely wondered
How it all could be
You searched for answers but none would do
In the face of such tragedy

"How could this happen? What did we do?
That we should suffer so?
What could cause those people to hate us so much?
That would make them sink to such a low?"

Still haunted by your pain
Of having loved ones stripped away
You demonstrate your strength and pride
By your presence here today

Your lives are monuments to us
And for all the world to see
The trail blazed by your elders
Will live on eternally

Black Wall Street Survivors
We pay homage to you tonight
We remember your parents with love and respect
And we celebrate their valiant fight

Black Empowerment with Attitude!

Their Indomitable Spirit against the greatest of odds
Was truly and surely a gift sent from God
Having labored and built Black Wall Street back then
They now are at rest, but they left <u>you</u> to win

So against all of the odds, you must continue to fight
And so too must we stand up for what's right

For yours is a righteous battle, grounded in sacrifice and pain
But God will give you the strength you need to go
on and to sustain

Yes, you are here, and we stand with you today
In the light of your Indomitable Spirit that will never
ever fade away

Peace, love, and blessings to you, **"The Survivors"**

*Written and read by
Jim Clingman, Oklahoma City, Oklahoma 02/23/07
Northeast Church of Christ's Tribute to the Survivors of the 1921
Black Wall Street Race Riot, Tulsa, Oklahoma*

AKA's and Omega's providing economic leadership
Sept. '06

BACK IN 1998 I SPOKE AT the organizing meeting of the Nashville Black Chamber of Commerce and, in addition to the occasion of Black folks taking control of their economic resources, the meeting was even more special for me because it was held in a building that the local Alpha Kappa Alpha Sorority built and owned. I was so proud to be speaking about economic empowerment within a glowing example of economic empowerment. In my speech I remember pointing out the fact that we need more such examples of ownership among our sororities and fraternities.

Here in 2006, I am pleased to see these organizations implementing real economic empowerment strategies. Guided by intelligent, conscious, and aggressive leaders, sororities and fraternities are using their tremendous collective leverage to effect positive economic change via real estate development, technology, financial literacy, entrepreneurship, banking, and other areas in which their members have expertise.

I recently came in contact with two of those leaders, and it was a pleasure to hear their plans and share their visions for helping to move our people into the 21st century of economic empowerment.

Barbara McKinzie, the President of Alpha Kappa Alpha Sorority, is a sister with whom I so thoroughly enjoyed talking. She has that rare combination of consciousness and commitment, under-girded by a wealth of talent and experience in finance as a Certified Public Accountant. It did not take long for me to see that Ms. McKinzie definitely understands not only what it will take to move us forward economically, she is also willing—and quite able, I might add—to support her words with action.

In her new role with the AKA's, the oldest and largest (200,000 members worldwide), Barbara will continue her quest to empower our youth by preparing them to be leaders and instilling in them her philosophy of "making excellence a habit." Ms. McKinzie has also adopted the theme, "Continued Improvement," which has to do with enhancing and strengthening our basic competencies, and encourages a "pay as you go, not after you get there" system among Black people. Now I like that.

One of the most impressive things Ms. McKinzie shared with me was her statement, "You can't give what you don't own." She gets it. She knows that in order for our people to be economically empowered we must be owners of wealth-generating assets. She cited the age-old, wrong-headed message that has gone out to our youth for years, "Get an education and get a good job." Instead of that message, Barbara strongly advocates for business ownership and business growth, which is indeed the proper economic message for our people. Barbara McKinzie is a blessing and a model for the brand of leadership we need. Congratulations to her and the AKA's!

The other leader I want to highlight is Warren Lee, newly elected Grand Basileus of Omega Psi Phi Fraternity, Inc. I met Brother Lee during a visit to Dallas, Texas, during which time he emphasized his commitment to the theme: "Economic Empowerment Leading to Social and Political Change." Warren, an entrepreneur himself, understands that by devising and implementing economic initiatives that establish and grow businesses, Black people will be empowered. He also knows how important home ownership is for Black people, who are at the bottom in that category, and that is where he is placing his emphasis.

Lee has adopted Dr. Claud Anderson's Powernomics philosophy, which is refreshing. Many of our brothers and sisters who claim to be leaders are reluctant to espouse and support anything that is all Black, despite the fact that their organizations and those whom they supposedly lead are all Black. How sad it is to be so conditioned that you would not support your own people unless other groups are involved. Warren Lee is just the opposite. He knows who he is and he is not ashamed or afraid to claim it.

Lee stated, "We have the capacity to be a lot better and to do a lot more when it comes to having a positive impact on Black people. It's not that we are against anyone; we are simply <u>for</u> Black people, and we will contribute what we can to the cause of Black economic empowerment." Lee's local Omega chapter in Dallas recently started an investment club called, "Omeganomix." Dallas entrepreneur and Omega man, Detrick DeBurr, describes it as "economics in the mix," which enhances economic literacy and builds wealth simultaneously.

In my call for and support of new Black Leadership, these two leaders fit the bill. There is a document making its way into Black newspapers, on radio talk shows, and around the Internet called, "Open Letter to Black America, It's Time to Bring Back Black" which poses some questions about our direction and, of course, our leadership. An excerpt from that letter states, "Enough is enough, Black people are in need of leaders who without apology are committed to the very real needs of Black Americans. We urge our leaders who feel trapped by their Blackness to go quickly to the task of providing leadership for other groups so that we can get away from their mis-leadership long enough to get out of our current political and economic ditch."

You will never know how good it makes me feel to know that Barbara McKinzie and Warren Lee are around. I know the Kappas, Alphas, Deltas, Zetas, Sigmas and any that I omitted, are doing similar things on economic issues. Please let me hear from you. Let's spread the word about this most important subject: Economic Empowerment.

There is an "I" in "We," but it's silent.
March '07

IN THE NORTHERN STATES, WE ARE not slaves to individuals, not personal slaves, yet in many ways we are slaves of the community...It is more than a figure of speech to say that we are a people chained together. We are one people—one in general complexion type, one in degradation, one in popular estimation. As one rises, all must rise, and as one falls all must fall. Having now, our feet on the rock of freedom, we must drag our brethren from the slimy depths of slavery, ignorance, and ruin. Every one of us should be ashamed to consider himself free, while his brother is a slave. Frederick Douglass

One conclusion I have drawn from working in the collective economic empowerment vineyard for years is that "We" fail because the "I" gets in the way. Black folks adore the statement, "I am because we are, and because we are, therefore, I am." Oh, that we would live that statement rather than merely recite it. Frederick Douglass and other ancestors knew they were all in this thing together, and that no Black man or woman would rise without the rest of us rising. Have we come so far since his time that we no longer believe in the collective? Have we achieved so much and risen so high as individuals that we have lost sight of our brothers and sisters?

Considering that we are so into words these days, I thought it appropriate to offer a change in how we perceive the word "We." Each of us should adopt the thought that there is an "I" in "We" and realize, as our forefathers and mothers did, no matter the level of anyone's individual success, he or she is still included in the "We." That way we can eliminate much of the ego that tends to separate us from one another.

The "I," when it stands alone, is dangerous. It is rife with self-aggrandizement, self-delusion, vulnerability, and sometimes self-destruction due to its tendency to make one think his or her success was obtained without the help of anyone else. But add the "I" to the word "We" and watch what happens. The "I" is still successful, and it uplifts the "We" by its individual success.

The "We" is strong. It overflows with self-reliance, self-determination, love, trust, respect, and cooperation. The collective aspects of success, whether one person attains it or everyone in the group attains it, fills the "We" with pride and the "I" with strength to do even more. Thus, I would assert to you that there is an "I" in the word, "We"—it's just silent.

The "I" is silent, not in the sense that it never speaks out or never does anything for itself as an individual, but rather it appreciates and respects the "We" so much that it is willing to make individual sacrifices to uplift the "We". Just as Frederick Douglass said, "As one rises, all must rise…" He understood his obligation to his people and acted upon it, irrespective of the fact that he had attained tremendous success and was "accepted" in social and political circles from which his brothers and sisters were rejected. Jackie Robinson said, "We might make it as individuals, but I think we have to be concerned about the masses of [Black] people." Both men understood the inside-outside game quite well.

While Douglass was unwilling to do what Harriet Tubman and John Brown did, he knew Black people needed a spokesperson, a protest organ, and he was not afraid to tell it like it was and speak truth to power, as he did in his famous July 4th speech: "What is it to me?" he asked. Although Douglass was an "inside" man he heaped praise on outsider, Harriet Tubman, by supporting her efforts to free our enslaved ancestors and by acknowledging Harriet's strength and commitment in a written tribute to her.

The inside-outside strategy worked well for those two stalwarts and with many other historical figures. What about us today? Are those on the inside so comfortable, and do they think they are not vulnerable to the same treatment the outsiders are receiving? Are the outsiders so envious of the "success" of the insiders that they spend their waking hours trying to bring the insiders down?

Black Empowerment with Attitude!

If we understood that there is, indeed, an "I" in "We" the battles Black people are fighting in this country would have been won a long time ago. Other groups practice the "I" in "We" strategy, even to the point that now we have so-called Indians expelling Blacks from their tribe, Blacks who have every claim to the rights and privileges of that tribe, privileges like tax abatement, land, reparations, etc. If Indians are now "dissin" us, we are really at the end of our rope in this country. They used to be on the bottom but have now parlayed a collective strategy into golf courses, casinos, and hotel ownership.

Group ego beats individual ego any day. Black people must begin to look at our group with the understanding that there is an "I" in "We" but it is a small "i"-and it's silent. To remind us, when referring to Black people, maybe we should spell it "Wie."

Wanna be free? Come go with me.
Feb. '05

I CAN HEAR HARRIET TUBMAN UTTERING those words. She risked her own liberty and her life as well, to help those who were still enslaved. She had the right message, just as David Walker had the right message in his famous Appeal, both to his enslaved brothers and sisters and to those who enslaved them. The message was simple. "If you want to be free, come and go with me." The opposite of that is, of course, if you want to be a slave, stay where you are. Isn't it funny how the same things that were spoken back then, still apply to Black people today?

Frederick Douglass shed light on what freedom is when he said the turning point in his life as a slave was deciding to fight back and not allow himself to be whipped by Edward Covey. After defeating Covey by fighting back, Douglass said, "I was nothing before ... I was a man now." The experience of fighting back made Douglass even more determined to be a free man. He described a feeling he never had before, a feeling of being released from the "tomb of slavery, to the heaven of freedom."

He went on to say, "My long crushed spirit rose, cowardice departed, bold defiance took its place; and I now resolved that, however long I remained a slave in form, the day had passed forever when I could be a slave in fact. I did not hesitate to let it be known of me, that the white man who expected to succeed in whipping [me], must also succeed in killing me."

Harriet risked her life by going back to rescue slaves. David Walker risked his life by writing his famous Appeal; he died shortly thereafter, some said he was poisoned. Frederick Douglass risked his life by standing up and physically fighting back against mistreatment. Accounts of similar actions by African Americans abound and certainly should be discussed in our homes and in our schools, especially during Black History Month.

More important, however, are the lessons we can learn from the strength and tenacity of our ancestors. We must look at their actions and utilize them in our daily lives. We must listen to them and hear their plea to us, their children, the ones for whom they suffered, survived, sacrificed, and died. They are still telling us, "If you want to be free, come and go with me."

We say the same thing today. Do we want to be free? If we do, shouldn't we follow those who are leading the way to freedom, rather than those who are keeping us enslaved? We know quite well that the "establishment" wants status quo, and we can look back in history and see how the system changed to accommodate the desires of the powerful vis-à-vis maintaining status quo. For instance, five years after the Civil War, according to Dr. Amos Wilson, the percentage of Blacks in prison went from nearly zero to over 33%. Even though Black people were so-called "free" the establishment still figured out how to enslave us, the 13th Amendment and its "exception" notwithstanding.

Take a look at the Civil Rights period. We fought for the right to spend our money wherever we wanted and, despite the resistance of the establishment, we finally won that right. (I said, "Right" not "Privilege.") The economic system quickly came up with ways to see that we could do exactly what we fought for. They started making all sorts of trinkets and clothing to sell to us, setting up jobs programs for us, building barracks-style and high-rise housing for us, and designing a state-of-the-art welfare system that would surely destroy our family structure, all in an ongoing effort to make us their economic slaves. We should have listened to and heeded Harriet's words.

So what do we do if we really want to be free? And, by the way, I can hear some brothers and sisters right now saying, "I <u>am</u> free; I don't need to do anything." They are obviously the remnant of those who told Harriet they would rather stay where they were than to go with her, and they are probably the reason she said she could have freed more slaves if they had simply known they were slaves. Nevertheless, for those of us who know we are still not free, what are we going to do about it?

First, I think we had better stop our mindless, blind, and lemming-like behavior when it comes to some of those we call leaders. They are enslaved, and they are busy trying to keep us that way. Then, we must find the Harriet's, Frederick's, and David Walker's among us who are willing and able to lead us to true freedom. Those among us who are dedicated to and have an understanding of where we must really go to obtain freedom are the ones we should be following and helping.

Those who are willing to make sacrifices like Marcus Garvey, those who are willing to stand up and speak out like Malcolm X, those who are willing to design and execute bold economic strategies like Reginald Lewis and Ken Bridges, those who are fearless and selfless like Medgar Evers, are the ones we need to follow today. They're saying the same thing our ancestors said: "If you want to be free, come and go with me."

Puzzling Stuff

"How strange it is to see men of sound sense, and of tolerably good judgment, act so diametrically in opposition to their own interest."

— David Walker's Appeal

Some things that take place in our society, especially when it comes to Black people, are amazing and even strange. I am never at a loss to find something to write about each week because so many puzzling things are happening all the time.

For the most part, those puzzling occurrences usually are detrimental to Black people, for instance, the social, economic, educational, and political disparities that are exclusively peculiar to our group, the games played on us by our public officials, and the way some of us treat one another. Why do we allow it? Why do we continue to fall for the same old contain and control tactics?

We have seen the same scenario many times over, but 140 years after the Civil War, in terms of ownership and control of this country's assets and wealth accumulation, we are still in the same relative position as we were prior to that time. Yes, we earn much more money, but we don't control it the way we should. We occupy high positions, but we fail to use that clout to help empower our brothers and sisters.

Although we are dominant in public sector positions, administering contracts, purchasing millions of dollars worth of goods and services, we seldom seek out our own people to whom we can direct some of those deals. We get elected to political offices by the thousands, across this country, but we soon fall into the trap of self-aggrandizement, greed, and ineffectiveness, living the lavish lifestyle and becoming the pigs that came to power in George Orwell's Animal Farm.

Puzzling? Very much so. But if we do an analysis of our history, we will see the causes and effects of a mindset that has directed some of us to seek validation from white people and advocate assimilation rather than nationalism, two of the main reasons for our inappropriate and puzzling behavior.

I do not believe we are a shallow, uneducated, child-like people that cannot put a relatively simple puzzle together. Much of the "system" under which we were enslaved and still controlled by today was devised by folks far less intelligent than we. I know we can solve this puzzle, but we must first realize that's all it is.

It may look hard, but there are really not as many pieces to this puzzle as we may think. I believe some of our people are so mired in the false promise of "equality" and negatively affected by the "illusion of inclusion" that they have come to accept and then seek the standards of others rather than establish their own standards based on their own culture and heritage. But I also believe that we are far too smart to continue in that vein.

Once we know better, we must do better—or no better for us. We are too intelligent not to be able to solve this puzzle called "Being Black in America." Read the following essays, put the pieces of this puzzle together, and start down a new path toward collective economic freedom.

Masochistic Black Folks
Jan. '05

"How strange it is to see men of sound sense, and of tolerably good judgment, act so diametrically in opposition to their own interest." — From David Walker's speech to the Massachusetts General Colored Association, as printed in Freedom's Journal. December 19, 1828.

IT WOULD NOT TAKE MUCH MORE for me to conclude that our people willingly submit to mistreatment, discrimination, and abuse by the establishment. Police brutality is running rampant across this land, from the brutal murders of Amadou Diallo and Patrick Dorismond in New York, Roger Owensby and Nathaniel Jones in Cincinnati, and the latest outrages, the killing of Kenneth Walker in Columbus, Georgia, and 13 year-old Devin Brown in Los Angeles, California.

Economic apartheid shows itself as "normal business practices" in our cities, as stadiums are built for millionaires, in our state highway and school construction projects and our federal government, as it goes about its business handing out no-bid contracts to Halliburton and Armstrong Williams.

Every week Blacks are treated like common animals, being beaten, choked, electrocuted, maced, cheated, exploited, and abused in any number of ways. Our solution is to march, protest, or start a protracted legal case that takes years to settle, despite the blatant guilt of the perpetrators. The latest in this tragicomedy is the outlandish scenario that took place in Inglewood, California, where a white cop was awarded $1 million after he physically abused a young Black man—on television no less. He must have injured his fist when he pounded the young brother into submission.

Here in Cincinnati, the City Council debates whether or not the cops should be allowed to electrocute 7 year-old children with their new toys: Tasers. Can you imagine that? They actually have to decide on shooting 50,000 volts of electricity through a 35 pound child, and since the overwhelming majority of those youth who have already been tasered are Black, you know what that means for our 7 year-olds.

Notice: Black conventioneers, Black college football and basketball teams, and music festival patrons coming to Cincinnati despite the boycott, leave your children at home. You may be able to survive 50,000 volts, but not your children. Remember, this is the same city administration that participated in putting 500 Black families out of their homes under false pretenses and sanctioned the killing of Nathaniel Jones. If they would do this to their own residents, you can imagine what they would do to out-of-towners.

One definition of masochism is "liking or inviting misery." Black people, in many cases, simply lie down and take the abuse heaped upon us. Yes, we yell and scream, but so does a masochistic person. Maybe we are like the little boy who constantly hit himself in the head with a hammer. When asked why he did it, he said, "Because it feels so good when I stop." Our abuse stops from time to time, usually around MLK's birthday, when we hold hands with guilt-ridden white folks and feel, just for a fleeting moment, the pain has stopped. That euphoria soon wears off, the beating starts once again, and we long for it stop again, because it "feels" so good when the pain subsides.

As David Walker must have asked in 1828, "What's wrong with us?" The same question applies today. We continue to give our money to companies that have absolutely no interest in our welfare. We give our votes to baby-kissin' political candidates who couldn't care less about our children's future, as they cast their votes to use tasers on 7 year-olds. We turn our children over to teachers who only want to educate them to grow up and work for their children. If that's not a form of masochism, please tell me what it is.

Are we once again acquiescing to the paternalistic pretense of those who want to keep us "in our place?" Have we fallen so deep into the pit of dependency that we can only hope for a brief respite from our pain and suffering, and even say "thank you" when they stop abusing us for a while? And, are we sadistically imitating our captors by abusing one another?

I shudder to think how other folks really see us, the most educated Black people in the world, with more annual income than many countries. As David Walker must have, I also smile at the thought of Black people taking a real stand against injustice and economic discrimination. What a day that would be! When, once and for all, Black folks say, "This is as far as we are going; it ends right here, and we will use our financial weapons to wage war against those who mistreat us," our freedom will be complete.

If white folks' attention is what we crave, we would get much more of it by withholding our dollars from them, and by redirecting more of those dollars toward our own businesses. Until we do that, in a concerted and determined manner, and until we do more to secure our economic future by educating our children and creating jobs for them in our own businesses, the police abuse will continue, the economic discrimination will go on, and Blacks in this country will go down in the annals of history as a broken people who not only took the abuse but, in some cases, invited and welcomed it.

Freedom is another word for "nothing left to lose;" just ask Patrick Henry.

Puzzled People
March '06

THE LATEST ALLEGATIONS AGAINST ANOTHER SO-CALLED "Black Conservative," Claude Allen, while they are quite sad and disturbing, are also an indication of something more, something larger, something strange. We have seen the likes of Armstrong Williams, Rod Paige, Clarence Thomas, Condoleezza Rice, and even Colin Powell, to some extent, fall prey to the wiles of folks like Jesse Helms, Strom Thurmond, Trent Lott, and both of the Bushmen. Under Ronald, "Let 'em eat ketchup" Reagan, there was Samuel Pierce, the lone Black face in the cabinet and the guy whose name Reagan even forgot.

And there was another Clarence (Pendleton) who was appointed by Reagan to head the Civil Rights Commission where he provoked criticism by taking stands against several established tenets of civil rights reformers. He made the switch to the Republican Party in 1980, coming to Reagan's attention when he was the only one of 150 Urban League officials to support Reagan's bid for the Presidency.

There were other Black folks, all of whom apparently found some reason to support Reagan's "Voodoo Economics," or "Papa Doc" Bush's "Thousand Points of Light," and now "Baby Doc" G. Dubya's litany of ridiculous missteps and bungled acts of war. I don't get it; how do these "puzzled people" come to their supportive conclusions? Is that just the way of politics? Is it just about choosing sides between the elephants and the donkeys, no matter what their leaders do?

I know there have been some lock-step Black folks traipsing after Democrat Presidents too, doing any and everything they request of them, even serving as lapdogs and sycophants. I find that equally reprehensible, but when compared to the other side, and the trouble the Republicans have caused for us, the so-called "Black conservatives" from the last 30 years take the cake.

Black Empowerment with Attitude!

Puzzling? You bet! Some of you "older" folks out there might remember the Temptations' album called Puzzle People, of which I am reminded when I think of these Black neo-cons. Why would and how could a highly intelligent person like Condi Rice be so enamored with George "What, me worry?" Bush? He's the Bobby McFerrin of politics, walking along his merry way, singing, "Don't worry, be happy." He is this nation's Nero.

What is the rationale for someone like Colin Powell to do the bidding of a dunce? What would make any Black person think Strom Thurmond and Jesse Helms had their best interests in mind? Is the political lure that strong for Black folks? Will we sell our souls to be accepted in white-controlled political circles?

Do our political activities and involvement debilitate us to the extent that we would lose our self-esteem and self-worth, and sink to a level of constantly having to prove that we are intelligent, capable, and qualified? Why would Claude Allen, if he did what he was accused of, put his life and his family's life in such jeopardy for a few trinkets? What was he trying to prove—to himself? Maybe hanging around with Bush and his gang of thieves, Cheney, Rumsfeld, and Rove, rubbed off on Allen. Maybe he rationalized that since they stole things so should he, in order to measure up.

Carter G. Woodson wrote, "The new Negro in politics, moreover, must not be a politician. He must be a man." These puzzled people, many of the Black folks in politics today, reflect the conditions the Temptations sang about on their album. That genre of music wasn't called "Psychedelic Soul" for nothing.

Today, nearly forty years later, some of these "Negroes" in politics, as Carter Woodson called the ones in his day, seem to be ensconced in a psychedelic state of mind. Their perception is distorted, they are hallucinating, they are in altered states of awareness, and they are reminiscent of folks in the 1960's who took hallucinogenic drugs. In the case of some of these current Black conservatives who just love themselves some George Bush, it's the proverbial "purple Kool-Aid" scenario.

The Puzzle People album contained socially conscious songs that spoke to the condition of Black folks in the United States in 1969, which could also be applied to our situation today. Those songs described the injustice against Blacks by the prison system; they spoke up for Black power, as did other songs during that era. Cuts like "Don't Let the Joneses Get you Down," "Slave," and "Message from a Black Man" gave us insight into ourselves and those who did not have our best interests in mind. Some of our misguided and misled politicians, on both sides of the aisle, ought to start listening to those old songs; maybe they will find out who they are and what they should be doing for their people.

Claude Allen is an obvious prime example of another puzzled person. If the allegations against him are proven, what a shame it will be that Allen chose to do something stupid for who knows what reason. Was he trying to prove that he could outsmart the system? Was he pulling a prank that he could go back and brag about to his cohorts and maybe even to his boss? Was he suffering from the "Rage of the Privileged Class," as described by author, Ellis Cose?

We may never know the answers to those and other questions that will surely arise as this incident unfolds, but I would put forth the contention that we do know one thing. Claude Allen is a puzzled person and a puzzling person, and I base that simply on his alleged actions, and his political relationships, both past and present.

Free at last! Finally! For real this time!
June '05

JUNE 19, 1865 IS COMMEMORATED BY Africans in America as the day the last slaves were freed. For many Black folks Juneteenth, as it is now called, is our Independence Day, that final nail in the coffin of the worst treatment ever put on a people. Juneteenth was the culmination of the prayers, hopes, and dreams of our enslaved relatives, the notice that finally gave them their freedom, despite recalcitrant cotton plantation owners who were not about to allow our ancestors to go in peace. Freedom was in the air on that day in June 1865, and millions of Black people still celebrate that freedom today.

This year I am speaking in Columbus, Ohio at their Juneteenth celebration, and I am pleased and honored to do so. It is my hope that the brothers and sisters will come out and participate in this event in even higher numbers than they would if it were a concert or a football game. Yes, there is an admission, but there are also admission fees for amusement parks, theaters, music festivals, sporting events, et al. At those events you get entertained; at the Juneteenth event in Columbus, you will get educated, informed, inspired, and I hope infected with a consciousness that will cause you to always support your brothers and sisters in efforts such as this one.

Juneteenth is about freedom. I ask again, "Are we really free?" Many of those ancestors in Texas, upon hearing the good news, left with nothing but the clothes on their backs. They left to seek for themselves, as Richard Allen stated 100 years earlier. They took the risk of being killed or even enslaved again, despite so-called emancipation. They were willing to go out into a land about which they had no knowledge and get something for themselves. They were not about to continue to "work for their former masters for wages;" they knew full well what that would mean.

The trick of emancipation has pervasively perpetuated itself in this country, especially in our children's textbooks, thus, it is incumbent upon us to learn as much as we can about what really happened and what the Proclamation was all about. It is also important for us to know the words of General Orders, Number 3, read by Major General Gordon Granger on that day in June 1865. Many of us celebrate Juneteenth but have no idea of the details of the celebration.

We should know and teach our children that the Emancipation Proclamation did not free the slaves; approximately 800,000 slaves were not covered by the proclamation, and the rest were in states that had seceded from the Union, so those states simply ignored Abe Lincoln's order. The power of words is important, however, and even though the 13th Amendment was not ratified until December 1865, when the brothers and sisters in Galveston heard the words, "all slaves are free," they took it from there.

One hundred and forty years later, we should ask ourselves, "What are <u>we</u> celebrating? Our ancestors celebrated physical freedom. Shouldn't our celebration be about psychological freedom by now? Our brothers and sisters celebrated the right to leave and explore new lands and new opportunities. Is it not our obligation to celebrate ownership of income-producing assets and having realized the opportunities our parents and grandparents passed on to us? They celebrated life in its simplest form when their chains were broken. With all of our excess, are we celebrating their lives, their sacrifices, their pain and suffering on our behalf?

My call to you this year is as it has been for many years now. Celebrate the freedom of our ancestors with the understanding that they wanted us to be free as well. Have we done our jobs the way they did theirs? Are we free if we continue to allow crooked greedy politicians to use us as political pawns? Are we free if we continue to settle for the economic crumbs from the master's table in the form of parties, football games, concerts, and dysfunctional programs that only demonstrate and perpetuate our dysfunction?

Are we free if we continue to allow our brothers and sisters to be beat down, shot down, and abused by racist police officers? Are we free if we continue to allow our children to be shot down by their peers, as we impotently look on and do nothing but complain about it? Are we free if we allow drugs and guns free access into our neighborhoods? Are we free if we allow our children to be mis-educated by teachers who only teach our children to grow up and work for their children? Are we free when we settle for minority programs, pass-through contracts, and 20% allocations for subcontracts, rather than development and control? Are we free if we allow our most heralded leaders, especially our supposed moral leaders, to traipse after immoral acts and attach themselves to immoral people?

When you celebrate freedom this year, ask yourself, "Is it for real this time?" If it's not, commit to doing something to get your freedom. Gordon Granger died in 1876; he will not be returning with new general orders for our freedom. We must write our own general orders, and start our march, albeit very late, toward true freedom.

Black Leadership—Serving us or serving us up?
Nov. '06

> "Black America has an overclass that is charged with the responsibility of maintaining the racial status quo. This Black overclass is wedded to the white power structure and is opposed, therefore, to any independent thoughts or actions which might unite Black America. The overclass is commissioned by white organizations and governments to keep Black Americans powerless by allying externally with other groups rather than allying internally with members of their own race."

— Dr. Claud Anderson, <u>More Dirty Little Secrets.</u>

BLACK LEADERS, WHY HAVE YOU FORSAKEN us? We have always stood beside you, and oftentimes we stood in front of you, willing to die if necessary, to protect and defend you against our enemies. Despite all of the sacrifices we have made on your behalf and all of the support we have provided to your efforts, you have forsaken us. You have abandoned us. You have relinquished your position as authentic leaders and opted for a watered-down, tepid, caricature of Black leadership that continuously succumbs to a white dominant society. Instead of standing up and speaking "truth to power," you cower in the face of adversity. Instead of refusing to be bought, you eagerly cut selfish deals that only maintain status quo, which, for Black people, is a prescription for failure.

You have accepted subordination, a "less than" description of our people; you have abdicated your role as spokesperson and warrior for Black people by allowing others to define you; you have accepted the label of "minority," a term connoting deficiency; you even promote diversity and multiculturalism, but outside of rather than within our own race. You advise us that we must help everyone else, but you fail to lead us toward self-empowerment.

Black Empowerment with Attitude!

What a tragedy to propose that Black people, who have virtually no collective power, should engage in the struggles of other people prior to winning our own battles. Even sadder is the fact that you, Black leadership, suggest we do not love others because we refuse your call to action. Some of you even use the oxymoronic term, "Black racism" and the canard of "reverse discrimination" if we don't follow your illogical directives.

We are offended by Black politicians who rush to the podium to publicly proclaim "I am not a Black politician; I am a politician who happens to be Black, and I will work for all of the people." How strange it is that we never hear any other politicians make such a statement. We are insulted by Black leaders who turn their backs on the very ones that elevated them to their lofty perches. We are disgraced by Black political leaders who have sold out, settled in, and succumbed to a corrupt political system. Why have you forsaken us, Black politicians, after being in office for decades and accumulating wealth for yourself and your families, why have you turned your backs us?

Black intellectuals, why do you lecture us on the economic problems we face but seldom, if ever, build institutions or start initiatives that will solve the problems you decry? Surely you have the intellectual capacity to lead us to higher economic heights, with all of your degrees and oratory skills. Marcus Garvey did it without degrees, but you hold yourselves up as our intellectual leaders, making high-priced speeches before throngs of Black people, and have yet to come even close to what Garvey and others did, without the trappings of an ivy-leagued education or a professorship.

Black religious leaders, why have you gone the way of the moneychangers? Your influence is the strongest among Black people, but you misuse it for your own self-aggrandizement, building edifices that showcase your power to persuade Black people to put up <u>and</u> shut up when it comes to their money. You live royally but keep telling us every Sunday, and two or three times during the week, that "somethin' is about to happen in this place," "God is gettin' ready to bless somebody here tonight," "It's your season; the anointing is coming." Why have you forsaken us in exchange for filthy lucre and political favors?

Have you ignored the greatest leader's words, found in Matthew 20:27 and 23:11? "…he that is greatest (or chief) among you shall be your servant"

After we have supported, promoted, and even forgiven Black leadership for your missteps and transgressions against us, you have ignored our needs, you have collaborated against our interests, and you have engaged in actions that keep "the patient" sick, as Booker T. Washington noted.

You continue to lead us in circles, rather than where we must go, and it seems you do not understand the negative effects your brand of leadership has on us. How is this possible from intelligent Black leadership? Why do you pursue an integration/assimilation strategy that pushes Black people toward the bottom rung of the economic ladder? What sense does it make for you to remain silent in the face of continued mistreatment of your people? Or, are we "your" people?

Why have you forsaken us, Black leaders? Why have you become hypocritical in your actions toward us? Why have you feathered your own nests at the cost of our blood, sweat, and tears? Why have you not provided real solutions to our problems, not just in words, but also in deeds? Are you not capable? Are you unwilling to sacrifice for your people? Are you reluctant to do what DuBois asked of you? Have you disregarded Carter G. Woodson's plea for "servant leaders"?

We don't know what your answers are, but we do know that we are tired, and we must have a new brand of Black leadership. We cannot afford to wait for you any longer. We love you, but we must move on now.

The Tsunami after the Tsunami
Jan. '06

NOW THAT THE FIRST TSUNAMI HAS subsided, another one has been visited upon the same people. It's the "Money Tsunami." Just after the huge waves hammered the islands, cities, and beach resorts, billions of dollars immediately began to wash onto those same shores. Money came in so fast they didn't know how to handle it. But not to worry, I am sure they have figured it out by now. All that money being raised was a sight to behold.

The vaunted G-8 countries began their high stakes competition; little children raised money; and corporations vied to see who could give the most. Even our President dipped into his pocket, albeit, not too deep into his pocket, and came up with a whopping $10,000! Of course, that had to be lead news story. After all, aren't "Bible-believers" supposed to broadcast our charity? Or, is it the other way around? (Pardon me while I check Matthew 6:1-4.)

This country and others, now coming up with billions of dollars, have looked on for years as Africans have suffered tremendous hardships. There was no outpouring of funds and military support from this country when nearly a million people were being slaughtered in Rwanda, but folks in Hollywood are about to make a lot of money on that tragedy with its new movie "Hotel Rwanda." People dying in Sudan and Congo seem to have no effect either. With all of the money being spent in Iraq for a war that should never have been, a billion per week, you would think we could break off a billion or two to save lives in Africa rather than to kill people in Iraq?

Oh, I'm sorry. Most of the *jack* being squandered in Iraq is going to Halliburton. Sorry, Dick (Cheney). Didn't mean to get in *yo bidness*. Hey, maybe you can figure out how your former company can get a piece of this Tsunami action. Need infrastructure? Need meals on wheels? Halliburton to the rescue. What do you think, Mr. "vice" President?

The *crazy* money being raised and sent off to Asia, some $6 billion and counting, graphically portrays a few aspects of our so-called global society. But even more distressing is the lack of Black consciousness by many *brothas* and *sistahs* in the U.S. for their relatives in Africa.

First of all, as I stated above, we have watched people in Africa suffer several Tsunami-like disasters and have done little to help them. For instance, in response to the news about the tragedy in Asia, globalafrica.com reported the following: *"It has been common knowledge … that an African child below the age of five dies every three seconds on the [African] continent. That means <u>every week</u> 201,600 African children don't get to celebrate their 5th birthday. Every year ten and a half million (10,483,200) African children perish, some through curable and preventable diseases such as malaria, small pox, chicken pox, measles, whooping cough, dysentery, malnutrition, and others through combinations of neglect, starvation, poisoning, political mismanagement, local wars and deliberate genocidal policies of criminal, puppet governments. Of course, we are not taking into consideration another twenty million…annual deaths. This means, in human terms, Africa is haemorrhaging (sic) from a disaster much greater in scale than two Asian Earthquake Tsunamis each and every week, year in and year out…"*

So much for the "Diaspora" Black people hold so dear. The reaction by many Black folks to the Tsunami disaster simply mimicked what the establishment was doing. I heard no questions about Africa nor did I read any coverage on the condition of the people living there. Brother Colin Powell never mentioned it in his defense of what Bush was not doing and had not done. (I won't even go there with Condoleezza Rice; even though it would not take long, it's not worth the time.) Folks were highly interested in finding out what happened to one of Oprah's regular guests, but several high-profile Black folks in the media never uttered a *mumblin'* word about the fate of their brothers and sisters in Africa.

A sight to behold was the National Basketball Association players offering $1,000 per point scored to the Tsunami relief effort. The guy that was hated a few weeks prior because of the melee in Detroit, Jermaine O'Neal, led the way with $55,000 for his 55-point performance. Several players got in on the act, scoring points and making pledges. Who knows how much they ended up sending? Now here's the thing. As we all know, most of the players in the NBA are Black. Will someone tell me where they were for the Rwanda, Sudan, and Congo disasters? Other than Patrick Ewing, Alonzo Mourning, a maybe a few more, where were they when their fellow NBA player, Dikembe Mutombo, announced he needed help to build a hospital in his native Kinshasa?

We have gotten so used to following the establishment and have forgotten about our own people, here and abroad. Not to diminish what happened to the people of Asia, but Africa has a Tsunami everyday; where's the U.S. government? Too busy looking for oil in the Motherland perhaps. Where are Black Americans and Black athletes and entertainers? Too busy waiting for white folks to show us what to do perhaps, and trying to get in touch with their agents, most of whom are white, to get permission to donate their own money.

Some of our people need a Tsunami of common economic sense followed by a Tsunami of Black consciousness.

Note: "In July 2000, [Antoine] Walker — then a Boston Celtic — was the victim of an armed robbery along with NBA center Nazr Mohammed as they sat in a vehicle waiting for a restaurant on Chicago's South Side to open. Police said at the time that three men approached and demanded cash and valuables, which included a $55,000 wristwatch." Associated Press, July 11, 2007

A $55,000.00 wrist watch! Puzzling? You decide.

Profit and Loss Statements
April '05

THOSE FAMILIAR WITH ACCOUNTING AND BUSINESS practices, and even many who are not, understand what profit and loss are all about. If you have a small business and apply for a loan, they ask for your P&L Statements; they want to know if you are making money or losing money. Collectively, if Black people in the United States check our P&L Statement we will not like what we see. It will reveal a startling fact. Everyone else is profiting from our dollars, and Blacks are talking a huge loss. If businesses conducted themselves the way we conduct ourselves, vis-à-vis reciprocity in the marketplace, they would be out of business in a heartbeat. How long will Black folks survive if we continue in the same vein of demanding rather than supplying?

We are spending billions of dollars each year with virtually no return. Their profit, our loss. Black people are buying everything everyone else makes, no matter how ridiculous the item is and no matter how fast the item depreciates. Their profit, our loss. Our people are in love with numbers and names on athletic jerseys, rims that keep spinning when the car stops, soft drinks that embarrass us with their commercials, and fast food restaurants that sell Black History to us—with fries, of course. Their profit, our loss.

Black people acquiesce to the so-called "powers that be," rather than stand up like men and women and fight against what we know is detrimental to our people, especially our children. The media messages and the control of so-called Black Entertainment Television, which has now made yet another move to dumb-down its audience by canceling the 11:00 P.M. news, are indicative of our plight. Talk about mission creep; Viacom has it down to a fine art and a science. Their profit, our loss.

Black Empowerment with Attitude!

We look on as immigrants move their businesses into our neighborhoods, mumbling and complaining under our breath but crouched at the start-line ready to race to their stores to buy their products. Their profit, our loss.

We stand by, even in towns where we are the majority in population, while projects funded by our tax dollars are being doled out, yet the lion's share is always given to outside developers, contractors, and workers. The most ridiculous thing is even when we get control of a project some of our people ask, "What's the 'minority' portion of this project?"

A prime example of this "inappropriate behavior" is occurring right now in Cincinnati, Ohio. Check this out: After wresting control of 60 acres of prime real estate by putting some 500 Black families out of their homes (132 of those families had to go into homeless shelters) under false pretenses and lies, the City gave the property to two adjacent Black churches to carry out the rest of their dastardly scheme. The two Black churches, having not raised a hand to stop the takeover or "defend the oppressed," immediately went to work by giving a significant portion of the deal to a white developer.

To add insult to injury, the two Black churches then brought in a white-owned company to build the houses, despite there being a Black faith-based housing developer in that same neighborhood. The company they brought in has annual revenues that exceed the aggregate revenues of all Black businesses in Cincinnati.

As if they had not rubbed Black faces in the mud enough, the white builder, with the help of Black "economic inclusion" experts, puts an article in the local Black newspaper calling for "minority" subcontractors to work on the project!

As I say on my radio show sometimes, "Do we practice being this stupid, or does it just come naturally?" Why do we, even when we get control of economic development projects, continue to play the minority game and act as though there are no Black folks who can develop land and build houses? As Dr. Claud Anderson always says, "Black folks can't even do wrong right." But Steven Biko said, "The greatest weapon in the hand of the oppressor is the mind of the oppressed." Massa doesn't even have to be in the room or in charge of the deal, and some of us will still do his bidding anyway. Carter G. Woodson was so correct in his comment regarding, "If you control a man's thinking…" Their profit, our loss.

Is there a Black CPA out there somewhere who is willing to do an annual report on our people? Is there an accountant who will show us exactly what our profit and loss statement says about how we spend our money and how we allow others to exploit us? Is there a bookkeeper available who will tell us that it makes no sense to turn over our own projects to white males (the ones who already get 70%-85% of all the contracts anyway) when we finally get control of those projects?

Sadly, by the moves we make and the ones we fail to make, Black people make profit and loss statements everyday, but the result is always the same, "Their profit and our loss."

Have you made your covenant yet?
March '06

ANOTHER STATE OF THE BLACK UNION has come and gone, and now we have something we can use to economically empower Black folks in America. We have something of substance, something meaningful, something both the Democrat and Republican National Chairmen support. And then there's the new book, The Covenant; it's selling like ice cream on a Sunday afternoon, making a lot of money I'm sure. What could be better? We finally have an agreement, a treaty of sorts, which could well be the elixir we have been seeking to cure the ills of Black people.

Admittedly, I did not watch the televised panel discussion. Didn't need to. I already know the State of Black America. As I said in a 2005 article, I am more concerned about the Fate of the Black Union; the state of the Black union stares us in the face everyday. I did not watch the show, but I have heard and read the reviews. They tell me Minister Louis Farrakhan upbraided some folks. Other than that excitement, and except for a few newcomers, was it the same folks saying the same things for the, what is it now, fifth year in a row? If so, by now we should have a pretty good handle on our state of affairs.

The questions now are: What are we doing? What are we going to do? But haven't those always been the appropriate questions? I pray there will be something of substance that comes from this affair. After all, if Black America's best and brightest, those "exceptional" men and women, who for nearly five hours shared their intellect and expertise, if they cannot lead us to salvation, who can? Who will? I almost forgot. On the Covenant website, it says "It is not our intent to define, determine, or prioritize these issues, nor to conclude how they are to be remedied. That's where you come in." I guess I just answered my questions.

Of course, no one is going to save us but us, those who are willing to sacrifice, to fight, to speak up and speak out, and those who are unafraid to stand up and be counted as Black. So the onus is on us. Black people must make a covenant with Black people. Made yours yet?

Have you made your covenant with individual Black politicians—and white ones too—who have your best interests in mind and do everything they can to bring home the political bacon to Black folks? Rhetoric from Howard Dean and Ken Mehlman, notwithstanding, do you really believe that either political party is going to operate on behalf of Black interests?

Have you made your covenant with Black developers and construction companies, especially those who build churches? Since we are talking about a "Covenant," don't you think Black churches should have covenants with Black people? Many Black church buildings are being built by non-Black companies. That's shameful! That's not good stewardship. Can't we at least make covenants between Black congregations and Black builders?

Have you made your covenant with Black bookstores and publishers in America? It sure would have been great to see Covenant books leaping off the shelves of Milligan Books, in Los Angeles, rather than so many being sold by "you know who." Of course, "you know who" can take books on consignment, while Dr. Rosie Milligan has to pay up front for hers.

Have you made your covenant with Black youth? What are you doing to help them overcome some of the numerous problems they face in this society? Have you started your Boycott Prisons campaign yet? Are you helping those who have been incarcerated and are now back home?

Have you made your covenant with Black Nationalist thinkers and activists who work collectively and cooperatively in support of Black people? I am sure you saw those Latino Nationalists marching in various cities across the country in protest of the immigration proposals. They were not marching for "minorities" or Haitians; they were marching for themselves.

Black Empowerment with Attitude!

Have you made your covenant with Black organizations and institutions that are working on your behalf—not faking it, not perpetrating, but really working to improve the conditions Black people face in this country? I dream of fearless Black organizations that will step out and publicly declare who they are and for whom they work. The organizations of other groups have no problem declaring allegiance to and advocating for their constituents.

Have you made your covenant with Black America? I made mine a long time ago and will honor it until I die. To some of you it may a novel thing to do; it feels good, and it sounds good, but remember, it's the "doing good" that counts. Corporations and politicians will pay for and support rhetorical jousting by Black folks; but will they pay for our freedom? You got it!

Make your covenant with Black people today, that is, if you haven't already, not with empty words and pontification but with action. It's long overdue.

Trying to run away from Blackness
June '07

AS THEY SAY IN NEW YORK, "Fa-get about it!" It's sad to see some of our brothers and sisters making every attempt to deny who and what they are. We hear it in their statements, we see it in their actions, and we feel it in our relationships with one another. Plain and simply, some Black folks are trying to run away from their Blackness. They do it in all sorts of ways, but it's mainly to appease white people in hope they will see a "different kind of Black person." That's how O.J. Simpson used to be characterized, before they showed him the doorway back to his Blackness—even though he still has not taken the hint. Now it's being said about Barack Obama: "…he is not black in the usual way," said one white commentator.

We have some serious psychological problems, obvious vestiges of our conditioning and maintenance over several generations, but trying to run away from what we are is the height of madness for Black people; besides, it's rife with futility. It is also shameful considering the legacy left to us by our forebears in this country, and even before we arrived here. Are they lying cold in their graves now, having sacrificed themselves for our true freedom, for a cause from which we now distance ourselves?

Obama's statement, "…There is no Black America" is indicative of a fear that we will be alienated from white people if we do not give deference to them by suggesting that we are really not Black, but rather we are "neutral." It seems to me white folks would want us to be who we are rather than pretend and play silly games. When it's all said and done, they will make their decisions about us based on <u>their</u> respective social paradigms and parameters anyway. So why are we scared? Why try to run away from Blackness?

Black Empowerment with Attitude!

Obama tells Blacks not to vote for him because he is Black, which is highly commendable to say, especially for his corporate donors and the Washington status quo. It is also a very condescending statement to make and suggests Black people aren't sophisticated enough to decide based on qualifications. (On second thought, that may indeed be the case) But have you ever heard white candidates tell white folks not to vote for them simply because they are white? We always have to make other people feel comfortable, don't we? Obama knows full well that millions of Blacks will vote for him simply because he is Black, but to tell us not to do so brings credence to the contention that he really is "not black in the usual way."

If being Black doesn't mean anything, if there is no Black America, why do Black folks get excited about Bob Johnson, Tiger Woods, Serena and Venus, Oprah, Shani Davis (Olympic Speed Skater) Dominique Dawes, and Debbie Thomas? Why are we constantly discussing the possibility that Obama could be "the first" Black President (John Hanson notwithstanding) if Blackness means nothing in this country, or if it does not even exist? Yes, Barack, there is a Black America, as well as all those other Americas too, just as there are 50 separate states rather than one country with no internal borders.

One of the main problems with Black people is that some of us are too busy embracing diversity rather than embracing our own Blackness first. Who else other than Black folks do you hear promoting "diversity" and allowing themselves to be called "minorities?" When is the last time you heard an Italian person denounce the "Little Italy" communities across this country? When have you seen Chinese people decry China Towns? When have you heard Hispanics say, "Down with La Raza, we are one America"? Blacks are the only ones trying to run away from who we are, and that is embarrassing, unconscionable, and cowardly. It also speaks volumes about the self-hate among our people, which causes much of the crime we in our neighborhoods.

Newsflash! You cannot run away from being Black! You can't get promoted from being Black; you can't move away from being Black; and you can't get enough money to change your Blackness (Sorry, Michael). Wherever you go, there your Blackness will be also. Whatever you do, your Blackness will do it with you. So you may as well settle in and get down to business for your people, just as others have been doing and continue to do in this country—just as we used to do in this country, prior to "integration."

The United States is a myriad of nations within a nation, not just one nation as the politicians would have you believe. That's utopian rhetoric, Pablum for Black people, because we are the only ones who buy the hype. White folks are circling their wagons right now at the specter of being outnumbered by so-called "minorities." Hispanics are carving out their piece of the economic pie by working in support of one another.

So-called American Indians, after having raked in billions from the hotels, casinos, and golf courses, are now branching out to other business ventures, off the reservation. Koreans, Vietnamese, and Chinese are making moves to control more industries. Pakistanis and Indians are buying all the businesses they can find. What are Black people doing, collectively, to improve and solidify our position in this nation of nations? We are trying to run away from our Blackness, which will only cause us to disappear.

Why is nationalistic action bad only when it is promoted by Black people? The groups I mentioned, as well as Jewish people here and abroad, are all nationalistic; Joel Kotkin calls them "Tribes." So what's it going to be, Black America? Nationalism or nihilism?

The Chinese Connection
April '07

LET ME GET THIS STRAIGHT. WE have a Chinese furniture company labeling one of its sofas "[N-Word] Brown." We have a Chinese Sculptor being awarded the rights to carve the proposed $100 million Martin Luther King Memorial. And while Master Lei Yixin is carving the MLK stone, his Chinese brethren will continue carving out a large piece of Africa by developing the land, purchasing the oil, and selling Africans everything they want and need. What's wrong with this picture? To most Black folks in America, it seems the answer is: Nothing.

The sofa issue could be mitigated by the possibility that in the Chinese city of Guangzhou, from where the sofa was shipped, the N-Word could be just an effort on their part to emulate a colloquial U.S. expression. The Chinese are capitalists; they want the money. I can't believe they would intentionally do something to alienate what might be the largest consumer group in the world in terms of disposable income. I don't know; they may have thought the N-Word was a term of endearment; some Black folks do.

Nonetheless, the "N-Word Brown" sofa fiasco will have a brief shelf life and will soon fade into the annals of "shock news" stories. Purchases from China will go on and we will be back to business as usual in a month or so. Whatever the case, I can give the Chinese furniture label a free *ghetto pass* this time. Now if the color of the MLK memorial is done in lush tones of N-Word Brown, I will definitely have a problem.

Nice segue. Let's talk about this MLK memorial. I don't know if you saw the article written by one of the country's most renowned artists, Gilbert Young. The article, titled, **"A Chinese Martin Luther King?!"**

(www.kingisours.com) expresses Young's outrage at the lack of a Black designer (The Roma Group, http://www.roma.com, was selected for that) and a Black sculptor to complete the project (Lei Yixin was elected for that $10 million honor).

As a result, Gilbert Young says, "So let's see—that leaves the digging and hauling, which in some folks' eyes may be appropriate because this nation was built on the backs of Blacks. I, for one, am not willing to bob my head and grin over the fact that some Black subcontractor will be employed to move the dirt. Nor am I willing to allow my children's children to visit a memorial that will not reflect African American art and culture and artistry."

Black people are always busy trying to be "inclusive" with our projects while, at the same time, we are being "excluded" from projects controlled by others. I don't know what's up with those in charge of the MLK Memorial, but I gotta go with Gilbert Young on this one. He questioned the, "…travesty of justice in having the 'national treasure of China,' Lei Yixin—that's Communist China—sculpt the center piece of the most important African American monument, in recognition of the most important African American movement in the history of the United States. A movement that never could have taken place in China."

Maybe they should put the memorial in China, especially since some of the quotes to be inscribed on it speak directly to the oppression in that country.

I must be missing something here, because it just does not make sense. Uh oh, I thought of something Booker T. said, "Beneath everything lies economics." Could this be about the money? Of course, it could.

Another nice segue. China boasts the world's second-largest cache of foreign exchange behind only Japan; it is on pace to see its reserves soon climb past $1 trillion. China virtually controls the U.S. and has made significant economic headway in Africa especially during the past 25 years. Consider the trade deficit with China, the rise of the Euro and the fall of the Dollar, the manipulation of the Yuan by the Chinese, the escalating oil consumption by China, and the sheer power ensconced in China's 1.3 billion consumers. They tell me even the stone for the MLK Memorial will be imported from China!

Since China loves Black folks, according to Yang Zhou, a hotel manager in Sierra Leone, who said, "'Africa is a good environment for Chinese investment, because it's not too competitive," and when you consider the economic impact of doing deals with China, especially among the heavy-hitters who have already donated millions to the MLK Memorial, the dots get connected.

But let's get back to Black folks. If we want to make a Chinese Connection, then let's do it, but let's do it with some leverage. To simply channel profits to them at the expense of Black artists, designers, all in the name of inclusion and the flimsy rationale of Dr. King being "international" in his reach and in his message, will not give us the leverage we need to build our own Chinese connection—one that will benefit our children prior to benefiting everyone else's.

When I saw Andrew Young and Jesse Jackson crying alligator tears at the groundbreaking of the MLK Memorial I thought it was in remembrance of MLK and what he did for us. Maybe I was wrong; could their tears have been in response to the most of the funds being collected for the memorial going to China rather than to Black folks?

As usual Black folks get to participate in the emotional side of things, putting shovels in the ground, making speeches, and crying, while other folks stay in the background waiting for the money to start rolling out. We get excited about the sizzle, and they dine sumptuously on the steak. Please, stop the madness and Bring Back Black! (www.bringbackblack.org)

Amos Wilson was right; "We are, indeed, out of our minds." June '07

FILE THIS ARTICLE UNDER, "YOU GOTTA to be kidding me!" Dr. Amos Wilson's words, quoted by Kwa David Whitaker, in his outstanding presentation titled, "The Wake-Up Call," rang in my ears when I heard about the latest in a series of self-deprecating, self-denigrating, and self-hating acts of Black-on-Black economic violence by a Black organization. Of course, Amos Wilson was not disparaging Black folks just to be negative; he loved his people and would do anything to help us achieve economic empowerment and "Afrikan consciousness" as he put it. While Wilson and Whitaker used those words to awaken our people, it seems we see more and more black (small "b" intended) people committing acts that are directly reflective of a "sick people."

Prior to the most recent act of economic treason, we had the Chinese Connection, which involves the $10 million contract awarded by Black folks to a Chinese sculptor to carve the National Martin Luther King Monument, and the awarding of the project design contract to a white-owned firm. It was unconscionable that a Black organization would not see that a Black Sculptor and Designer got those contracts. But, Amos Wilson was right; we have lost our minds. "Massa, is we sick?" "No, 'we' ain't sick, but you sho is."

Now, as if the MLK Statue was not bad enough, the NAACP National Convention is going to Detroit, a city with 80%+ Black population; Detroit, with its Black Mayor whose mother chairs the Congressional Black Caucus; Detroit, with its history of Motown, Muhammad's Mosque No.1, New Bethel Baptist Church, Rosa Parks, and Coleman Young; Detroit, with strong Black folks like Kwame Kenyatta, Joann Watson, and Theo Broughton; the NAACP is going to Detroit, and during its convention will present an Authors' Pavilion, which will not be managed by a Black bookstore! (Sorry for disturbing you, Brother Amos.)

A representative of the National Association for the Advancement of "Colored" People, when asked about the Authors' Pavilion contract with a non-Black book store, responded with an equally outrageous excuse: They were not aware of Black bookstores, distributors or publishers in Detroit. Can you say, "The Shrine of the Black Madonna"? It's only been there for 35 years or so, and has locations in Atlanta and Houston.

Is our NAACP telling its Black constituents that no one in the National Office knew about the Shrine? Are they saying that no one in Baltimore, where they are located, knew to ask one of the largest distributors of Black books, Brother Nati, at African World Books? Have they not heard of Maryland/DC-based Karibu Books, whom they could have called to get information on Black book stores in Detroit?

Are they saying they never heard of Haki Madhubuti and Third World Press, or Lushena Books, both in Chicago? Would they have us believe they know nothing about Milligan Books in L.A., whose owner, Dr. Rosie Milligan, annually presents **Black Authors on Tour** in the same town where the NAACP held its Image Awards? What about Nia Books, Amber Books, and Cush City Books? Puleeeze! Give us a break! This is absolutely ridiculous and, even though I should not have to say it, it's also unacceptable.

Black bookstores, publishers, and distributors all over this country are struggling to stay open. Why in the name of all that is sensible, all that is logical, all that is reasonable, all that is respectable, all that is ethical, and all that is conscionable, would a Black organization not use a Black bookstore or distributor in Detroit, or even some other city, to present its Authors' Pavilion? "We didn't know," won't get it. Can you say, "The Internet"?

Where does this leave individual book vendors? Well, I spoke to five Black book dealers from across the country; they have been priced out of the NAACP Convention market, whose booths cost more than $800.00 each. They cannot afford to go to the convention now because they will not have the right to sell certain books, and the NAACP will certainly not allow more than a couple of book dealers to be there as vendors. One bookstore owner was told, "You can sell bookmarks." What?!!!

This situation is insulting, and it speaks to the psychological conditioning that still rules some of our people. How can any Black person, who works at a Black organization and has just a hint of intelligence and knowledge of self, take a convention to a Black city, and not at least consider the possibility of there being a Black bookstore in that Black city that could organize and manage a Black Authors' Pavilion? I'm at my wit's end on this one, brothers and sisters.

So what now? Unless things change real soon, and I doubt they will, Black folks who attend the event should not patronize the Pavilion. You can still purchase the showcased authors' books from the Shrine of the Black Madonna or another Black bookstore in Detroit. You must refrain from supporting this asinine move by the NAACP National Office. And here's the toughest recommendation: Those Black authors participating in the Pavilion should refuse to do so. But, assuming that won't happen, I would ask that they at least put in a good word for Black bookstores with the NAACP, O.K.?

It is ironic and sad that the words, "We have met the enemy and he is us," are attributed to a comic-strip character named Pogo, placed on a poster by Walt Kelly in 1970. In 2007 Black people are indeed our own worst enemy, and in the words of another Kelly (Jim), the actions of the NAACP National Convention come "straight out of a comic book."

Who and what are we fighting?
July '06

I HAVE BEEN DOING A GREAT deal of soul-searching lately, on a spiritual level as well as a physical level. Having studied much of the history of this country and the role of Black people in building it and sustaining its wealth for centuries, as well as the deeds of some of the white folks who set this thing up and those who continue to do anything to maintain status quo, I began to ponder the question: Who and what are we fighting?

We are daily witnesses to warring factions, gang slayings, increasing violence in our streets, and some of the most heinous crimes committed against children in our history. The weather has drastically changed in the past five years to the point of causing major catastrophes with wind, water, heat, and forest fires. The elements are rebelling against us as we continue to pollute our land, our living space, and as we seek new places to live on the moon and on Mars in outer space. Much of the strife we face can be traced right to our front door. Who is in charge? Who is running this country? Who is running this world?

I watched a video about the assassination of John Kennedy recently and was emotionally moved at the mere thought of this country's leaders doing what they did, not only to JFK but also to MLK, RFK, Fred Hampton, and Malcolm X. It made me want to give up my quest of trying to move Black people to collective economic change, because the foe we face is so treacherous.

Who is this monster we are fighting? Is it even rational to think we can defeat him? Is it logical to think we can ever get even? I certainly believe that we are fighting against those "principalities and powers and rulers of the darkness of this world and spiritual wickedness in high places." That said, I truly believe, just based on what I have studied and what I see today, that we are fighting the devil himself.

There have been men in this country who have occupied high places, ravaged other countries, and trampled the rights of people in this country. We still have men in high places doing the same things today. I used to ask how they could do the things they do, how they could sleep at night, and how they dealt with their consciences. I no longer ask those questions because I know who we are fighting, therefore I know the answers.

For instance, the Enron debacle was one for the annals of time. All of a sudden Ken Lay has a heart attack, after he is convicted and looking at 20 years in jail. His very close relationship with Dubya, coupled with the strange and unresolved "deaths" of the past, gives credence to the possibility that Lay is not dead. Who knows? Maybe they fixed that situation like they fixed the Kennedy thing.

With enough money, ignorance, and fear, anything can be "fixed" in this country, and with the help of the media, some of whom collaborate with the liars, the people will believe anything and continue to mimic the thousands of wildebeest on the Serengeti Plain. Instead of acting collectively and fighting together against the lion, we wake up everyday hoping and praying that today is not our day to get eaten.

Brothers and sisters we are in a fight for our very existence, but victory is possible. The odds are great but so what, we can still prevail if we stick together. If Black people would just stop trying to "be equal," stop trying to assimilate, stop trying to change hearts, stop going along to get along, stop pretending, stop apologizing for our Blackness, stop hating ourselves, we would cause a sea-change in this country and at least live the rest of our lives as real men and women who are willing to fight rather than die as hogs (or wildebeests), as Claude McKay wrote.

Yes, we are fighting some of the most evil forces on the face of God's earth; just study and analyze the history of this country and you can draw no other conclusion. They have committed so many evil acts over the past four centuries, but they won't get away. A due date is coming. In the meantime, Black people must realize that we are indeed inside the "belly of the beast." We are a nation within a nation and we should conduct ourselves accordingly. Presently we do not, and that must change.

If we continue down the road we are presently on, we will most assuredly fail. Black folks in the U.S. must acknowledge our collective situation and then be willing to contribute whatever we can, as individuals, to change it. Status quo is a prescription for failure. Laurence J. Peter said, "Bureaucracy defends the status quo long past the time when the quo has lost its status." Why are some of us defending the evil that we face? Things could hardly get worse than they are right now.

Like other groups, we must settle on a common denominator that will bring and keep us together despite our many surface differences. That commonality is that we are Black people of African descent. If we hold that reality high and close to our hearts, we will find new hope, new love, and a new spirituality that propel us toward the greatness of those ancestors we celebrate. Don't let the devil get you down; he is simply being true to who he is. The greater question is: Are you being true to who you are?

Note: In 1919 there was a wave of race riots consisting mainly of white assaults on black neighborhoods in a dozen American cities. Jamaican-born writer Claude McKay responded by writing the sonnet, "If we must die," urging his comrades to fight back. It had a powerful impact, then and later.

> If we must die, let it not be like hogs
> Hunted and penned in an inglorious spot,
> While round us bark the mad and hungry dogs,
> Making their mock at our accursed lot.
> If we must die, O let us nobly die,
> So that our precious blood may not be shed
> In vain; then even the monsters we defy

James Clingman

Shall be constrained to honor us though dead!
O kinsmen we must meet the common foe!
Though far outnumbered let us show us brave,
And for their thousand blows deal one deathblow!
What though before us lies the open grave?
Like men we'll face the murderous, cowardly pack,
Pressed to the wall, dying, but fighting back!

Civil Rights vs. Civil Wrongs
Nov. '04

"All things are legitimate [permissible—and we are free to do anything we please], but not all things are helpful. All things are legitimate but not all things are constructive." **First Corinthians 10:23 Amplified Version**

"Everything is permissible—but not everything is beneficial. Everything is permissible—but not everything is constructive." **First Corinthians 10:23 New International Version**

"Just because you have the right to do something does not mean it is right for you to do it." **First Corinthians 10:23 Simplified Clingman Version**

WE CELEBRATED THE 40TH ANNIVERSARY OF the signing of the Civil Rights Act on July 2, 2004. For forty years, after fighting for "civil rights," Black people have the right to share rest rooms, restaurants, theaters, water fountains, and various other facilities and accommodations with white people. Unfortunately, after winning our rights, some of our leaders made us believe they were "civil privileges" rather than civil rights.

Most of those who fought that battle were brave, dedicated, committed, brothers and sisters, both Black and white, who were determined to make much needed changes in this country's policies toward the sons and daughters of enslaved Africans. They fought for choice, not privilege. They won the choice to sit wherever they wanted on public transportation and at whatever table they wanted in any restaurant. They won the choice to drink from any water fountain they chose, and they won the choice to shop wherever they wanted.

Freedom to shop wherever they wanted? Was that a right or a privilege? Was it a choice? I would say it was a right, a choice, but certainly not a privilege. So what have we done with our civil rights for the past forty years? In my estimation, we have exercised them as though they were privileges.

Some of our leaders during that time put so much emphasis on the "victory" they had won that it seemed to many, I suppose, that we should now take full advantage of our newfound freedom, our newfound privilege, by spending as much of our money as we could at those businesses that did not want us in their stores and restaurants in the first place. In the process of exercising our *civil privileges*, we abandoned our own businesses, walked away from our economic base, and deserted the very bastions of economic empowerment that would have propelled us to the heights we seek today.

Black people in this country, as it faces an impending economic meltdown, along with most of the citizens of the United States, are now suffering from a dearth of economic advantages, as opposed to pre-1964, when we at least owned and controlled the basic infrastructure necessary to take care of ourselves and to spend more of our money among our own businesses.

When we gained our civil rights we started committing *civil wrongs* against one another—and we continue that fatal trend today, forty years later. Yes, we have the right to spend our money wherever we choose, but it's not a privilege. We have the right, but that does not mean that it's right for us to do it. As the scripture says, it's permissible but not constructive, not beneficial.

Why do we continue to commit civil wrongs against one another? Are we still enraptured by the notion that we can enter someone else's business and show them how much money we have to spend? Are we willing to continue seeking the privilege of giving our money to folks who hold us in disdain? Or, are we willing to take an honest look at our past forty years in this country and admit that we have really messed up? Are we willing to make the changes necessary to move from the civil wrongs we have committed against ourselves and our children, and return to building and owning income-producing assets? If so, let's consider doing something about it right now.

Black Empowerment with Attitude!

There are several movements across this country, which I have written about many times, that Black people can-and should-use to reverse our civil wrongs. If you read my column on a regular basis, or have read my other books, you know what they are. You also know how urgent our economic transformation is to the future of our race. Thus, after literally forcing white folks and others to take our money, and after walking away from our own businesses, and virtually boycotting them for forty years, it is time for us to admit our civil wrongs and commit, once and for all, to using our money to help ourselves.

We have made every other group in this country wealthy. I did not say rich; I said wealthy. We insisted they allow us to cavort with them, to patronize them, to sit with them, and to mingle with them, all the while they were figuring out how to take advantage of our desire to do so.

Now we spend the vast majority of our money with those same folks and we wonder why they continue to treat us the way they do. Don't you think we are smart enough to see that we were played and that we have even played ourselves? If so, let's change it. We won the right to choose by winning our civil rights, but we lost our economic base by committing civil wrongs against one another.

Elitist Hip-Hopcrisy
April '07

I HARDLY KNOW ENOUGH ABOUT THE Hip-Hop industry to get real deep about this; my students at the University of Cincinnati do what they can to keep me up on the genre and who is running things. But I can see with my own eyes some of the contradictions within the industry and the folks that control it. Is the latest "epiphany" regarding the words being used by rappers and even the suggestion to ban some of those words coming from the heart or is it coming from the pocket?

Aside from the fact that protests of rap lyrics have been made by others for years now, we act as though it's the first time, now that Russell Simmons has come out with his proposed ban. Simmons is on television shows discussing the virtues and vices of rap lingo, and has gotten "religion" after all these years.

Mind you, he was explicit about his position. He said he was not trying to actually "ban" the words; he was proposing those words not be played, that they should be bleeped out. Of course, I don't know what would be left to listen to in some of those rap songs if you bleep out the "bad" words. It would be like watching one of those movies on BET where every other word is bleeped out.

Has the Hip-Hop phenomenon reached its pinnacle? Has it achieved its highest point of approval and is now on the way down, now that Simmons has taken a different position on the lyrics? I am not the one to answer those questions, but I believe there is a change brewing. Why? Money, of course.

When a television host suggested to Simmons that Hip-Hop was on the way out, Russell laughed and said, "Don't tell my investors that." It was a funny line, but it spoke volumes. It gets us to the real issue behind this multi-billion dollar industry. Who is behind Simmons and who is behind the rap industry, which is now the Black complaint *du jour*?

Black Empowerment with Attitude!

What most of us see as Hip-Hop are guys in big jackets, baggy pants, hiking boots, gold and silver teeth, and baseball caps, and don't forget about the ladies in thongs. They are the generators of billions in cash to the ones behind the industry, the shadowy figures who only come out to collect their huge profits.

There are a relative few who make the money Simmons, Jay-Z, and Puffy, Diddy, or whatever he's calling himself these days make, and there are fewer still who do anything positive with what they make. The high-stakes game room is controlled by someone else. Even Simmons answers to someone else, and it's not Ben Chavis.

Now that hundreds of millions have been stashed in Simmons' account, he is on tour espousing the virtues of linguistic political correctness. He is the Dali Lama of the Black experience, talking about the inner self and the force within, and so much more. I used to think he had a speech problem because he would only say, "Thank you, and goodnight" on Def Comedy Jam. How wrong I was about him.

An important point to consider is that, once again, Black people are being led, and misled in some cases, by media moguls who are only interested in cash flow—from Black folks' pockets to their bank accounts. There have been many other Black people protesting the language in rap music for years. I recently wrote about the new documentary film titled, <u>Turn Off Channel Zero</u>, that decries such language as well as the visual experience of some of the rap videos. No big media response to that. As I said, when Simmons spoke out you would have thought it was the first time anyone had.

The Hip-Hopcrisy runs rampant, in my opinion, within the ranks of the Black elite. "Now that I have made a half billion dollars on these words, I think we should stop using them." BET's Debra Lee, in an interview, boasted about BET and what great work it does by bringing us the kind of programming we want to see. She said she gets feedback from her teenaged daughter who watches the shows on BET; you know, so they can bring us the shows we want to see, like Beef, American Gangster, and degrading buffoonery, and, oh yeah, those great videos that Russell Simmons is railing against now.

Will Puffy or Diddy with his diamonds, Jay-Z with his champagne, Fifty-Cent with his bullet wounds, Snoop Dogg with his golden chalice, and the rest of them with their cars, trucks, grills, 24-inch rims, and chinchilla coats, take Simmons' path and get religion about the words they use—now that they have made their money from those same words? Will the executives continue to exploit the industry and continue to hide? And will the corporations looking to sell Black folks everything from soda pop to gym shoes continue to slither around and find ways to make their billions from the Hip-Hopsters too?

It seems we have totally bought in to what Nino Brown said about things not being personal, just business. We have been lulled to sleep by the shining cars and fists full of dollars being displayed by the rappers. And we have fallen, once again, for feel-good, couch-talk reflections and introspection from the Hip-Hop elite.

One thing we can be sure of though. Amid this episode of Hip-Hopcrisy, at least one of the elite will remain "true to da game" as they say. When commenting on Don Imus' remarks about the sisters on Rutgers' basketball team, Snoop admitted he <u>was</u> talking about b's and h's by saying, "We're talking about ho's that's in the 'hood that ain't doing sh--, that's trying to get a n---a for his money." No Hip-Hopcrisy in the Dogg, folks. I guess that's what's called "keepin' it real."

O.K., Martin, you can go back to sleep now.
Jan. '07

SORRY FOR WAKING YOU UP EVERY year to celebrate your birthday, despite the fact that you would not be welcomed at some of the celebrations on your behalf. After all, your fiery and provocative rhetoric concerning the economic condition of your people is not what the sponsors of those celebrations want in return for their support.

No, they don't want to hear you call for a redistribution of wealth in this country, higher wages, equity in public sector contracting, and certainly not a word on stopping this ridiculous war in Iraq. As I recall, you spoke against the Viet Nam War exactly one year prior to being assassinated. Oh yes, in your final speech you also told your audience to boycott various products in response to unfair treatment in the marketplace. No, Martin, it would have been a waste of your time to have made the rounds to those Kum ba ya hand-holding celebrations of your life.

Many of the folks that attended MLK events, as they have for years, were only interested in "keeping the dream alive." They are not concerned with carrying on the work you started and moving it to the next level; they merely want to revisit what you did and what you said, mourn your loss, and then go home and wait for next year's MLK Day.

Despite your being an action-oriented leader, many of our so-called leaders today are content to just talk the talk. And you know what, Dr. King; every year it seems the number of folks who "marched" with you increases. Too bad most of those same folks didn't go to jail with you.

Yes, there were lots of celebrations on your birthday, but most of them did nothing to make your dream a reality; their objective was to merely keep your dream "alive." I guess as long as we keep the dream alive we don't have to do any work, make any sacrifices, take any risks, make any waves, or disturb the status quo, right? But wasn't that just the opposite of what you did?

Before I forget, let me tell about the celebration I attended in Philadelphia, put on by the African American Heritage Coalition. No, it wasn't one of those hand-holding hymn-singing affairs; it was a serious event put on by some serious dedicated sisters and brothers, all in your name but also in remembrance of the question you posed in 1967, "Where do we go from here? Chaos or Community?" And guess who was there. Remember Dr. Walter Lomax, the brother who attended to you that time you got sick on the road? He still has that newspaper photo of the two of you. When he showed it to me a few years ago, I kidded him by saying, "You saved Dr. King's life!"

I had the honor of being the keynote speaker for the event in Philly; it felt so good to be among brothers and sisters who were committed to taking the action steps necessary to move our people beyond your dream and into the reality of Black empowerment. I used your question, but I changed it just a little; I hope you don't mind. I asked, "Where do we go from here? Complacency or consciousness? I wanted to know if they would continue status quo or finally do something about our condition.

I told them that naming streets after you is great, but let's not stop there, especially if Black people don't own anything on those streets. Besides, I know you didn't do what you did to get your name on street signs; rather, you did it so <u>we</u> could get our names on things like deeds, businesses, development contracts, and other assets. You would be appalled to know that most of those streets named in your honor are not even safe for our children to walk and play. I know that hurts you, but I thought you should know.

Of course, I left some challenges in the City of Brotherly Love. I gave the audience a list of things they could do the very next day to start down the road to economic empowerment. That's what you were telling the people that night in Memphis before you were killed wasn't it? Forty years later and I have to give the same message. That's wild! Do you

Black Empowerment with Attitude!

think we will ever get it, Dr. King? And if we "get" it, do you think we will ever act upon the economic empowerment message? I sure hope so.

Anyway, as I said, the event I attended was just the right kind for me. I'm not in to the traditional celebrations where we get together simply out of obligation and just for show. I figure if we cannot come together on your birthday for more than recanting the "I Have a Dream" speech, we should stay at home. I mentioned to my audience in Philly that I could not picture Dr. King, if you were still alive, going somewhere every year and reciting that same speech for forty years.

I was encouraged in Philadelphia, and I want you to be encouraged too. There are some folks there who are seriously moving in the right direction for our people. I think you would be proud to know them.

But you go back to sleep now, and continue "your" dream. You may be disturbed again on April 4th, but that won't last long either, so don't worry about it. Please get a lot of rest before that date next year though, because it will be the 40th anniversary of your assassination. You're really going to get a workout then. Give Coretta a big hug for us; and we'll see you again next year, on Dr. Martin Luther King, Jr. Day.

America's Melting Pot: Blacks are the only ones melting.
June '06

WHAT WILL IT TAKE FOR BLACK people to stand up against centuries of unfairness and mistreatment? I know we're tough and can take a lot of abuse, but c'mon brothers and sisters, we don't have to continue proving our toughness by submitting to and even participating in the destruction of our own people. Where is Chancellor Williams when we need him most? Have we not been hurt severely enough? Are we still waiting for the crucial blow that will finally make us fight back? Well, the longer we wait the less effective we become, and the smaller and more insignificant we become as well.

This melting pot thing has definitely played us for chumps. Every other group is doing its thing by building wealth for themselves. Black people are busy melting away, soon to become invisible and a "non-people" as Albert Cleage told us we would become if we continued down the yellow brick road of social integration without an economic foundation.

We are engaged in silly discussions about Democrats and Republicans, as if we have any say in what happens politically in this country, and as if the rulers of these parties care about what we think. They put us in political trick bags by inviting us to their parties and allowing us to run for office only after we have pledged allegiance to one party or the other, again, as if that means anything in terms of real political power for Black folks.

Some of our Black politicians are so scared of offending their white handlers that they never put forth any agenda that is pro-Black. In some cases they are even ashamed to be Black. They seek our votes and move into their plush secure political offices, while we melt away in a society that has two things on its mind: money and power.

The silly Black electorate goes along with these do-nothing politicians, both Black and white, by falling into the trap of endless and mindless dialogues about issues that mean absolutely nothing when it comes to the economic wellbeing of Black people. We engage in high-brow political conversations, again, as if our rhetoric will change things, and as if we have real political power in the first place.

We wrap ourselves in the agendas of others and subvert our own interests for the silliest and flimsiest of reasons. For instance, in Ohio the discussion is now centered on the governor's race. Like our neighbors in Pennsylvania, we are faced with a political choice between a Black Republican and a white Democrat, the Blacks being Ken Blackwell and Lynn Swann, respectively. I can't imagine what the rationale is in Pennsylvania for electing Lynn Swann, who said George Bush is the "most qualified and most credible candidate to fulfill the role as president of the United States." But in my hometown of Cincinnati, Ohio, the rationale being promulgated in support of Blackwell is, "Let's make history." That's what they said about Doug Wilder. How are you Black folks in Virginia doing these days?

Black people should have had enough of just "making history" by now. Heck, Condoleezza made history, y'all, but what have we gotten from that? You would think Black people could come up with a better reason than that to elect a governor. Another silly political platform is gay marriage. What in the world does this issue have to do with the economic uplift of Black people? Nothing. But we will vote for folks simply because they espouse a Constitutional Amendment that defines marriage.

Newsflash! To all of you Black right-wing religious zealots, all of you empty-headed political pundits, and especially you wannabe political office-holders, the marriage amendment has already been written, passed, and instituted by God a long time ago. He sanctioned the first marriage and His word does not change; He does not need help from George Bush, Bill Frist, or anyone else with defining what constitutes a marriage. The arrogance of those who promote this amendment nonsense amazes me. Although most of us know it's only a diversion and an attempt to regain the Republican base, we fall for it anyway.

The immigration issue has been reduced to discussions about Black people disliking Latinos. How silly is that? This issue is about Black people loving ourselves enough to stand up for our own rights, which have been trampled not only by the establishment but by other groups that have come to this country. They walk on the legacy left by our relatives who suffered and died to get their "rights," as we silently do our best Stepin Fetchit impression and move to the end of the line—once again.

Here's the deal, Black folks, and I do mean "Black folks." You cannot allow these shallow-minded, unconscious, conniving, political hacks, and "misleaders" to cause the destruction of the Black race. We have made mistakes by trying to assimilate, by trying to make others love us, and by buying into the minority game. We are suffering the consequences of silly political slogans and disingenuous politicians who want to be Black only when it comes to getting the Black vote. That is our fault; nobody else's.

We must turn from being Stepin Fetchit and become Lincoln Perry, the man who "played" that role but was much smarter than people thought. He invented his game and played it well; he controlled his game. When are Black folks going to control our game? Right now we are out of control, and melting away fast in this melting pot called the United States. The sad part is that there are other blacks (intentional small "b") aiding in that process, and we cannot allow them to get away with it. Just like the brothers and sisters do in Detroit, "Call 'em out!"

Economics Stuff

"Because the Negro does not own and control retail establishments in his own community, he is unable to stabilize his community... The Negro must pool his capital in order to help himself... This will enable him to solve his own problems."

— S.B. Fuller

This subject is obviously close to my heart. Economics is the engine that runs this country—and the world! It affects virtually everything in our day-to-day lives, having been the impetus for the establishment of this nation. So why is economic empowerment still just a minor blip on the radar screen of Black people? You would think by now, after being traded for food and provisions by the captain of that Dutch ship in 1619, and after being formally auctioned and sold, and after being made to work from dawn to dusk—for free, and after creating much of the tremendous wealth of this nation, that Black people would realize, understand, and act upon the fact that economics runs this country, and we are still running behind. We are in last place, falling further and further behind the other groups who live here, apparently in acceptance of an inevitable last place finish when it's all said and done.

Among the questions that come to my mind is one that is captured in the following article, "Are we serious?" Do we really understand the dire consequences of refusing to build a collective economic future for our children? Have we been so well conditioned and programmed that we just don't know how to begin to catch up to the pack?

Some of our actions and activities, when it comes to our resources, both intellectual and financial, suggest that we have fallen for the ultimate shell game, the proverbial bait-and-switch sucker play. We thought we had something when white folks made promises and passed regulations on our behalf. We sang and danced in the streets when integration finally came around. We celebrated (and still do) when "the first" Black person got that certain position. Yes, we bought the economic fool's gold, and now we are in last place.

The economics stuff we need to know and respond to has kept me writing a weekly article on economic empowerment for 13 years! That's 676 articles, not counting the extra magazine articles and specialty articles written over the years. And guess what; they just keep on coming, without repetition, because there is always something to write about when it comes to economics in this country. That's why this subject is so important and why Black people must take it a lot more seriously than we have for the past 45 years, since 1964 or so.

Were we serious when we abandoned our economic base in return for the "right" and perceived privilege to help build someone else's? Were we serious when we gave up the education of our children and turned that function over to those who cared very little about us? Were we serious when we stopped supporting one another, when we started to neglect economic empowerment and, as T. Thomas Fortune described, devoted our "infant energies" to politics?

The most important question is: Are we serious now? Today is all each of us has, right now, this moment, to answer that question. And we must answer it positively, not with rhetoric only but with action. The action we must take is serious, therefore, we must be serious about it by not allowing outsiders, provocateurs, and hustlers, to lull us to sleep, move us off point, or take us off mission. We must resist the temptation to believe the hype of corrupt, lying, self-serving politicians, pontificating, self-aggrandizing, pay-me-to-get-to-heaven preachers, and bought-and-sold-out *afrocentricksters* who talk the talk but never walk the walk.

I say, "Enough!" But what do you say, brothers and sisters? What do you say? "Do you want to get serious," as Regina Belle asked in one of her songs? Do you want to get serious about economic empowerment and change the status quo? Do you want to get serious and move beyond the mundane, "stay in our place" position we've occupied for centuries?

Speaking before the National Urban League (2007), Barack Obama said economics is the way to erase much of the racial animus in this country. I take it he meant "Black" economics, or Black people getting a firmer grip on our economic situation, to which I strongly agree, not because I am concerned so much about the "race problem" but because I am concerned about our economic problem and our children's future. You should be concerned as well. Now it's your call. Please make the right one.

Are we serious about economic empowerment?
Nov. '05

ARE WE PLAYING TO WIN, OR are we playing just for the sake of playing? It appears that Black people are content with our third string status in the two most important team sports in this country: Politics and Economics. We have seen the results of being "bench-warmers" (or is it "booth-warmers"?) in the political game, and now, despite so many of our so-called leaders hailing economic empowerment as the most important issue facing Black people, there are few results coming from all of their bombastic rhetoric. Black people, collectively, remain in the same relative economic position as in years past.

In politics we have seen the first string team get virtually all of the resources. We have seen them convert public money into private money, via laws they bring forth and pass, and we see them steal whatever is leftover or allocated for the less fortunate, via no-bid contracts, fundraising campaigns after hurricanes, and under-the-table deals. We have a President, a "vice" President, and a just plain goofy Secretary of Defense, who are more interested in building someone else a "New Iraq" than they are in rebuilding our New Orleans. Politics? We are on the sidelines, brothers and sisters, not even in the game.

In the economic arena we have seen a new form of apartheid, via "minority" and "economic inclusion" programs. We have seen a new millennium affirmative action program that is reminiscent of the one started and maintained for the first 250 years of this country's existence; a program that allows white people to get 99% of the resources and the rest of us get, not what's right, but what's left. And, we have seen black gatekeepers stand in the way of Black progress, getting their meager payoffs along the way. Are we playing to win? Hardly.

So the question is: Are we really serious about our economic freedom? Of course, this question is directed to those of you who are consciously aware of our predicament and willing to step up and do what must be done to change our situation. There have always been and there will always be a group of our brothers and sisters who will sell out, act as fronts and pass-through businesses, and even seek a position on the opposite team. But the rest of us must answer the question, and then act upon our affirmative answer.

I watch television in sadness on so-called "Black Friday" when there, leading the throngs to get into the stores to spend their money, are my brothers and sisters. Knocking one another down and even trampling those who fall in the rush; they actually run to spend their money, playing right into the hands of the merchants. It is a "Black" Friday indeed.

I listen in sadness to Black folks who complain about store owners selling bad meat and inferior products, yet continue to support them in their effort to suck the lifeblood out of Black households. I ache when I see vacant storefronts in Black neighborhoods, which could be stores of our own, that only serve, for the time being, as props to hold up our young men as they lean their lives away everyday.

Are we serious about our economic freedom? All indications say we are far from serious about it. When we allow ourselves to be mistreated, some of us even volunteering for that mistreatment, we cannot be serious about our economic freedom.

Even when we were in bondage and relegated to slave labor, thousands of our ancestors continuously sought and eventually won their freedom, both physical and economic. Even in light of the ominous specter of maiming, torture, mutilation, and murder, many of our ancestors ran for freedom and even fought back, in the face of overwhelming odds, against men who held absolutely no regard for Black life other than how much work they could get from that life. Despite the threats and likelihood of death, there was a Gabriel Prosser, a David Walker, a Harriet Tubman, a Denmark Vesey, and a Nat Turner. And for you white folks who read this, there was also a John Brown.

If you are serious, you must dismiss the empty rhetoric of pandering politicians, the transparent ramblings of self-righteous religious pretenders, the oratory of warmongering money-grubbing government officials, and the unbounded pronouncements and musings of speechifying intellectuals. If your leaders are only talking about the problems and have nothing to show for their monologue, such as a genuine plan of action, an institution they have established to deal with the problems they decry, or a movement that will help you economically, you must not follow them.

If you are serious you must understand the difference between Black leaders and "leading Blacks," as Drs. Julia and Nathan Hare tell us. You must know that some of your leaders are really misleaders, chosen by the establishment to do its bidding. You must take Carter G. Woodson's advice to heart, who said, "We must have servant leaders." And, if you are serious, you have no choice but to change your behavior, economically, politically, and socially, in a radical way, if you are truly playing to win.

If you are serious, grab somebody of like-mind and start doing the things that will lead to economic freedom. If you are serious, throw off the old paradigm of Black leadership.

If you are serious, be a leader, not a lemming.

Black sales force not benefiting Black people
Nov. '06

HAVE YOU STOPPED TO THINK ABOUT the fact that Black children across this country are being used as a sales force, par excellence, selling all sorts of products from candles, to cheese, to sausage, to candy, to cookies, to magazines, and almost any nonperishable item you can imagine. Millions of Black children are going from door to door, soliciting their parents' fellow employees, and ordering items for their church members. They are "encouraged" to sell various items to raise money to pay for school activities. Girl Scout cookies notwithstanding, it's time Black people get in on this windfall.

In our public school systems, especially in urban areas, Black children comprise a large percentage of the student population. Every year there are programs and projects that require outside financial assistance; teachers set up deals with companies for the students to sell products, with some portion of the profits going back to the students' projects. Have you ever wondered to whom the balance of those profits go?

If you have ever purchased any of that high priced chocolate candy or those cheese rolls and crackers, you know how lucrative a situation like that can be for a manufacturer of those products. How can we turn down a little girl staring up at us in church or at our front door saying, "I am trying to go to Disneyland; would you help me by buying something out this catalog?" Every year I tell myself "no," but every year I end up with a refrigerator full of cheese and sausage that I don't eat, a freezer full of cookies I will never consume, more candy than I should ever eat, and more magazines than I have time to read.

In addition to our children being used as a nationwide sales force, and a very good one at that, Black businesses get little or no fruit from our children's labor. Can you imagine the money Black photographers could make taking the students' pictures every year? What about the uniforms, the class rings, the food, and the construction of the school buildings? There are many opportunities for Black folks to get in the game, especially in school systems where Black children comprise the majority of students. Why shouldn't the parents and relatives of the children who occupy the classrooms include themselves in the business side of that school system?

Growing more frustrated by this every year and, as always, looking for ways to economically empower ourselves, here's what I did. I contacted Ricky Fyles of Farley's Coffee, Inc. in Seattle, Washington (www.farleyscoffeeinc.com) and asked if he would develop a special coffee to help raise funds for our Entrepreneurship High School. Everybody either drinks coffee or knows someone who does, so why not sell coffee as a fundraiser item and help a Black owned company at the same time? Hmmm.

In his usual expeditious manner, Ricky had the label design back to me in a couple of days and was ready to start roasting, blending, and packaging shortly thereafter. He called our special coffee the "Scholars Blend" and made a very fair deal with us on the profit split. Man, did I feel great! Our students could now sell a Black product and get the funds they needed to help with their extra curricular activities, and a Black company would benefit as well. "What a novel concept," I sarcastically thought, "We should do more of this."

Is this something that only Black students can do? Of course not. All students participate in fundraising; it's just that the overwhelming majority of the products they sell are from non-Black owned companies. There is no reason that some of those products sold in our schools, both public and private schools, should not be from a Black company, no matter what the student population percentages are.

Black folks have been creating wealth for everyone else for centuries. It is way past time that we take more initiative to create wealth for our people, especially where we live, especially in our school systems, especially among our children. If your child is being used as a salesperson, in addition to the CD or MP3 Players, the field trips, the band and dance uniforms, and baseball jerseys, don't you think there should be more of a return to the overall Black economy for their labor? Whoa! Free labor? Why did I go there?

There is nothing sinister about this, folks. I am simply advocating Black economic empowerment via the activities in which our children are already participating. Empowerment, not exploitation. A national sales force would be great for any Black consumer product company. Imagine how quickly Farley's Coffee, Inc. would become a billion dollar business if its coffee were being sold, along with everything else being sold by our children, to millions of parents, employees, and church members.

You would look into that child's beautiful eyes and melt, "All right; I'll buy a couple of pounds." And guess what! Either you or someone you know would consume the coffee; it wouldn't be taking up space in your pantry and eventually discarded like some of that other stuff you buy every year from those sweet little children.

Next to oil, coffee is the number two selling commodity in the world. Purchase some of your coffee from Farley's Coffee, Inc. this year. Get one of their gift baskets to give for Christmas or Kwanzaa, and set up a fundraiser for your school or any other entity with which you are working. Look for other Black owned companies to support with our national student sales force, and let's do more with the money we have, for ourselves and for our children.

The Black Hair Care Tragicomedy
July '06

THE SADDEST PART ABOUT THIS ISSUE is the fact that we could see this one coming. Now that it has hit its mark, right between our eyes, maybe the pain will be severe enough not only to get our attention but also to hold our attention long enough for us to rally our forces and fight back. The Black Hair Care Industry (BHCI) has, once again, become a hot topic among folks other than Koreans.

Now that an investigative documentary has been produced about the industry, obviously shocking Black people once again, maybe some of us will resolve to do something to reclaim at least a portion of that vertical market. After all, the last time I checked, no one is using Black hair care products except Black folks.

The documentary discloses information, none of which was news to BHCI insiders, about the ownership of stores and distribution of hair products sought and bought by Black people. The main point of the report centered on the fact that Koreans own and control, and I do mean control, the overwhelming majority of the distribution and sales of Black hair care products, which include shampoos, conditioners, oils and creams, and those fashionable hairpieces our sisters love to wear.

Some Black folks have seen this coming since the 1980's, especially in light of the infamous but prophetic comments by then Revlon executive, Irving Bottner, and the subsequent "funeral" and boycott of Revlon Products headed by Jesse Jackson. Man, where is Jesse now? We sure could use another funeral.

Nevertheless, as we looked on, and in some cases collaborated in the demise of Black control of an industry that brags about Madame Walker, Annie Turnbo-Malone, Anthony Overton, S.B. Fuller, and many other Black hair care pioneers, the Koreans have used the past 20 years or so to build their businesses and create wealth for their families. Oh yeah, we still get to look good, and we are quite willing to pay for it, but is looking good better than "doing good"– for yourself?

The three questions again come to mind: What? So what? Now what? At this stage, since we have ignored the "so what?" stage, we must deal with the "now what?" What are Black people going to do, if anything, about this situation? In the video, there are calls for boycotts, which could be done simply by buying your products at Black owned stores that get their products through Black owned channels of distribution. Oops, I almost forgot; we don't have very many of those, do we?

But, we do have a few, so let's start with them. We also have an organization, called BOBSA, the Black Owned Beauty Supply Association (see bobsa.org or call 650 357 0073). Every venture begins with a first step, so our "now what?" step must be taken from where we are, with what we have, and with whoever will go. If Black people are serious about slowing down the Korean Black Hair Care Express and revving up an economic engine of our own in this industry, we had better get busy buying from one another, expanding the Black channels of distribution we already have, creating investment pools to build warehouses and wholesale facilities, and all the other things it takes to become "players" once again.

BOBSA is advocating for those changes and more, but it needs help from you, the consumer, on two fronts. BOBSA needs you to become a working member and supporter, and it needs you to commit to redirecting your spending. In addition, if you are serious, you should locate every Black hair care products store in your area and ask the owners to support BOBSA by becoming members. From that effort a nationwide database can be developed and posted on BOBSA's website, and no matter where you are in the country, you can find a Black owned store from which to purchase your products.

Now these suggestions are not coming from an expert in the industry; there are folks who know much more about this than I. Call upon them and get their ideas; use them as consultants to help recapture a portion

YOUR market. Do everything it takes to hold on to what is probably the last vestige of an industry developed and maintained by Black people.

It is, quite frankly, shameful, as I think of the great brothers and sisters I teach about in my Black Entrepreneurship class, that we have allowed this to happen. Nothing against the Koreans for taking care of their business and beating us out of our own game, but are they really that much smarter than we are? Are they more capable of running this business than we are? Are they that much better at marketing to our people than we? Oh, it's about the money isn't it? It always is. Do they have more money than we? Or, is it that they use their money collectively to help their group a lot more than we do?

Now we're getting to the meat of this issue, right? We can come up with all the excuses and reasons for being behind in the race for an industry in which only Black people competed for years, but we cannot truthfully say that we are consciously disturbed enough, collective enough in our thinking, and willing to make the sacrifices necessary to do what other groups do to build their wealth. Watch the video and you will see how it's done, just in case you have forgotten.

I end with this challenge. Make a commitment and then follow through on that commitment to purchase Black manufactured hair care products from Black owned outlets. Let's write a happy ending to this tragicomedy. One more thought: Don't envy the hair that Brandy wears; buy your own, from your own.

Note: In 1949 Black beauticians expressed concern that whites were pushing their way into the lucrative beauty shop business. The following is an excerpt from industry leaders at a national conference.

"The old line beauticians were losing a long-waged battle to keep the $450,000,000 beauty business in tan hands. The move [is] for non-colored promoters to buy up beauty shops and rent out booths…they have moved into the actual operating end. This year's convention saw two-thirds of the

Black Empowerment with Attitude!

demonstrators white, or merely having colored to front for them…whatever the blame the fact remains that a highly profitable field is surely and not so slowly being taken out of our hands." — Excerpt from: **The History of Black Business, **Juliet E.K. Walker

The African American Trade Deficit
Sept. '04

THE MORE I SEE THE STATISTICS relating to the so-called Black Economy and Black Buying Power, the more desperate my message becomes and the more insulted I feel. How can we get so excited about having an annual aggregate income of more than $700 billion while we are at the bottom of every economic category in this country? Do you feel insulted, maybe embarrassed, about the fact that Black Americans create vast wealth for others at the expense of creating and retaining wealth for ourselves? Can we look our children in their eyes and assure them that we, as a collective body, will leave a strong economic foundation upon which they can stand? Black America is operating at a huge deficit. We must change that.

Just as the government gets a bit antsy when the U.S. trade deficit goes awry, Black folks in the United States should feel the same about ours, and we should finally do something about it. Our trade deficit is horrendously out of kilter, and it's getting worse everyday. Oh yes, I almost forgot, we are currently enthralled with who will be our next President, and it's difficult to draw our attention away from that circus, isn't it? But can't we walk and chew gum at the same time?

Black Americans cannot afford to neglect our trade deficit, and continue to allow it to spiral out of control, while we discuss politics as usual and prepare to cast our votes for two guys who either don't care about us or take us for granted. What a choice, huh?

Well, we have another choice, brothers and sisters. We can choose to redirect more of our $700 billion toward our own businesses; we can choose to start and grow more businesses; we can choose to create more jobs for our children; we can choose to teach our children how to be entrepreneurs; and we can choose economic freedom over economic enslavement and modern-day sharecropping.

Black Empowerment with Attitude!

I read an article by the so-called Black Conservative, Larry Elder, in which he stated, "...despite slavery, Jim Crow and racism, the progress of American blacks is simply astounding. Black America, if divided into a separate country, ranks No. 16 in Gross Domestic Product, ahead of Australia, Turkey, Thailand, Argentina, the Netherlands, Taiwan and South Africa."

A little Economics lesson is in order here. The broad components of Gross Domestic Product (GDP) are: consumption, investment, net exports, government purchases, and inventories. Consumption is by far the largest component, totaling roughly two-thirds of GDP.

Let's see now, Blacks save and invest very little, as evidenced by our median net worth per family, which is one-tenth that of white families. Exports? Not much going on there either, although our brothers and sisters in Africa and the Caribbean eagerly await the day when we get our act together and start taking care of business. Government purchases? Well, we have a lot of government jobs, if that counts. And finally, our inventories are not much to speak of either as we don't seem to care much for ownership of wholesale businesses, warehousing, and distribution channels.

Now let's look at consumption. As the definition of GDP tells us, consumption is the largest of its components, totaling roughly two-thirds of GDP. Consumption? Yeah, now we're speaking our language, right? Now Blacks folks really make the grade. We have that consumption thing down pat. Two-thirds of GDP? Nah, we can do much better than a measly 66%. Our consumption from businesses other than our own is as high as 95%!

No, Mr. Elder, I don't think we can use Black GDP to show how far we've come in America. Quite frankly, it's embarrassing. I'd be willing to bet that Taiwan and Thailand export a whole lot more than they import; we can look around our homes at labels and tags and see that. Comparing our GDP to that of the Taiwanese, and the rest of those 14 countries, is a real joke, even if we do earn more money than they earn. We may rank 16th, but we'd have a huge trade deficit.

Yes, it feels and looks good when we use that line about Blacks being the 10th, 12th, or the 16th richest "country" in the world. It's balm for our injured souls, consolation for our wounded psyches, and ammunition for those who say, "We've come a long way, baby!" But what good is it doing us if we consume everything someone else makes, fail to save a minimum of ten percent of what we earn, have no import/export relationships with brothers and sisters who live in Africa, the richest land in the world, and fail to set up and support a Black owned and operated distribution channel?

What good does it do us to have $700 billion if we are in a constant trade deficit with the other groups in this country, i.e. Koreans, Indians, Vietnamese, Lebanese, et al? What good does it do for us to brag about how far we have come when, relatively speaking, we are no further than our grandparents were two generations ago when it comes to business and land ownership?

The Black trade deficit is way out of balance, and we had better get busy fixing it before we become totally dependent on *"foreigners"* to supply our sustenance. No one can take care of us better than we can take care of ourselves. We proved it once upon a time; we can do it once again.

The Negro in this country must become, in a more potent sense, a producer of wealth as well as a consumer. He must become more of a business man and must enter all avenues of industry. Even now, in almost every part of our country, there are industries that mean our life-blood, that are fast slipping from under us. From being the head and center of these industries, [as we once were], we are too fast being relegated to the ragged edge of the most important. I repeat that we must, as a race, enter business, for we are constantly being required to measure ourselves by the side of the business world, and by this test we rise or fall. **Booker T. Washington**

Let's Boycott Boycotting
Nov. '05

AS WE CONTINUE TO CELEBRATE THE life of Rosa Parks and the Montgomery Bus Boycott that was started because of her defiant act, let's take a look at boycotts and maybe even reevaluate Black folks' participation in and support of them. After all, the very person whose life we celebrate and are now planning, in some circles, to erect a statue in recognition of, the "Mother of Civil Rights," was the lightening rod for the most famous boycott called and sustained by Black people. As we reflect on Rosa's life, shouldn't we also reflect on the power of boycotts?

The term boycott comes from a fellow named Charles C. Boycott, an Englishman who managed the estate of the Earl of Erne in County Mayo, Ireland. In defiance of an outcry for land reform and lower rents called by members of the Irish Land League, Mr. Boycott refused to lower the rent, and he evicted his tenants. In response, the people refused to have anything to do with Boycott and his family, leaving them isolated and without workers, service in stores, servants, and even mail delivery. Boycott was boycotted and his name was adopted to signify that kind treatment.

While other groups have initiated similar treatment against transgressors, white folks came up with the term boycott and still use it quite effectively today. Black folks effectively used it to obtain civil rights, public access, and reciprocity in the marketplace; but the success of our boycotts today is questionable at best.

Consider: A boycott was called by white folks, via television personalities and others, against France for its failure to support the Iraq war, thus, causing a loss of some $300 million. Most recently, the Governor of Alabama called for a boycott of Aruba because the family of the missing girl, Natalie Holloway, cannot get justice.

White folks obviously feel that one of their children, missing or possibly killed on this popular island, is a serious enough occurrence for them to withdraw their money until they get justice. They also know that boycotting is the ultimate punishment and the most effective way to get what they want. Will whites get what they want? Yes. Why? Because it's always about the money.

Now consider this: Black folks in Cincinnati, Ohio called a boycott of the city's tourism and entertainment industry because their children were being abused by police officers and in some cases even murdered. A boycott was called in order to get justice for the families of Timothy Thomas, and then Roger Owensby, who was choked to death by police officers prior to Thomas being killed, and even later for Nathaniel Jones, who was also killed by police officers. In addition, the boycott was called because of the city's economic apartheid system, in which Black people were constantly discriminated against in public development projects.

Did Blacks get what they wanted? No. Why not? Too many Black people continued to spend their money in the boycott zone of Cincinnati instead of withdrawing their money from it. If Black people would do what white people do, when it comes to boycotts, we would be just as successful as whites are, which begs the question: Are we really serious about boycotts?

Imagine the irony of the National Organization of Black Law Enforcement Executives (NOBLE) agreeing to hold its 2006 convention in Cincinnati, Ohio, where five Black men lay cold in their graves, unjustifiably killed by police officers. Why would a Black law enforcement organization bring millions of dollars to a city where these incidents took place? How will we ever win justice if we continue to finance injustice?

We come up with all sorts of reasons for not boycotting, not the least of which is the "who it will hurt" excuse. The Governor of Alabama knew there were white folks from the U.S. who had business interests in Aruba. White television and radio commentators must have realized that their brothers and sisters in the tourism industry might suffer as a result of calling a boycott against Aruba, but that didn't stop them from calling for it.

Black folks don't fully follow through with the boycotts of today, as opposed to the Montgomery Bus Boycott where brothers and sisters sacrificed to get what they wanted. Boycotts called by Blacks also suffer because in many cases some Black "leader" will take some money from white folks to put an end to the boycott. (I wonder if the government of Aruba offered the Governor of Alabama or the talking-head commentators some money; and I wonder if they took it.)

Compare: One missing white girl. The answer: boycott the entire island of Aruba until justice is won. Five dead Black men. The answer: boycott Cincinnati until justice is won. What's the difference in the two scenarios? Not enough Black lives taken or what?

It is obvious, as we look back at recent boycotts called by whites and Blacks that white people are definitely more serious about getting what they want than we are. And when you add the reasons for boycotts called by both groups, we can also see that white folks understand the economic implications of boycotting a whole lot better than we do.

Just as the people of Ireland boycotted their Boycott, Charles C. that is, maybe Black people should consider boycotting the boycott for a while, until we learn how to conduct and support them properly.

The Fate of the Black Union
April '05

EACH FEBRUARY WE LEARN ABOUT THE State of the Black Union, the condition, the position, the status, and the circumstances of Black people. With that in mind, let's now look at the Fate of the Black Union. Let's look at our destiny, our chances, our luck, and our lot. Knowing the State of our Union, and not being fully engaged in doing something to improve it, logically suggests a strong need for us to know the Fate of our Union.

Union? That word denotes coalition, alliance, harmony, accord, unity, amalgamation, coming together, and unification. Union? Doesn't that word also connote one-for-all-and-all-for-one? Wouldn't you think that for Black folks the word, "Union," would be used for more than just its marquis value? I sure do, but it sounds good, doesn't it? And you know how we love hype.

Anyway, what about our fate? I assert that our fate is inextricably attached to our present state. And judging from what I have seen and heard over the past five years about the state of Black men, Black children, Black families, Black churches, and Black folks in general, our fate is all but sealed. Why? Because all we seem to do is talk about our state; it seems to me that anytime prominent, educated, intelligent, national leaders get together for two days to discuss the state of Black folks, there should be some immediate action steps set forth for the people to follow, that is, unless, as the President always says, "The State of the Union is secure!" Or, "strong," or "better than ever," or whatever lie he decides to tell us every January.

For years now, we have heard Black "leaders" give numerous pronouncements regarding our condition and offer absolutely no direction, no action steps and, thus, no positive results from their discussion of the state of our union. Seems to me they are wasting their talents by just getting together on television to discuss our issues and then leave without doing anything about those issues except making plans for the next year's discussion. Surely all of our Black intellectuals can come up with something we foot soldiers can do to improve our lot. We are listening. We are waiting. (Where is Harold Cruse when we need him most?)

Here's what we know. Black families have been all but decimated; Black children are being mis-educated and taught to grow up and work for the children of those who are teaching them; Black people have the highest infant mortality rate; Black women have the highest increase in HIV/AIDS; Black men are the least employed; Black men—and women—occupy most of the prison cells in this country; Black people have the lowest home ownership rate in this country and the worst housing; Black people have the fewest businesses per capita; Black families' median net worth is ten times lower than white families; Black politicians have no real "power" in government; Black businesses have the lowest annual revenues; and Black people top the list of victims of police brutality.

What else do we know? Black people attend church services more than other groups; Black congregations build multi-million dollar edifices; Black people rank among the highest consumers of travel and tourism; Black people spend billions to attend music festivals, football games, and conventions; Black people earn more than $750 billion per year; Black people have accumulated trillions of dollars in intellectual resources; Black people have risen to the highest heights in corporate America; Black people earn billions in entertainment and athletics; Black people have thousands of elected officials and comprise a huge voting bloc; Black people are survivors, and have been since we were brought to this country; Black people have a heritage of community, entrepreneurship, and self-help; Black people, throughout recent history, have shown what we can do when we work together in support of one another.

That's the state of our union. Now, what is the fate of the Black union? Despite the tremendous resources and talents we have been blessed to accumulate, Black folks are busy squandering them at a mind-boggling rate. Some Black business executives get to the top and all of a sudden forget about the rest of us; some Black politicians get elected and instantly become invisible when it comes to Black issues; some Black entertainers and athletes are so busy seeking the approval of others that they forget about their own; some Black ministers are more interested in stadium-sized church buildings than they are in helping those who sit in those buildings every week; and some of our Black intellectuals are content with giving speeches rather than writing strategies to help Black people move forward.

The fate of the Black union ominously awaits us. It is paradoxical that we have so much and yet do so little with it. Many of our leaders are ensconced in vying to see who is the most im-po-tent, I mean important, and have no time to serve anyone but themselves—and their former masters, of course. Many of our "everyday people" are so busy racing the rats and spending what we have on "nonsense," as Maria Stewart said. We complain about other folks' businesses being in our neighborhoods, but we don't start our own businesses, and we refuse to make the sacrifices necessary to enhance our feeble economic position.

The State of the Black Union is in our minds; the Fate of the Black Union is in our hands.

Muestrame el Dinero
May '06

DO YOU REMEMBER WHEN MEXICAN PRESIDENT, Vicente Fox made the following comment? "There is no doubt that Mexicans ... are doing jobs that not even blacks want to do there in the United States." He made that comment to a group of Texas businessmen in May 2005. Jesse Jackson and Al Sharpton telephoned Fox to voice their displeasure, to which Fox responded by inviting both of them to Mexico to "join forces" on working for immigration rights and civil rights for immigrants in United States, according to CNN.

Fox at first refused to apologize for the comment, saying his remark had been misinterpreted. But later said he understood the African-American community has worked hard to fight against discrimination and that as a result of that fight the Mexican community in America has benefited greatly.

Jesse Jackson replied that he was sure the President had no racist intent and suggested the two meet to discuss "joint strategies between blacks and immigrant groups" in the United States. Fox agreed to set up a visit to Mexico by Jackson, Sharpton, and a group of American black leaders.

Black people have very short memories. Does anyone know what has happened since those comments were made and since that invitation was extended and since those Black "leaders" were supposed to go to Mexico and work things out? Now we have this brouhaha regarding illegal immigrants and what to do with them, and for the most part Black leaders are not even in the discussion. What does all of this really mean? What has happened since May 2005?

I participated in a press conference ("Choose Black America") on illegal immigration, held at the National Press Club, on May 23, 2006, during which time I spoke about the economic ramifications of this topic and how it negatively affects Black people in this country. I noted our hesitancy to enforce the law when it comes to the corporate raiders who hire "illegal" immigrants and pay them well below the going wage, all the while filling their own pockets with even more profits from this "New Jack Slavery."

I suggested this is an economic issue, not a political issue, and not a race issue, as many would have us believe. It is an economic issue when corporations and people who enter this country illegally are able to get away with illegal activities. What else could it be?

Just in case you cannot read Spanish, the title of this article means "Show me the money." That's exactly what's happening folks, not only with the corporations but with some of our so-called Black leaders as well. As the title of the Jacksons' book says, "It's About the Money"

I think I am safe in saying that somewhere sometime, in some backroom the statement was made by someone, "Muestrame el Dinero," because that's what this immigration thing is all about. But why can't Black people see it for what it really is? Why are we engaged in conversations about "helping" the immigrants get their civil rights? Why have I heard brothers saying things like, "Let's not get into a fight with Hispanics," and "We have to strengthen our alliance with Latinos and support them."

When did you last see Latinos, or any other group for that matter, standing with Black people on, say, reparations for the work our parents did to help these groups attain what they have, as Fox acknowledged? What about their support for us during Katrina? Why were there no marches in the streets then? Where was this alliance when Black men and women were murdered by police officers, when Black people were being profiled, and where is it now as Black people are unfairly incarcerated, denied equal access to housing, to bank loans? Where is the unified support for Haitians who are sent back to their country? And where is this alliance now, as millions of Black people languish in perpetual unemployment?

Frederick Douglass said, "The old employments by which we have heretofore gained our livelihood, are gradually, and it may seem inevitably, passing onto other hands. Every hour sees the Black man elbowed out of employment by some newly arrived immigrant whose hunger and whose color are thought to give him a better title to the place."

Booker T. Washington said, "Now is the time, not in some far-off future, but now is the time, for us as a race to ... do our part in owning, developing, manufacturing, and trading in the natural resources of our country. If we let these golden opportunities slip from us in this generation, I fear they will never come to us in like degree again. Let us act ... before it's too late, before others come from foreign lands and rob us of our birthright."

David Walker said, "How strange it is to see men of sound sense, and of tolerably good judgment, act so diametrically in opposition to their [own] interest." To paraphrase Dr. Earl Trent, author of "A Challenge to the Black Church," Blacks are taught to "love everybody, especially whites and other groups," but we are not taught to "love one another," especially ourselves.

Illegal immigration has leaped to the forefront of the public discourse as though it just arrived; it has been going on for decades, but Black people, and the issues that keep us at the bottom of the economic heap, have been around for centuries. I say, "first things first." Black people had better help themselves, with or without the alliances and those who acknowledge that our struggle has helped them, even though they paid no price for it.

The 13th 14th and 15th Amendments were written for Black people, not minorities, and until we stop playing in the minority game, Black people will continue and will forever lose. And the constant refrain of Muestrame el Dinero will ring throughout the land, for everyone else except us.

Animal Farm—The Black Version
July '05

YOU MAY REMEMBER ANIMAL FARM, THE 1945 classic written by George Orwell. Many in my generation had to read the book in high school. Over the years, I have come to see the relevance of the message in Animal Farm, even more as I look at the condition of our people.

The book is centered on the dissatisfaction of farm animals who felt they were being mistreated by Farmer Jones. Led by the pigs, the Animals revolted against their human masters, and after their victory they decide to run the farm themselves on egalitarian principles. The pigs become corrupted by power and a new tyranny is established. That famous line, "All animals are equal, but some animals are more equal than others" still rings true, even among Black people.

Is white racism the bane of Black society? Or, is Black *"classism"* more debilitating to our progress? I just finished reading The Head Negro in Charge, by Norman Kelley, reminiscence of E. Franklin Frazier's Black Bourgeoisie, and Harold Cruse's Crisis of the Black Intellectual, which also reminded me of Orwell's book. I highly recommend his book to all of you. Brother Kelley makes his case with an unapologetic, equal-opportunity, callout session of some of our Black leaders, their penchant for self-aggrandizement, and their individual prosperity rather than our collective economic progress.

But back to Animal Farm. As he looked back on his Talented Tenth concept, W.E.B. DuBois realized his "exceptional men" saw their position at the top of the Black food chain as an end rather than a means. In other words, once they reached the pinnacle of what they deemed to be success, they made no attempt to reach down and pull the other 90% up. DuBois lamented that he had underestimated the "power of [their] selfishness over sacrifice."

In our current state, because we have not rallied our "best and brightest" Black folks, or should I say because they have not rallied themselves around using their tremendous wealth of intellectual—and financial—resources to help their people, we continue to languish and our economic fate is all but sealed. No, I am not blaming the entire "state" of Black folks on the Black elite, Cosby's remarks about the "lower economic" class of Blacks notwithstanding.

What I am drawing upon is my personal experience with those Blacks (oops! I should have used a small "b"—I apologize) who repeatedly stand in the way of their brothers' and sisters' collective economic progress. With all of the status reports coming out for the *umpteenth* time, which tell us that Black Americans are still at the bottom of every economic category, my experience with the opposing side of Cosby's "lower economic" people brings me to the conclusion that class has caused major schisms among our people.

If you honestly assess our situation, you will find that many of those who benefit from the battles fought by the "lower economic" people often disappear when their resources are needed by those who fight for them everyday. You will also see Orwell's famous line relative to equality running deep within this elite class of black folks. Many of our brothers and sisters think they are more equal than others of us.

The sobering reality is that if these upper class elites get caught in the wrong place at the wrong time, or if they get themselves into trouble with the law, or if they do or say something their white superiors do not like, they will get their wake-up call. They will see that they cannot be promoted from being Black; they cannot move away from being Black; they cannot graduate from being Black' and they cannot get enough money to change them from being Black.

The most important thing is that we cannot, should not, and must not deny who we are, and we should understand that if anyone is going to lift us out of the muck and mire, it will be us, by the "work of our own hands." Since we comprise only 14% of this nation's population, it is only logical that we must work together, rich and poor, old and young, light-skinned and dark-skinned, straight-haired and curly-haired, upper and lower economic groups, to obtain and sustain our collective economic freedom.

To think and act as though some of us are "more equal" than others puts us in the same category as the pigs who, after the revolt by all of the farm animals, took control and ended up treating their brother and sister animals just as badly as Farmer Jones did. The pigs failed to realize that they were farm animals as well, which was the common factor that brought them together to revolt in the first place. They soon forgot how they rose to power and status.

Our common factor is Blackness, not just on the outside, but a Blackness that is dictated and supported by our consciousness, our culture, and our commitment to future generations. We must not get hung-up on who has the most intellect, because if the intellectuals are only talking and not getting some dirt on their hands trying to solve our problems, their words ring hollow.

We cannot make deities of our rich and famous simply because they have a lot of money, because if they are not using some of their money and influence to move us forward then they are merely Black folks who have a lot of money. Also, we cannot make superstars of slick-talking, fashion-plate pastors, because they will lead us to their own prosperity and leave ours behind.

No matter what you have or what you know, you are not "more equal" than any one of us.

Gas Prices—Complain, Restrain, and Sustain
May '07

HERE WE GO AGAIN WITH ANOTHER "Gas Out Day" on May 15, 2007 and a plan to "hurt" Exxon/Mobil, a company that earned (or did they steal it?) a $36 billion profit in one year, the highest ever in the history of America. Here we go again with the hand-wringing but yet accepting the straight-up thievery by the likes of guys who receive $400 million in annual salary and stock options. Here we go again ignoring the fact that our so-called politicians, while they are so concerned about the security of Iraq, don't have that same level of concern for the people of this country who are steadily being ripped-off by greedy, immoral, unethical oil barons. Here we go again.

There are a couple of plans floating around the Internet to counteract this new form of "highway robbery." One plan says we should not pump gas on May 15th. Question: What difference does it make if the gas thieves get our money on the 14th the 15th or the 16th of the month? So we skip a day, then what? Back to business as usual?

The other plan has been around for a couple of years. It suggests we stop buying Exxon/Mobil in order to drive their prices down. With $36 billion in profit for one year, you better believe Exxon/Mobil can stay in the game much longer than we can. Besides, they sell gas to other local outlets, thus, we could be buying their gas anyway.

Jesse Jackson's latest plan is to purchase oil company stock and ask them for jobs for "women and minorities." A lot of good that will do at the gas pump. I prefer Brother Cedric Muhammad's (blackcoffeechannel.com) call for "economic militancy to compliment political activism."

This gasoline situation is a planned get-richer-than-rich scheme by the few oil companies that run the industry. They make billions while the consumer gets gouged. Where I live there is a BP, a Speedway, a Shell, and a Marathon station all within 100 yards of one another. Did they all get the same phone call at the same time saying, "Raise your price to $3.19"? It's funny how they all get the same call to raise their price to the same amount, but they don't seem to get the same call when it's time to lower their prices. One went to $3.09, one went to $3.12; you know the deal.

Collusion abounds in the gas industry and we are the prey. The executives of these companies have no ethical constraints and no concern for their consumers. They are nothing less than criminals who have not yet gone to jail.

Where does this leave the consumer who is struggling to find the ends, much less to make the ends meet? Was it Tip O'Neill who said, "All politics is local"? Well, all economics is local too. Let's organize efforts in every city to refrain from buying gasoline at two or three particular outlets. We should do so until their prices drop to a point where it will be beneficial to switch back to their stations; and I don't mean a price drop of a few pennies.

The stations we sanction will either lower their prices to draw us back to them, or they will go out of business for lack of support. Once we put some of these stations out of business we will see a change in the way others treat us as consumers. Yes, it will take some sacrifice and inconvenience, but $4.00 or $5.00 per gallon gas will be a greater inconvenience and cause even more sacrifice.

Consumer action is the only thing that will curb these crooks' behavior, and we have to do it on a local level. How in the world do we expect to hurt Exxon/Mobil on a macro level? All Exxon has to do is give a donation to some Black folks for a conference or buy a few banquet tables at a Black event, and they are back in our good graces.

If we want lower prices for our gas we must be willing to fight. Basic economics tells me that when supply is high, price goes down. Well, let's increase the supplies of a few local gas stations, by refusing to purchase from them, and watch their prices go down. Then let's return our business to them and refuse to purchase gas from the other thieves. At least we can pick the thief we want to do business with and get a few concessions at the same time.

Finally, there are other things we must do, but you already know what they are. In summary, as we complain about them we must exercise some restraint in our own lives. Cut back on trips, stop buying those "gas hogs," carpool, walk, ride a bike, ride the bus, and cut back on other activities, which will have a negative impact on industries and businesses that are not in the gasoline business. The more folks who hurt, the more folks who complain, the wider the pain is spread, the quicker the remedy will come.

You and I know this gasoline game is nothing but a worldwide shell game. Hugo Chavez knows it too, and now that he is taking more control of his country's oil reserves, our "leaders" are telling us to expect even higher prices, as if we don't know they only want to further demonize Chavez. I think Black folks should be cutting a deal with him. Maybe we could get some brothers and sisters to open gas stations and pump Chavez' gasoline at a much lower price than we are paying now. That way we could benefit on both sides of the economic equation. Anybody out there have connections with Brother Hugo?

Complaining alone will not bring gas prices down; we must be willing to show more restraint in our consumption, we must be willing to sacrifice, and punish the crooks in the gasoline business. We must do this on a local level and, rather than going back to sleep when prices drop, we must sustain our actions and keep up the pressure year round.

Spreading the pain of high gas prices
May '07

LET ME SEE IF I CAN say this a little stronger than I did the last time. Economics is local! Until we make a point of doing more than complaining and calling for symbolic gestures to protest high gasoline prices—along with conservation, of course, Exxon/Mobil, Conoco Phillips, Chevron, Shell, and British Petroleum will continue to laugh at us and do whatever they want with their prices. Just as the crooks at Enron did in California when they caused an artificial hike in energy prices, the gasoline crooks are doing the same thing to us now.

Until we get serious in our outrage and really do something drastic, like causing a few gas stations to either close or lower their prices due to the excess supplies they will have when we refuse to purchase gas from them, we will continue to get ripped-off. I know the local stations, for the most part, do not control this, but who else do you deal with when it comes to gas prices? Like George Bush and his crew say about the tens of thousands of innocent Iraqis killed thus far, "The casualties of war."

For the life of me, I do not understand why we continue to come up with empty, meaningless, gestures to let crooks know we don't like their actions. Don't you think they already know that? Gas Out Day, May 15th, on which I did participate by not buying gas, was symbolic and really meant nothing to the gasoline industry thieves. Where I live, the price per gallon on May 14th was $3.19; on May 15th the price was $3.29. Gotcha!

The gas crooks just raised the price in the correct anticipation that many would still need gas, thus, they made even more profits on Gas Out Day than they would have on any other day. And just think what they made on May 16th. Knowing that we consumers are so undisciplined and dare not ever inconvenience ourselves by organizing a real gas out effort, they played us for the suckers we are-again. Now, just one week after May 15th, they are paying us back for our temerity of trying to retaliate against them; they raised prices even higher, to $3.49-$4.00+ per gallon.

I can see them now, like that TV commercial with the fat-cat bankers eating shrimp and playing golf while they chide a small business owner who wants a loan, "Well show those stupid consumers who's the boss. And our excuse, this time, despite oil prices being low, will be that our refineries need repairs." After all, they suffered damage during Katrina. "But that was two years ago," said the stupid consumers. "Don't bother us with minor details," the fat-cats responded, as they continued to count their $72 billion in profits.

We love Martin Luther King so much. Every year we repeat his "I Have a Dream" speech and his "I've Been to the Mountaintop" speech. Since we love him so much and believe in what he said, let me see if I can get us to DO something he said. Read the following excerpt of his "Mountaintop" speech on the evening before he was killed.

"Now the other thing we'll have to do is this: Always anchor our external direct action with the power of economic withdrawal. Now, we are poor people, individually, we are poor when you compare us with white society in America. We are poor. Never stop and forget that collectively, that means all of us together, collectively we are richer than all the nations in the world, with the exception of nine. Did you ever think about that? ... That's power right there, if we know how to pool it.

We don't have to argue with anybody. We don't have to curse and go around acting bad with our words. We don't need any bricks and bottles, we don't need any Molotov cocktails, we just need to go around to these stores, and to these massive industries in our country, and say, 'God sent us by here, to say to you that you're not treating his children right. And we've come by here to ask you to make the first item on your agenda fair treatment, where God's children are concerned. Now, if you are not prepared to do that, we do have an agenda that we must follow. And our agenda calls for withdrawing economic support from you.'

And so, as a result of this, we are asking you tonight, to go out and tell your neighbors not to buy Coca-Cola in Memphis. Go by and tell them not to buy Sealtest milk. Tell them not to buy—what is the other bread?—Wonder Bread. And what is the other bread company, Jesse? Tell them not to buy Hart's bread. As Jesse Jackson has said, up to now, only the garbage men have been feeling pain; now we must kind of redistribute the pain. We are choosing these companies because they haven't been fair in their hiring policies; and we are choosing them because they can begin the process of saying, they are going to support the needs and the rights of these men who are on strike. And then they can move on downtown and tell Mayor Loeb to do what is right."

Can't you see what King was doing? Can't you see how his words are instructions for us today? Can't you see that we must use the power of withdrawing our dollars, not for just a day, but for the long haul? Spread that pain, not only within the local industry but in entertainment, restaurants, recreation, and the like. As many people as possible should feel the bite of gas price-gouging.

Organize an effort and refuse to purchase gas at just a few local stations, especially those that are corporate-owned, and, as the pain starts to spread, sit back and watch what happens next.

We Demand; They Supply
June '04

"If there had been no poverty in Europe, then the white man would not have come and spread his cloths in Africa." **Asante Proverb**

"But I must own, to the shame of my own countrymen, that I was first kidnapped and betrayed by some of my own complexion, who were the first cause of my exile and slavery; but if there were no buyers there would be no sellers." **Ottobah Cugoano, 1787**

(Both quotes taken from, The History of Black Business in America, by Juliet E.K. Walker.)

IT SEEMS THE REAL LAW OF supply and demand, when it comes to the so-called "Black Community," is "We demand, so you had better supply." And, according to recent statistics, the original principles of supply and demand do not apply to our consumer group; we will pay the price no matter how high it goes, as a matter of fact the higher the better, and we don't seem to care how low or how high the supply goes; we want our stuff and we want it right now. What a dangerous twist on the basic law of economics. Too bad it doesn't also apply when it comes to Black support of Black owned businesses.

Can you imagine what suppliers of the Black consumer market must be saying as they hear and see us demanding they supply more and more stuff for our conspicuous consumption habit? I can hear them laughing now, as they gleefully count their daily receipts from demand-crazed Black purchasers of 24-inch rims that keep spinning when their truck stops, Black tourists who are always willing to turn their money over for the finer things life, such as top-shelf liquor, suites and meetings in hotels we don't own, and admission to events we do not control.

We demand everything and supply very few of our own material desires. We demand that Arab grocery stores in our neighborhoods sell us good meat and treat us courteously, but we fail to take advantage of the same opportunity they exploited by starting our own grocery stores. We demand the latest designs for our nails, and decry the Vietnamese for taking over the industry in less than ten years, while many of our sisters walk past the Black owned nail shop on their way to do business with someone else.

We demand the best service and response from a Black business person, paying attention to every detail of their business practices, and yet we go into major department stores each week knowing we are being watched because we are Black.

We demand "concessions" from convention bureaus in exchange for our tourism dollars, and they supply us with everything we demand, such as sumptuous banquets fit for Henry VIII, chauffeur-driven limousines, and fruit baskets in our rooms. In extreme cases we allow them to invest, say, $400,000 in pitching and wooing us, as was the case with the National Baptist Convention U.S.A., in exchange for a $21 million return on their investment! In the publications they bragged about landing such an economic plum; a Black preacher even said "This is good for the African American community."

We demand reciprocity in the marketplace; they supply donations to our annual dinners. We demand fairness and equity from our tax dollars; they supply "economic inclusion goals" for "minorities" that never come to fruition for Black people—and we fall for it every time.

We demand better schools with all the bells and whistles, and they build them with our tax dollars passing the economic benefits on to their companies and their families. We demand all the accoutrements in the finest prisons anywhere in the land, and they supply us with a prison industrial complex second to none—while reaping billions, of course, building them and supplying their needs. As we demand 25% set-aside programs, they supply padded construction contracts to their friends and relatives and sweetheart deals that add millions to their wealth. Oh yes, they throw in the usual token contracts to the same token "minorities;" and the beat goes on.

Black Empowerment with Attitude!

A Black construction company owner told me the situation in his city was so terrible that if Jesus paid them a visit He would think white folks were our slaves, because they were doing all of the work in Black neighborhoods. That's funny, but the same would be true where I live as well. We have a billion-dollar school construction program in progress, and you can count on one hand the Black workers on the individual construction sites—right in the middle of 100% Black neighborhoods!

Yes, we demand and they supply. Our demands are so vehement and urgent that we have become personified profit margins, across the board, for virtually every business area in this country. We demand to be served, and we are being served up by our timid, weak, greedy, so-called leaders. We demand to be treated properly, but oftentimes mistreat one another. We demand all of the things we need and want in life, but we are reluctant to supply those needs and wants to ourselves.

Other groups in this country are using us to create wealth for their families by supplying what we demand. Black people must decide to get on the supply side of this economic equation; we must decide to take control of more of our resources and stop selling them to the lowest bidder. We must decide to create a demand for our supplies by supporting our own businesses and growing them into bigger and better businesses.

There is no reason, except for lack of will, that Black folks could not have several billion-dollar businesses. How? By simply supplying more of our own demands for food, clothing, shelter, entertainment, and all the other niceties of life that we love so much.

James Clingman

Black Economic Insurance Policies
Oct. '04

NO DOUBT YOU HAVE HEARD ABOUT the various insurance companies being sued because they misled and cheated Black consumers. I remember my great-grandmother religiously paying her few cents on her debit policy in the 1950's; every Saturday when the agent came to the door she handed him the payment and he wrote it in a little book that she kept. Of course, when she died there was no money at the end of that policy. What was it that made our elders care so much about paying those premiums? You may not have noticed, but we do the same thing today.

Why are some of our people still paying for "policies" while not receiving anything in return for their money except a promise? To what kinds of policies am I referring? Well, there's the one that signs us up for, say, $25.00 per month, and then promises to be there when we need a legal service. There is also the kind that promises good health if we would just pay a small amount every month, or the one that offers us millions of dollars in return for a mere $29.95 per month, of course, you can pay it in a lump sum if you choose.

These are the modern-day insurance policies that are sold to Black people—and others, of course, that for the most part are never used or redeemed. These policies never pay off, not even when you die. We pay the premiums into a pool of reserves that create and maintain wealth for other people but never translate into wealth for our people. Sure, there are the "success stories" they always parade out for potential policyholders, but the chances are slim to none that a cancelled check, such as the one they always let you see, will ever be in your bank account. Yet we sign up to pay for a policy we trust will pay-off one day and carry us to that promise land of riches we dream about.

Black consumers pay into an array of "policies" owned and controlled by non-Black companies or individuals. Some may be good and some may pay-off, but the point is that we do it and promote them as if they belong to us and as if they actually will help our people. They may help YOU as an individual, but as for the Black collective, I don't think so.

I remember Brother Ken Bridges telling me that after reaching the highest level in a nationally known multi-level organization he walked away from it. "Why would you do that?" Ken and his wife were asked by friends and associates. Ken told me that after he discussed with top management the possibility of adding some component that would help empower Black folks, and being turned down, he left the organization.

He left because the policies they were selling had no positive, long term, collective economic effect on his brothers and sisters. Sure, Ken and his family were earning a tremendously good living, but he was concerned that there was no way the masses of Black consumers could truly benefit from what he was involved with. He knew that ownership of income-producing assets such as distribution channels, manufacturing concerns, and other businesses were necessary for Black people to move forward collectively. Ken also knew, as Martin Delany told us, that our economic prosperity had to come from the work of our own hands.

Ken Bridges was a rare brother, a Marcus Garvey type brother, who put the welfare of his people before his own, so I am not suggesting that every Black person will or even should do the same as he did. What I am suggesting is that we consider the ways we are spending our money by taking a look at the "policies" we pay for very month, and start putting more of our money into policies that Black folks write. Let's pay some premiums to ourselves for a change.

Just as we pay for our life insurance policies to pass something on to our families, especially our children, when we die, we should also be willing to pay on a collective policy that will strengthen and sustain our children and their children long after we are gone. Our conspicuous consumption of everyone else's products and services are essentially economic insurance policies for those who own the businesses we support. If we would support our own businesses and pay more of our premiums to them—to ourselves—we could build an economic future for our beneficiaries.

Beware of so-called Black leaders who stand up and promote Black support of companies that require us to pay premiums on "insurance policies" sold by everyone else. Beware of them, especially if they do not also promote Black owned companies that have the same kinds of "policies," "memberships," "monthly purchasing plans," etc. You should at least question why they are advocating for non-Black businesses and not advocating for businesses owned by their brothers and sisters.

Black people must not repeat the mistakes of the past by paying monthly "insurance premiums" to everybody except ourselves. Monthly payments to Black businesses, through purchasing and memberships, and monthly payments to Black organizations via local investment and loan funds for OUR businesses, will lead us to collective economic prosperity. Let's leave some paid-up "collectible insurance policies" for our children.

Dumb Stuff

"Black purchasing power is now at [$750 billion]...but Black economic influence and its benefits aren't commensurate with this purchasing power."

—Marian Wright Edelman

C'mon now, you have to admit that some of the things we do are just plain dumb, right? I sit and wonder sometimes how we get into some of the situations we discuss so much. I jokingly and lovingly ask the question: "Did we go to school to get this way, or did it just come naturally?

We may not want to freely admit it, but stupidity is present when it comes to various situations in which we find ourselves. Of course, we can find stupidity within all groups of people, but the name of this book is "Black" Empowerment.

Like many others, I have done some stupid things in my life, and I wonder how I am still around after committing some of the dumbest acts ever. When I think about it, I actually feel scared, even though it's all in the past. The reward of being stupid, if we survive our stupidity, is learning from it. Have we learned anything from the dumb things we have done to our economic status in this country? Have we learned from the mistakes we have made?

During the days of segregation, Black people did some stupid things, but at least we had our own economic base, our own safety net, to rely upon. Having established benevolent societies, cooperative purchasing associations, banks, colleges and universities, girls and boys clubs, orphanages, insurance companies, food co-ops, and everything else we needed to survive, we gave ourselves a little cushion, a little space to make some mistakes.

Now, with far fewer collective resources than we had prior to 1965, we cannot afford to be stupid in any area of life, most especially economic empowerment. As we take a look at some of the dumb stuff we have done and still do, let's make a commitment to stop it; let's make a commitment to change the way we do business—with one another especially, but also with the world.

As you read these next essays please take an honest look at yourself and at us as a people. Do an assessment of our progress, past and present, within the entire spectrum of collective and cooperative opportunities available to Black people. Take a close look and see if there is room for vast improvement in how we conduct ourselves in this land of the "free." If your assessment agrees with and maybe even proves the points made in the following section of this book, then get busy to help make appropriate changes.

Let's renew our strength and rebuild our communities. Let's put an end to the dumb stuff and get on to the practical and necessary work that lies ahead.

Chasing the Illusion of Equality
Aug. '04

"SEEMINGLY, OUR BIGGEST OBJECTIVE IS TO *be equal, but this is not the answer to our issues. The problem is that they want to keep us striving to be equal to take our minds off of the real problems, and if we never discover the real problem they can keep the control and keep us right where they want us.*" This quote was taken from an e-mail I received from Celeste Wakely, a member of the Blackonomics Million Dollar Club (BMDC), regarding knowing our history and acting upon that knowledge. She stressed the importance of using what we know about economics to elevate ourselves rather than spending all of our money to elevate others. Her assessment of our continued quest for "equality" hits the mark.

What does this "equality" thing mean to Black folks anyway? The Urban League boasts of an "Equality Index" that shows us what we already know: That Black folks are still behind whites in economic terms as well as other areas. Well, that's been in force since we came to this country. Whites had an affirmative action program that entitled them to everything and entitled Blacks to nothing. For years, the Urban League has also published a letter from its President, titled, "To Be Equal." I don't know what it means, but that's the title; it sounds like an aspiration, a goal, or a petition of some kind.

As Celeste says, we keep chasing "equality" with absolutely no chance whatsoever to attain such a lofty ideal, while other groups never even mention being "equal" with white folks. They just come to this country and get busy making money by starting businesses and capturing segments of industry, especially those in which Black folks spend millions of dollars.

White people go about their business, handing out tokens of appreciation for our loyalty every now and then, sponsoring all the entertainment we can stand, with the ultimate goal of cutting off all rational communication among Blacks and by keeping our attention focused on anything that has do with singin', rappin', dancin', and tellin' jokes about one another. Oh yes, they want us to concentrate on playin' games, jumpin' real high in those new gym shoes, drivin' shiny cars and trucks, and drinkin' soda pop and liquor too. They want us to keep stylin' and chillin', and don't forget about the killin,' y'all.

All of this negative, meaningless, and diversionary behavior, as Black people go about the business we feel is really important: Gaining equality. You'd think we would know by now that equality s nothing more than a *nirvana pipe-dream* that will never be realized. Even more importantly, Black people in America should put the quest for equality on the shelf, permanently, and get busy on a quest for economic empowerment.

Whites own and control the vast majority of the resources of this country. As the Urban League annual report points out—every year—there are widening gaps between Blacks and whites when it comes to family net worth, wages and employment, home ownership, criminal justice, bank loans, and the list goes on and on. Yet, we chase "equality." Whites claim "reverse" discrimination and graciously allow Blacks to be "economically included" in taxpayer funded projects. Yet, we chase "equality." Whites treat Black life with irreverence and kill us for reaching for cell phones. (Is that why we kill one another so easily and in record numbers? Trying to be equal with them?) Yet, we chase "equality."

Whites run the political system, the economic system, the social system, the educational system, and the legal system. Do we really believe they are about to help Black people "To Be Equal" with them? How naïve are we? Or, maybe it's a question of how lazy we are. We should be doing the things that a nation within a nation does to develop and maintain its own economic foundation. You know, like the Vietnamese who went to what used to be called Westminster, California, which is now called "Little Saigon;" In case you *Sistahs* haven't noticed, they control the Nail Industry now.

But there is some good news on the Black front. Have you heard about the project in Detroit? I am told the City Council voted 7-2 to bring in Dr. Claud Anderson and his Powernomics business development program. It's a drop in the bucket at $30 million, but it is a start and could be the precursor for many other initiatives across this country for Black people. It is also a great example of nation-building. After all, Detroit's population is overwhelmingly Black, isn't it? (I also heard that the celebrated young Black Mayor of Detroit made an unsuccessful attempt to stop the project. Is that true, Detroiters? Why?)

All things not being equal, chasing the illusion of equality and trying "to be equal" with white folks is an exercise in futility and keeps our attention diverted from other more important issues for Black people in this country. But, since many of us will probably continue to try to "measure up" and meet the standards of others, when it comes to economics among demographic groups and consumer segments, let's just forget about "equality." Maybe "parity" is a better word.

An update on "Maroon City," Dr. Claud Anderson's Project in Detroit:

As of the Spring of 2007, Dr. Anderson's project was scrapped after he discovered that "neither the City nor the State owned the site they were selling [to him], therefore, the company could not issue clear title or provide title insurance." (Read the entire article and Dr. Anderson's letter to the Detroit City Council in the Summer 2007 edition of the Harvest Institute Report—www.harvestinstitute.org.

Dr. Anderson decided it was futile and a waste of time and financial resources to continue to pursue the project, which would have resulted in a Black economic enclave in the Black city of Detroit. So much for Black political leadership.

All is not lost, however. Dr. Anderson took his business venture to Maryland's Eastern Shore and has opened the "Nation's first seafood factory," according to the Harvest Institute Report. "WaterLand Fisheries is a vertically integrated, Black owned business that will raise a variety of top-quality fish indoors in state-of-the-art tanks, in environmentally controlled conditions." Take that, Detroit!

Considering all the fish and other seafood that Black folks consume, maybe this is just the beginning of a number of business ventures Black people will establish. Now all of you restaurant owners and food stores get on the horn and call WaterLand to get your place in line for "fresh homegrown" seafood. With all of the chemicals and pesticides being found in our "imported" fish, Dr. Claud Anderson's venture looks absolutely wonderful, and it is literally just what the doctor ordered.

Dumbing-Down Black America
May '06

MUCH OF WHAT I HEAR, SEE, and read in Black media these days is an insult to Black people. Entertaining to some, no doubt, but still insulting. Knowing that very few positive messages are coming from so-called "mainstream" media, you would think our Black media would take up the slack and do more to uplift, enlighten, and educate our people rather than acquiesce to the desires of those who control the vast majority of the media outlets in this country.

You would think that, at a very minimum, Black owned and operated media would make a firm commitment to smarten us up rather than dumb us down with silly, meaningless, empty messages and images that only capitulate to the status quo. You would think... But, as Brother Glen Ford of Black Commentator once chided me for wrongly assuming that Black-owned media are really Black conscious media, and for suggesting we secure more of the same, Black media ain't necessarily Black, is it?

Like many of our Black politicians, much of our Black media are really doing a job on us by keeping a wide range of Black folks, especially our children and young adults, uniformed, misinformed, and just plain dumb. Watch that white-owned outlet we call Black Entertainment Television; listen to some of the conversations on some of these so-called Black radio stations; read some of the absolute junk in some of our pseudo-Black newspapers, magazines, and websites. You will see that we are, as our elders used to say, "Going out of the world backwards."

Having been a guest on many radio shows, and a several television shows, across the country, I can attest to the fact that there are media hosts who do not fall into the dumbing-down category. I desperately want to name them for you, but I know I will omit someone. If you really want to change the messages going into your brain, you can find them; it's not that difficult to do.

One of the first things you can do is use your critical thinking skills to determine the validity and usefulness of what you listen to on these shows. Don't just settle for the entertainment aspect. As a conscious person, ask yourself what the benefit is to listening or watching certain material. Remember: "Garbage in, garbage out." If we are getting a daily mega-dose of nonsense, of falsehoods, of non-educational clap-trap and slap-stick, it's no wonder we are so far behind in serious aspects of economic empowerment. It's no wonder we seldom follow through with initiatives that will make us stronger, as individuals and as a collective.

In case you didn't know, as Booker T. Washington once said, "There are some Negroes who don't want the patient to get well." Even today, there are those among us who want us to remain psychologically crippled; they want to keep us dancing to their beat and buying what they are selling. They want us to keep on bobbing our heads and shuffling our feet and guffawing throughout the day, oblivious to our plight and totally without a clue on how to fix it.

Thus, we get a barrage of jokes, self-deprecating comedy, and exploitation on television. We are on the receiving end of mindless "beats" that are pounded into our brains by 1200 watt speakers in the backseats of our cars. We are fed some of the most useless rhetoric, much of which is not even factual, by brothers and sisters on the radio who obviously have no idea what they are talking about. And, as we read our Black newspapers, we are ensconced in a lifelong dream of hitting the number, getting psychic readings, or checking our horoscopes before we make a move.

Even in the spiritual marketplace, we are the subjects, or should I say fodder, of hucksters who want to sell us God's blessings, as if they have cornered the market on His grace. It's fascinating that on Sunday mornings we can find a white "preacher" on BET selling us a quarter-ounce vial of miracle water that will cure sickle-cell disease, all for the low cost of $206.00. Of course, if you send him more money, well, you know the deal.

Black Empowerment with Attitude!

Brothers and sisters, isn't it bad enough that we are being dumbed-down by white folks? Why do we except the same thing from our own people? We must do better than that. Take politics. What do you think of the statement attributed to the ex-footballer, Lynn Swann? "I certainly believe that George W. Bush is the most qualified and most credible candidate to fulfill the role as president of the United States." Now, I didn't hear Swann say that, I just read that he said it. But if he did say that, in light of what we have experienced over the past five years from the Bushman, why should anyone, Blacks especially, vote for Swann to be their governor?

We had better take stock of what is going on in this country, right in our own backyards. There are Black folks who control media outlets that do not operate in the best interests of Black people. Why would you support them—in any way? They do not want us to get well, nor do they care if we ever get well. The next time you find yourself wasting your valuable time ingesting their mind-numbing potion, remember this saying: "When the ax enters the forest, the trees view the handle as one of their own." Just because it's Black on the outside, doesn't mean it's Black on the inside.

Buffoonery, Exploitation, and Taboo
Jan. '07

THAT'S WHAT BET MEANS TO ME. The so-called "Black" entertainment network, owned by Viacom, is immersed in at least 20 hours per day of videos, hype, jokes, Black-folks-in prison movies, expletives, "Beefs," gangsters, and even snake-oil selling preachers offering blessings in a bottle. And we wonder why so many of our youth act the way they do. Admittedly, BET is not the entire problem; but it's sure not <u>any</u> of the solution either. Impressionable youth are being negatively programmed everyday by this money-machine called BET, and all most of us do is complain about it.

It's true that parents should keep their children away from TV trash and teach them better; but we also have an obligation to confront the perpetrators. How do we do that? Glad you asked. Stop buying the stuff their selling, and let those who are selling it know your feelings about the negative programming. Also, write to them and let them know your dissatisfaction.

Remember when BET at least had several programs that were informative and helpful to Black people? News, interviews with folks we respected and appreciated, Lead Story, Bev Smith, Tavis Smiley, George Curry at Emerge Magazine, Jazz. At least our children could learn something of value from it. Old BET aired some ridiculous stuff too, but it wasn't as stupid as most of it is now.

Does that mean Viacom sees us as stupid, blind, conspicuous consumers who will go out and buy everything they advertise on BET? If we continue to buy the gold chains and medallions, "grills," spinners, plasma screens, cars, gym shoes, guns, athletic jerseys, champagne, liquor, and all the other things they see during the daily BET video orgy of excess and nothingness, the answer is obvious.

Black Empowerment with Attitude!

I think Viacom not only believes we're stupid, they believe we're stuck on stupid. They pipe in garbage, and we lap it up. They insult us and our children, especially our young women, and we insult ourselves by participating in our own exploitation,. And the monotonous beat goes on and on like the drumbeat of a new Bataan Death March.

Yes, I do remember when I was young and impetuous, and how I liked to watch things that were not necessarily in my own best interests. An honest assessment of my young life would reveal many of the same vulnerabilities and excesses as the young men today, relatively speaking. Each generation has its demons. But when we know better, we must do better—or no better for us. Many of our young people are sitting in jail right now because they followed through on something they saw on television. It was their choice, for sure, but that is no excuse for us, the adults who know better, not to speak out against things that influence their choices. My bad choices as a child do not exempt me from the responsibility of helping the younger generations make good choices.

Because this society is all about money, power, and material gain we are scraping the bottom of the garbage pit when it comes to providing our children with reasonable, attractive, and lucrative alternatives to much of the behavior we often get on their case about. Black people remain at the bottom of every economic category in this country, yet we allow our children to sit for hours watching Buffoonery, Exploitation, and Taboo, vicariously living the bling-bling life of the rich and famous.

Meanwhile, they cannot speak in complete sentences, and when they do you can't understand what they are saying. They know nothing about their history and culture, and their Black consciousness is nonexistent. They drop out of school by the thousands, and you and I both know what awaits them after that, right? Our youth need all the help they can get—from us—and a major part of that help must be our willingness to speak out against attempts by profiteers and biased media to brainwash them. Then we must be willing to economically punish those who use our young people as crash dummies for their own economic empowerment.

And you know what else we must do? Those of us who are supposed to be men and women, adults in every sense of the word, must portray the proper examples for our youth. If we tell them Buffoonery, Exploitation, and Taboo are bad, and they see us watching it, what kind of message are we sending to them?

I don't know about you, Black folks, but I am hurt and saddened by what I see in our youth, much of which emanates from media like BET. I know our young people are into a lot of other negative behaviors; I know they are running rampant in the streets and hurting one another. But I also know that, wherever and whenever I can, I must use whatever resources I have to try to save just one at a time. In order to do that, I cannot be afraid, neither can I be tepid in my response to folks who strive to mislead and exploit our youth.

Does all of this sound quixotic? Maybe it is; but our young people are worth it. Just as you and I of the older generations learned in our later years, we must pass on those lessons to our young brothers and sisters so they too may "get it" in their later years, if not sooner.

The supporters of BET will tell me about all the jobs and entertainment opportunities BET has provided over the years, and that's true. But can't BET do the same thing in a more positive way? It sure did years ago. Ask Donnie Simpson.

Stop allowing your children to be programmed by Buffoonery, Exploitation, and Taboo.

Media Bias vs. Media By Us
Aug. '05

DURING AN APPEARANCE ON AMERICA'S BLACK Forum, which dealt with selling Black owned businesses to white companies, we discussed, in particular, the sale of Essence Magazine to Time-Warner. I made the point that it is vital for conscious Black Americans to own and control media outlets in order to tell our own stories and to report the news from a Black perspective.

We complain a lot about the portrayal of Black people by dominant media outlets, but we continue to support them, and we continue to sell our media or use our own media to perpetuate stereotypical images of ourselves. Isn't it bad enough that for years we have been subjected to negative images of ourselves by others? Doesn't it make sense for us at least to make an effort to stop it?

A glaring example of this is the following observation by Frank W. Quillan, in 1910: "When a Negro commits a crime the newspapers always emphasize his race connection by such headlines as 'A Big Black Burly Brute of a Negro' does such and such, and the whole race gets a share of the blame; while if the crime is committed by a white man, race is not mentioned, and the individual gets the blame." Have things really changed from that scenario?

Nearly 100 years later Black folks in this country are still subjected to the same treatment in dominant media. But we already know that, don't we? The points I want to make in this article are two recent observations, which you may have also noticed, in USA Today.

The first was a story on how folks in Lexington, Kentucky perceived George Bush; it was titled, "Taking the Pulse of Bush's America." The writer interviewed several persons, and several photos accompanied the piece. The striking part of the article for me was the photo of a

Black woman talking to her granddaughter in front of a housing project called Bluegrass-Aspendale. The caption under the photo of 2 year-old Amoni Price and her grandmother, Jackie Price, stated, "Drugs, Crime, Vacancies…"

The subliminal and obvious messages in the article jumped off the page. I searched the article for comments from Jackie Price but found none; thus, they used a photo of a Black woman and associated that photo with the most negative aspects of the piece, and did not include comments from Ms. Price in the article. Some may think this is a minor concern, but the power of pictures cannot be overstated. Also, the article reminded me of Frank Quillan's words in 1910 which, by the way were referring to my hometown newspapers in Cincinnati. No surprise there.

The other observation I made is even more important. We have seen the accolades heaped upon John H. Johnson since his death; we have heard his story of starting with $500.00 in 1942 and creating the $500 million empire, Johnson Publishing Company. We know he was an icon in this country and his rise to the top was and still is one of the most significant feats in our history. Again, USA Today, on the same day it did a two-page feature on Peter Jennings, gave a relatively small space and, quite honestly, short shrift to John Johnson. We can debate the issue of who made the more significant contributions to this society; it's a relative perspective anyway, but I think it's incontrovertible that Johnson's accomplishments exceeded those of Jennings, especially when we consider the barriers Johnson faced.

Nonetheless, the real issue is how the two were treated in the same issue of the paper and, I might add by the dominant media in general. That is why Black people must own and control our media and the messages that come from them. For this very reason, our children cannot read about the Riot that took place in Tulsa's Black Wall Street in 1921 and other historically significant events that occurred to their relatives. It is why they do not read about the tremendous strides of Black business owners during the early existence of this country. An African saying is appropriate here: Until the lion writes history, the hunter will always be glorified.

I am not suggesting that Jennings was not a good man, a good reporter and Journalist, and a good news anchor. What I am saying is the John Johnson story was an opportunity for dominant media to display what it always says it is: Unbiased, fair, balanced, and all that other nonsense. Where are Emerge Magazine and George Curry when we need them?

What do I expect from them? Nothing. I do not expect dominant media to treat the images of Black folks any differently from the way it treated us in 1910. If they do, it will be a blessing, but I do not expect it. That is why we must support our own media, and I mean our own "conscious" Black media. Additionally, we must maintain what we have and capture even more outlets; we must grow those businesses by merging and forming strategic partnerships with one another; and we must resist the temptation to capitulate to offers from people who do not care about us when they come calling to take over what few media outlets we have. Quite frankly, were it not for a few radio shows, most Black newspapers, and a few magazines, positive Black images and fairness when it comes to Black news would be virtually nonexistent.

Our children know very little, if anything, about A.G. Gaston, Annie Turbo-Malone, S.B. Fuller, Joe Dudley, Dr. Walter P. Lomax, Sarah Washington, and other Black men and women, living and deceased, who have made monumental strides in the business world. This is in large part due to the dominant media and their lack of attention to these kinds of role models. It seems that our images have been reduced to dunking basketballs, running touchdowns, and making music videos.

We can overcome "Media bias" with "Media by us."

Rewarding Friends and Punishing Enemies
July '05

BLACK FOLKS HAVE IT ALL WRONG; we reward our enemies and punish our friends. We complain, demonstrate, and protest against the same folks we give our money to, in what amounts to payment for our own oppression. Those who stand up, speak up, and sometimes make the ultimate sacrifice in support of Black people, we run away from, deny, castigate, and even participate in shutting them up and shutting them down. We must reverse this scenario if we are going to make it in this country.

Many of us have experienced the negative aspects of standing up for Black people, and I am sure most of us have wondered why we have to fight against our own people in order to help save our race. But remember Harriet Tubman and Marcus Garvey, just to name two; they had the same problems. Remember Denmark Vesey, Gabriel Prosser, John Brown, and Nat Turner; Black folks told on them. So it is not surprising that we still do the same things to our warriors today. Thus, individually, we will continue to experience similar struggles among our people.

But how about the collective? How can we reverse the very sick practice of further enriching those who would just as soon wipe us off the face of the earth, at least move us out of this country, rather than simply speak to us on the street? How can we come to the point where we are, at a minimum, considered an economic and political threat, rather than some monolithic voting bloc just waiting to be exploited? How can we be perceived as something more than a humongous ATM machine where merchants can come and withdraw all the cash they want, no questions asked and no reciprocity given?

How can we reward our friends—politically and economically—with the resources we have at our disposal? And I do mean "disposal." I say we begin using the power of leverage a lot more than we do now. You have read several of my articles on the Collective Banking Group (CBG) and how well leveraging has worked for their church members. You probably know about cooperative food buying programs, collective farming organizations, and efforts by various groups that have prospered through the use of fiat money, that is, printing their own scrip ("Metros" by KemetWorld.com) to empower themselves via bartering. The examples abound.

I know you have information on political groups that have swayed major political decisions in their favor simply because they banded together. Look at all the think-tanks in Washington that lobby for what white folks want. Where are ours? Well, we have the Harvest Institute, but very few Black people support it. There is the Christian Coalition, the Moral Majority, the NRA, and all of those other groups that more times than not get what they want from politics. Where are our political institutions that bring home the "earmarks" for Black people?

All right, so where do we start? I will leave the political strategies to those who know more than I do about that area. As for the economic side, let's start with banks and insurance companies. I noted the CBG, which has set the example of how we can leverage our collective monetary resources via churches. Now when it comes to insurance companies, automobile and homeowners insurance, virtually everyone who pays feels the pain caused by these companies raising their rates simply because they can. They continue to rip us off, canceling our policies simply because we use them, and it seems there is nothing we can do about it. Well there is something we can do.

Just like the CBG only "allows" certain banks to do business with them, the same thing can be done with insurance companies. Groups can be formed in various cities that only deal with one or two insurance companies. Covenant agreements can be written and, if violated, the group no longer does business with that company. Leverage brings lower rates, greater benefits, and better treatment. The big three insurance companies are steadily raising their rates and canceling homeowners' policies. What are we going to do? Shall we continue to give them our money and just "hope" they won't cancel us whenever they feel the urge? We don't HAVE to do business with them, you know.

I can hear the Black folks now saying, "But I work for one of those companies; I can't participate in such an effort." That's fine. This is not for you then. This is for those Black folks who know that there have been reports describing how we have been discriminated against by banks, insurance companies, and real estate companies. If they have the nerve to tell the world they have mistreated us, and we stand by and do nothing about it, they have no incentive to change their ways. Again, this gets back to being willing to reward our friends and punish our enemies.

These insurance companies have rolled out their catchy phrases and slick television commercials about whose hands we're in, how good a neighbor they are, and whose side their on, and we lap it up like some kind of trained pet. We pay our premiums for years and have one claim, and they either raise that premium or cancel the policy. It makes no sense not to fight back, collectively, against this kind of treatment. The idea of Black folks forming groups to leverage good insurance rates is no different from teachers' unions, the AARP, and other associations doing the same thing for their members.

We had better take stock of our situation and realize that we are not liked by the folks who run this country and those who run major corporations. (Sorry if I burst your bubble) We must practice collective and cooperative economics and leverage what we have before we lose everything we have.

Black-on-Black Economic Violence
Oct. '04

"WHEN THE AX ENTERS THE FOREST, the trees view the handle as one of their own."

Where I live, there is constant hand-wringing in response to the physical degradation, retribution, and self-destructive behavior among our young brothers and sisters. We see homicide, suicide, fratricide, and everything in between. What are the causes of this madness? If you read Dr. Amos Wilson's book, Black on Black Violence, especially the parts regarding the economic side of things, you will see the correlations that exist between the physical violence and selling one's soul for a dollar or two.

You knew this had to get down to economics at some point, so let's jump right into it. I will not review Dr. Wilson's seminal work; he was a literary genius, and I would not do him justice. You need to get the book and read it for yourself, that is, if you really want to understand and then deal with the problem, rather than just complain about the symptoms. I will say, however, that Dr. Wilson did not place the entire blame for our self-inflicted violence on economics alone, but he did put both in proper perspective.

With that in mind, I want to talk about another form of Black on Black violence. It's Black on Black economic violence. While some of our high and mighty, socially elevated, Black "leaders" shamefully decry the physical violence taking place in "the Hood," they are busy cutting their deals and taking their cuts from deals made on the backs of their brothers and sisters.

Here's one example. Just when I thought I had seen it all, along came another in a long line of economic sanctions against a city, called by Black folks because they were not being treated right. In the spirit of the South African boycott that led to the demise of apartheid, buoyed by the memory of those who walked to work in Montgomery, established on the principles laid out in MLK's final speech in Memphis, Tennessee, inspired by the three year standoff in Miami, Florida, and motivated by Stevie Wonder's "Happy Birthday," which became the rallying cry against the State of Arizona, this new boycott was called.

This new boycott was against a city whose downtown white-owned restaurants closed during a weekend in which thousands of Black folks came to town to spend millions of dollars, a city that allows police abuse and brutality to go unabated with impunity, a city that spent billions in local and federal tax dollars with meager sums and benefits going to the nearly 50% Black population, and a city that denies First Amendment rights to "some" of its citizens.

Almost immediately after this boycott was called, out came the Black folks, with their smiling faces on brochures, saying, "We're on the Move," while subliminally suggesting to the world that everything was all right in this city, and Black people were as happy as *pigs in slop*. Of course, this massive PR campaign was done to stop the boycott; it was done in return for deals and perks given to Blacks who had their hands out and were obviously willing to do whatever the Mayor, Mister Charlie, told them to do.

The latest scene in this horror movie features five black (small "b") folks going on a mission to cajole the National Coalition of Black Meeting Planners (NCBMP) into believing this is a "new" city and that it is living up to its contrived "most livable" status. It is ironic that five of these black economic predators went out to solicit Black dollars for this city while five Black men lay cold in their graves, unjustifiably and wantonly killed by white police officers that have never been criminally punished nor ever will be in this city.

These five black people, one from the majority Chamber of Commerce, one from the Black Chamber of Commerce, one from the National Underground Railroad Freedom Center, one from, of all places, a local funeral home, all led by the "vice" Mayor of this city, had the temerity to ask Black people from across the country to bring their money to a city where Black people are grossly mistreated. Go figure.

Everyone has to answer to his or her own conscience, that is, if they have one, so this is for information only. I want both sides of the story to be told. My conscience will not allow me to be silent about the murders of five young men, however. I will continue to tell their story because they cannot, and just as vigorously as I work for economic freedom, I will continue to disclose economic injustice.

Montgomery Blacks boycotted for seats on buses; Arizona Blacks boycotted to get a King Holiday; South Carolina Blacks boycotted to get a flag removed; and Miami Blacks boycotted because Nelson Mandela was snubbed by public officials. The city I am referring to, of course, is Cincinnati, where Blacks boycotted primarily because of police violence against Blacks.

Looks like snubs, flags, holidays, and bus seats carry more weight for some black folks in Cincinnati than do the lives of five of their brothers, because this boycott has resulted in an even more dastardly brand of violence against Blacks: Economic violence committed by Blacks against Blacks.

A Letter to White Folks

"When it comes to the crunch, whatever the morality involved, Whites will stick by their fellow Whites."

—**Bishop Desmond Tutu**

I wrote this "Letter" as a follow-up to the "Letter" I wrote to Black people in 1999, which cited what Black folks had done for whites and others over the years. My initial thought was to recap all of the tragic occurrences and mistreatment perpetrated upon Black people since our arrival in this country, but that would have been a separate book in itself. Thus, I decided to write only about the last 100 years.

Just as my <u>Letter to Black Americans</u> caused some of us to be uncomfortable, my hope is that the <u>Letter to White Americans</u> will do the same, and that it will not only enlighten us but cause a ripple of change that soon will become a tsunami of goodwill.

It is important that our children know what took place in this country and "never forget" their connection and contribution to the tremendous progress in this land, as the first "Letter" pointed out They must also never forget the suffering, anguish, and torture our relatives endured simply because of their skin color.

This "Letter" provides an insight on pieces of our history that are seldom discussed. Read it and then share it with your children. They must be fully armed with the truth in order to deal with those who would teach them to believe that things weren't really "that bad" for Black people "back then."

Additionally, you may want to share it with your white friends and associates. C'mon, don't be scared. Discuss it, analyze it, and deal with its implications. Just as <u>The Letter to Black Americans</u> was not meant to denigrate Blacks, this Letter is not meant to simply dump on white people. Both Letters tell the truth, and that's the most important thing here.

My prayer is that we look closely at ourselves—all of us—in this country and as we acknowledge the good, the least of which has gone to Blacks, we also acknowledge the bad, most of which has been committed against Black people.

It's just the truth, folks. Let's all deal with it.

Dear White Americans (Especially White men)

SORRY FOR TAKING SO LONG TO respond to the now famous "Letter to Black Americans" you sent to us in 1999. We wanted to wait until all of our people had an opportunity to read your words of gratitude for all the things we have done for you in this country. That letter spread like wildfire, across the country and around the world, in newspapers and over the Internet. It was even printed in several books, and Fred Price, the noted Los Angeles minister, read it on his national television show and said it was "awesome." Let's pray this letter will get the same attention, acclaim, and response.

Your letter made some Black people angry, but the facts cited in it were more important, and we just had to face the reality of a past that was not very pleasant for our relatives. We agreed that what you were saying to us was true, so the next logical thing was to ask ourselves, "What are we going to do about it?" The Letter, also titled "Kudos to Black Americans," cited all the things Black people have done for everyone else in America since we first stepped foot on these shores. It was a "Thank You" letter, and it's only appropriate that we respond.

This letter, unfortunately, is not to say "Thank You;" rather it can be characterized as a call for introspection on your part, based on the past 100 years. That's right, just 100 years; we didn't want it to be too long. After all, it would take quite a long time to recount everything from the "Door of no return," to the middle passage, to the auction blocks, to the separating of our families, to the raping of our mothers, to the lynching, burning, torturing, maiming, and murdering of our fathers, to the charade of the emancipation, to denying our basic human rights, to two and a half centuries of free Black labor, and all of the other crimes you committed against Black people. Recounting 100 years is quite enough. So here we go. Hang on tight; it's gonna be a bumpy ride.

Black Empowerment with Attitude!

As we assess our situation today, three centuries since you arrived on these shores, we see a country that you have dominated. We see the results of egomania, greed, arrogance, disregard for human life, and disdain, especially for Black people. We see, at every turn, the results of your having been so steeped in having it all and using any measures to get it. We see your fingerprints on murderous acts, corruption, theft, lies, and deceit. You have been in charge of everything that has ever taken place in this country, and you are still in charge of everything today.

When we look at politics, we see white men making virtually all of the decisions. When we peer into our economic system, we see white men at the controls. When we sneak a peek at our educational structure, we see white men making the rules and passing them down to the rest of us. When we pull back the curtain that shrouds this nation's criminal justice system, we see white men in Black robes, white men in blue suits, and white men in uniforms dominating, controlling, and determining the futures of millions of Black people.

And when we watch the news, we see a preponderance of white men with microphones, sitting behind news desks, analyzing and giving their opinions and directives on where this country is going and how it will get there. In other words, you always have been, you are now, and you probably always will be at the helm of this ship of state (Hillary and Obama notwithstanding), and that is a privilege, not a right. After all, you are immigrants too. As a matter of fact, you are illegal immigrants. You came, you saw, you conquered, you stole, you killed. I wonder if those who lived here prior to your arrival felt your "invasion" was legal. Now you fight against the same thing. But, you know what they say. What goes around....comes around.

With privileges come responsibilities, and looking back over the years, yes, you have come up with some fantastic ideas and performed some outstanding feats, but you have neglected the awesome responsibility that comes with your power. You have done a lot of real bad things to a lot of people, but this is about what you have done to Black people. Let's take a closer look.

The 20th century ushered in the most progressive period for Black people in the history of America. Just 35 years out of slavery and our great-grandparents had established towns, built their own schools, carved out business enclaves in major cities, and had reestablished their entrepreneurial acumen throughout the business sector. All of that was done despite your continuous mistreatment of our people.

In 1900 Booker T. Washington started the National Negro Business League, characterized by W.E.B DuBois as having come along at the "correct psychological moment," and shortly thereafter you started your economic reign of terror against Black people in this country. It must have been due to how adept we were at establishing and growing our businesses. After all, if Black folks had their own businesses where would you get your workforce?

A little more than a decade later, you went to work and made some slick moves at a meeting on Jekyll Island, where you created the Federal Reserve, followed by the establishment of the I.R.S. Then your President, Woodrow Wilson, sacrificed the Lusitania ocean liner, along with its 1195 passengers, to draw us into the first World War, made a boatload of money for his friends, and even brought about a new world government (Now that sounds very familiar). Then Wilson invaded Haiti and demolished its constitutional system. He must have been subscribing to his Secretary of State's (Robert Lansing) belief that "the African race is devoid of any capacity for political organization and possesses an inherent tendency to revert to savagery and to cast aside the shackles of civilization which are irksome to their physical nature."

Any excuse, back then as well as today, for stealing money, land, and other resources, euphemistically called "interests" by your government, was fine with you. It's always been about your making more money, and you were on the move in the first 20 years of that century, making money "by any means necessary." Black people back then were also making money, by whatever means we had available to us.

Called the "Golden Age of Black Business," the first quarter of the 1900's saw Black folks taking care of business. Then you came along in

Black Empowerment with Attitude!

1921, with your tired *Black man touches White woman* excuse and dropped firebombs on the Greenwood District, known as Black Wall Street, in Tulsa, Oklahoma. Your mob massacred more than 300 people, shooting them down in the streets as they ran for their lives. Then you ransacked their homes and wiped out the entire Black community, destroying 600 businesses in the process. Although you promised reparations to the survivors of the Tulsa riot, to this day they have not received one dime for their families' losses. To make things even worse, you turned around and did the same thing in Rosewood, Florida, but at least they received a small sum of money for their mistreatment.

Why were you so mean and evil back then? Oh, I almost forgot. You did the same thing to Henry Boyd's furniture company in Cincinnati, Ohio-three times!-back in the 1800's, so what else could we expect in the 1920's, right?

A look at the 30's and 40's and we get a glimpse of things to come. Jim Crow, sharecropping, segregation, and the epitome of your hatefulness, lynching, were all the orders of the day. Sister Billie Holiday called us "Strange Fruit," but those brothers and sisters you hung from trees had names, they had loved ones, they had hopes and dreams just like you did.

In 1932, and for the next forty years, you committed one of your most racist and heinous acts by using hundreds of Black men in your infamous Tuskegee syphilis experiments. Why did you do that? Did you hate us that much? Yeah, you're right; you did apologize for it 65 years later in 1997.

During World War Two, we went to war for you, again, only to be treated like the three-fifths you declared us to be, and when we returned we still had to suffer degradation and insults from you, as we were placed beneath even the folks we had fought against—for you. How could you treat us that way, especially after everything we did for you and yours?

Maybe your actions of that period were the remnants of what caused you to brutally murder Mary Turner in 1918, down in Valdosta, Georgia. She was pregnant, but you doused her with oil and set her on fire. As she dangled from the lynching tree, you cut her baby from her womb and let it fall to the ground, where you proceeded to stomp the remaining life from its tiny body. What manner of man would do this? But then again, you did kill 200,000 or so in Hiroshima and Nagasaki, right?

On to the 1950's. After your dastardly, cowardly, and brutal murder of young Emmett Till, (again using the White Woman excuse) Blacks, and some white people, really got serious about fighting for our "civil rights." (Rather than civil rights, all we really needed was civility on your part, and we would have been much better off.) Things began to change in this country once again. National guardsmen, federal troops, and FBI investigators were sent to the south to make sure Black people could attend the schools of our choice, so we could vote, so we could earn a decent wage, and so we could be protected from being lynched if we made an attempt to exercise our rights. Remember Governor Orval Faubus, Sheriff Bull Connor, Governor George "Segregation now, segregation fo-eva" Wallace, and Lester "Pick Handle" Maddox (Probably related to "Pitchfork" Ben Tillman)? What a cast of characters they were!

Physical violence was the order of the day during that period, but it was soon augmented by something called "Urban Renewal," under the banner of "National Defense Highways," later called "expressways" or "freeways," to further destroy what Blacks had built. Running through or beside every Black community, these highways destroyed much of the commercial progress within those communities! This was the beginning of the end for Black communities. Was that your version of a chicken in every pot? With friends like you, who could ask for more?

Then came the violent 1960's. Black folks were truly mad by then; but so were you. We burned buildings; you killed people. We prayed in churches; and you bombed churches, killing four little Black girls—in a church! You made other attempts on the lives of many Black people and were successful in some cases. Old Byron De La Beckwith and Governor Ross Barnett down in Mississippi were determined to keep Black folks in their place even if they had to kill a few. You proudly bragged about getting that uppity Medgar Evers, and slaughtering those three young men, Schwerner, Goodman, and Chaney.

Talk about a piece of work, you guys took the cake back then; you even killed your own people! You killed your own President and covered it up with actions and lies that still boggle the mind! Remember Viola Liuzzo and James Reeb in Selma, Alabama? How about those innocent men, women, and children, walking across the Edmund Pettus Bridge, and you decide they can't proceed; you resort to cracking heads, and your actions were so brutal that they called it "Bloody Sunday." Do you ever feel ashamed of what you did? How do you sleep at night? That kind of behavior was "treacherous," "ruthless," and just plain "evil."

How much time was wasted on all that nonsense? How many lives were lost or ruined during those dark days? And for what? Who was it that said you can't stop an idea whose time has come? It was inevitable that we would finally get sick and tired enough to stand up to your mistreatment of our people; and it was inevitable that we would win that particular battle, even if part of the reason for your "accommodating" us was to save face. You guys really messed things up back then. Wouldn't you agree?

Little did we know that you were just getting started. Your cross-dressing FBI Director, J. Edgar Hoover, got in on the act with his COINTELPRO and started tapping phone lines, taking pictures, and spreading conspiracies about Black folks. How convenient it was that Lee Harvey Oswald, Jack Ruby, Sirhan Sirhan, James Earl Ray, and the three Black men convicted of Malcolm's murder came along during that time.

As cities burned, Earl Warren and other "good" white folks were busy trying to make sense of it all. They wrote a report on why the riots occurred, and recommended things you could do to avoid other racial uprisings. The answer was quite simple: You had messed things up and Black folks just got sick and tired of it. All we needed was civility from you, not rhetoric and reports. But you put on your "I feel your pain" mask and went to work, once again, to put us into another political trick bag, passing laws and starting programs to appease Blacks and to soothe your guilty conscience.

The worst year was 1968. Political upheaval, murders, assassinations, riots, and chaos in major cities became the norm all because, once again, you messed things up. Greed, paranoia, your quest for more political and economic power, the Viet Nam War, police beat-downs and shoot-downs, and a host of other misdeeds on your part created an even more divided and polarized country.

Don't point your finger at Black folks and try to blame us; you were in charge of everything. One had to look a long time before one could find a Black man or woman in a high ranking political position, Edward Brooke notwithstanding. Barbara Jordan should have been running things at that time; oh yeah, I almost forgot, she was Black. Forgive me for thinking such an outrageous thought. So, you had it all. You had the power, the money, the natural resources, and full control of the political system. And even with all of that, you messed things up. Lord Acton was right about absolute power corrupting absolutely.

The 1970's were a time of transition. By then you had figured out how to use that "integration thing" to your full advantage, and the Black dollars started rolling in so fast you couldn't keep up with them. You really didn't want us around, but since we refused to continue to live in our own communities and support our own businesses, since we insisted you take an even larger share of our annual income, you graciously accommodated us. Well, not "graciously" but you took our money anyway, with our help, of course.

Richard "I am not a crook" Nixon, Watergate, "cutting and running" out of Viet Nam, the Shah of Iran, Jimmy Carter, American hostages, inflation, gasoline shortages, Gerald "Oatmeal Man" Ford, G. Gordon Liddy, Charles Colson, Spiro T. Agnew, H.R. Halderman, John Erlichman, John Dean, and James McCord. We saw "politricks" in 3-D in the 1970's. You really showed your behind, messing things up yet again with your dirty tricks and deceitfulness. I gotta give it to you though; you got book deals, radio and TV shows, and contracts, and then you moved on to more high crimes and misdemeanors.

The vaunted 1980's ushered in the guy you called, "The Great Communicator," Ronald "Let 'em eat ketchup" Reagan. You wanted to feel good again, so you elevated a B-movie star from governor to President. (Looks like you're now planning to do the same thing with the Terminator) In return we got more bureaucrats and fewer air traffic controllers. We got more drugs and guns, to which Nancy told our children to "Just say no." (Easy for her to say; she was married to "Ronnie" and probably said "no" quite a bit)

Some 240 soldiers get killed in Lebanon and you get revenge with a "bold" victory over the tiny island of Grenada, "rescuing" some White students from the terror of those fierce Grenadian people—or was it really an effort to maintain control of the nutmeg crop? We got Iran-Contra and Oliver North. All the while, Daddy, "Thousand Points of Light" Bush waited in the wings as the vice President, fresh from his stint at the CIA and the Council on Foreign Relations.

As if what you already possessed was not enough, you got even wealthier. Wall Street was turning over so much cash that you were emboldened to make a movie about it to show the world how crooked and greedy you were, and how easy it was to cheat and make millions of dollars along the way. Once again, I gotta give it to ya, bro; you know how to work it. When you set this thing up with the Rothchilds, the Carnegies, J.P. Morgan, the Rockefellers, Nicholas Biddle, and all the rest, you knew it would last for centuries, as long as you lied, cheated, killed, extorted, bribed, and perjured your way through it. What a plan! What a world you have designed, which brings us to the 1990's and the New Millennium.

The final decade of the 19th century saw Bush-Clinton-Bush; they were large and in charge. Prison-building was in vogue. You had to find a place to put the ones who did not "just say no." The profits started to come in so fast that private companies got into the game, finding remote locations for new prisons and guaranteeing economic booms if allowed to build there. They even rediscovered that "exception" in the 13th Amendment of the Constitution, which allows slavery in prisons, and quickly figured out how to make more money. "Lock 'em up and throwaway the key," and "Three strikes" you're *in*—for life, were the moneymaking mantras of the 90's.

It was good cop-bad cop for Black people. Clinton, of course, was the good cop, a pimp, a "playa," a superstar. He was Goldie, Shaft, and Super-Fly all wrapped up in one persona—with a little Charlie "Yard Bird" Parker thrown in for good measure; so we decided to go with his flow. Just as you "felt" good with Reagan, Black folks "felt" good with Bill. Tit for tat I guess, or maybe it was more like "na na na na naah na," from us to you. He blew it though. Clinton watched the Rwandan massacre and did nothing.

Then we got the bad cop, George "What, me worry?" Bush, Jr.? He's doing the same thing, as the people in Sudan starve to death, that is, if they escape being slaughtered; and despite an abundance of *yellow cake*, the people of Niger are starving too. And he says he wants to help Africans? Yeah, right. George W. could have started helping Black folks by speaking with the family of James Byrd after three white men came up with a new way to lynch a Black man. It wasn't enough just to kill him, they tied Byrd to their pick-up truck and dragged him—dragged him—until parts of his body fell off! What in anyone's nature would allow him, not cause him but allow him, to do something so atrocious, so odious, and so wicked? And George Bush didn't even want to speak with Byrd's family!

We are stuck with a President who is the very worst you have to offer, at least we hope he's the worst, and he is wreaking havoc on this country and on the world with his impish ways, his outright lack of real concern for Black and poor people, and his evil, vindictive, spiteful nature. He's a spoiled brat who is playing war games with the precious lives of our young men and women, as if they were G.I. Joe stick-figures. By the time you read this letter there will have been more lives lost, more idiotic statements on his part, more corruption and scandals in his administration, and more lies and political paybacks on the part of his administration. He is shameful, and we are ashamed of him and his administration.

After that tortuous trek back in time, what is our current situation? Well, we have the warmonger, King George (Or is he that "Prince" your forefathers wrote about in the Declaration of Independence who was "unfit to rule a free people"?) Already in the 21st century we have endured two Presidential "selections" and face the high probability of an economic meltdown right here in the good ole U.S. of A. under his rule. He gives us a steady diet of Rove, Cheney, Gonzalez, Bolton, and Rumsfeld, with a little "Brown Rice" on the side. Or, did they give him to us? Whatever. He is the very worst of your presidential puppets thus far! But the fact that he is our "leader" just accentuates how low we have sunk and how blatant your lack of regard is for "the people."

Under George W. and his minions, liars all of them, we live in the most powerful country in the world but have one of the highest infant mortality rates, the highest number of incarcerated men and women, outlandish prices for life-saving medicines, some of the worse school systems, inner cities that rival third world villages, and the list goes on. And white men are still in charge.

We have racial conflict, economic disparity, and outright exclusion and discrimination in projects paid in part by our tax dollars. Black people still get beat down, electrocuted with Tasers, shot down in the streets, bitten by dogs, and in some cases we are still found hanging from trees, electrical towers, and in jail cells. All that's missing are the water hoses, but that's probably because you want to save on your water bill. Our country is choking on its own pollution, being poisoned by its own waste; we are destroying our natural habitats, and sending our young people off to die in an unnecessary war. And you, white men, are in charge.

You have pilfered the retirements of Average Joe workers, while paying yourselves millions in salaries and bonuses. You have managed to run up so much debt that it will take three generations to pay it down. Paradoxically, you have presided over the best country in the world and the worst treatment of a people in the history of the world. You have created a system of laws from which you are exempt but under which we must suffer. All of these wrongs have taken place under your rule, your watch, and though you may not think so, you have made a terrible mess of things.

You still enjoy the benefits of 250 years of a labor force for which you did not pay. You wrote all the rules and regulations for this nation, after you said you were being mistreated by a foreign King, and then ended up mistreating millions of other people living in your midst. (Is that where George Orwell got the idea for his book, Animal Farm? "We are all equal, but some of us are more equal than others.")

You strong-armed and commandeered all of the land, all of the natural resources, all of the political power, and all of the economic power, and killed many along the way, ascribing it to your Manifest Destiny. You wrote the laws for immigration and designed it so that only those who looked like you could freely be admitted, but yet solidly stood on the words, "Give me your tired, your poor, your huddled masses yearning to be free," which obviously did not apply to Black people, and even to this day do not apply to Haitians.

You created and maintained a system of affirmative action for yourself and your families for more than 300 years, but you felt 35 years was enough for those you had oppressed for those three centuries. By the way, that "minority" move was slick too. You got us again! And your women made off with the spoils. You're just too crafty for us; we can't compete with you on that level.

Many of your Presidents, while claiming to be devout Christians, stood silent and unmoved by the horrible treatment of various groups of people in this land of plenty. Even one of your most famous and beloved leaders, Thomas Jefferson, knew slavery was wrong, and even referred to that fact in the Declaration of Independence. Of course, that part was never included in your document of freedom, and even he continued to "own" slaves and use them for his personal comfort and pleasure. That Sally Hemings must have been some kinda fine sistah!

You created your own governmental system because you were oppressed, and then you proceeded to oppress millions. You complained about your miseries, but you imposed numerous miseries on others. You appointed judges and attorneys who would do your personal bidding rather than seeing to the people's interests. You have used corrupt government officials to pilfer billions of dollars from the public coffers. You have favored corporations and industries with which you have financial ties and personal interests, allowing them to "steal" as much money as they could carry, hide, and launder.

You are so greedy for filthy lucre that your financial institutions impose usury interest rates on those who can least afford them; you displayed your utter disdain for us when we were drowning, starving, stranded, hopeless, and homeless in New Orleans and surrounding cities; and you went right to work to assure that you and your people would get the billions of dollars necessary for rebuilding.

You have created and maintained a land where Black people can be killed by police officers with impunity, a land where Black life is still considered only a fraction of yours. This is the land that Black men, women, and children nurtured, making it possible for you to have much of the wealth you now enjoy, but you still refuse to pay for that labor. We'd better stop; this is sounding a lot like those whereas clauses in your Declaration of Independence.

Yes, we've slapped you around a lot but you deserve it, you've been slapping us around, literally and figuratively, for a long time, not to mention Native Americans, Chinese and Japanese Americans. But take heart; imagine how long this letter would be if we recounted all of your transgressions against us. If you would stop thinking white males have been ordained by God as rulers of the world, things would be much better for all of us. What is it that makes you believe it's all right to mistreat and abuse people?

Your lust for war is unsurpassed. Your arrogance is beyond measure. You strut your stuff around the world as if you own it and control it, and if others don't see things your way you just invade them, or drop bombs on them, assassinate their leaders, or sabotage their governments, or anything else you are big and bad enough to do. Such power, disrespect, and disdain for others ultimately come at a very high price, and one day you will surely have to pay that price.

Yes, you have much to reflect upon and certainly much to regret. You have much to be remorseful about and have done much for which to ask our forgiveness. Thus, we write this letter to you to bring it to your attention and, yes, to rub your face in it a little as well. But hey, it's like you've always told us to do, "Suck it up," "Get over it," "Move on." Besides, this probably won't bother you anyway; you've done this stuff for so long that you think it's right and proper. After all, you planned it and presided over all of it, didn't you? Sadly, you also revel in it.

White Americans, especially the white men out there, you have no one but yourselves to blame for the mess this country is in today. You have been in charge since this show started; you could have done the right thing back in 1776, even in 1619 for that matter, but you chose your selfish path, and now look at what you've done. You wrote the script to this tear-jerker; you produced and directed it; and even though Black people financed it with our labor, you commandeered all of the box office receipts.

Despite all of the pain, mistreatment, discrimination, and inequity we have suffered under your control, amazingly, we do not hate you. We do not long for revenge. We are not conducting secret meetings to plan for your demise, and we are not lying awake at night devising ways to hurt you. We simply want peace, justice, and empowerment for our people.

But, in the words of Ricky Ricardo, you still have some "splainin'" to do. You have to account for what you have done and what you are still doing. Let's hope and pray you change your ways before you have to account and do your splainin' to God. No one lives forever, you know, and nothing will last forever—not even this corrupt system you have built. We don't have much confidence that you will, but we hope you reverse your course before it's too late.

The responsibility for the state of this Union, as well as the fate of this Union, is all yours; you created and presided over the tragedy and mistreatment of Black people, and since you are unwilling to share the power, you'll have to clean it up all by yourself. So you'd better get busy, because as powerful and mighty as you think you are, there is one thing you can't do; you can't stop time, and your time is running out!

We end this letter with a line from your boy, Shakespeare, in his Sonnet 116: "If this be error and upon me proved, I never writ, nor no man ever loved."

Sincerely,
All Conscious Black Americans

Church Stuff

"Much of what we call freedom is not freedom at all, but simply permission given by an oppressor to become somebody. This is not freedom. If the source of your liberty is another person or a group, then you are only as free as they allow you to be. Freedom cannot be given by another."

— **Myles Munroe**

We boast about the United States being the most "religious" country on the face of the earth, that it is a Judeo-Christian society founded on Godly principles and precepts. We brag about being accepting of everyone's so-called "religion," and we hold our "religious" leaders in high esteem, hanging on to every word that is uttered from their mouths. All of this "religion" we possess, but on September 11th, 2001, and for a brief time thereafter, the national mantra became "God Bless America!"

It is quite obvious that God has already blessed America in many ways and with many material possessions; thus, America should be blessing God in return for His goodness and His mercy. The 911 tragedy was a rallying cry for all Americans to come together in defense of our nation, but Sunday mornings are the most segregated times of the year in this country, which was founded on Godly principles and precepts. Why is that? Are we just trying to fake it to make it?

And what about Black America? (Sorry Barack, but there really is a Black America) What is our "religious" mantra? Do we even have one? I am often perplexed at our unwillingness to deal with certain issues within a "religious" context. It seems some of our "religious" leaders (Or, are they mis-leaders?) refuse to go there because they have something to hide, or something to "protect" might be a better term.

Don't get me wrong, there are many outstanding economic efforts started and managed by Black "religious" leaders; it's been that way since we were freed to practice "religion" on our own. But, you have to admit there are some terrible instances of inappropriate behavior by many who claim to be "religious" as well.

We have seen all of the shell games, the bait-and-switch schemes, the blessings-for-sale televangelists, the snake-oil sales pitches and the, *"We have to check your W-2 statements before we approve your church membership"* plan. We have seen all the "gators" and shiny suits, long flowing robes, diamond rings, and gold bracelets; we have heard all the blessing-in-a-bottle rhetoric that permeates the airwaves. When it comes to what many call "religion," Black folks have been there and done that.

So where does that leave us? Well, the first thing we need to know about "religion" is this: "Religion that God our Father accepts as pure and faultless is this: to look after orphans and widows in their distress and to keep oneself from being polluted by the world." James 1:27

With all of the resources Black people have been blessed to accumulate since we were brought to this land, collectively we have very little to show for it, and we are not practicing our "religion" by using some of those blessings to bless others.

We always seem to be complaining about someone else's stuff rather than buying and controlling our own stuff. Yes, white folks do owe us, but we owe ourselves too. Yes, they own most of the assets, but we can purchase assets as well. Yes, there is media bias against Black people, but "media by us" can cure that.

God has given us so much to work with; He knew we would need it, just as He knew the Israelites would need resources when they left Egypt, so He told them to go back and get what they were due. During the forty years from 1965-2005, Black people have squandered billions of dollars on someone else's stuff; that does not sound like the Godly principle of Good Stewardship.

Prior to 1965, Black folks owned and controlled economic enclaves from coast to coast, many of which were started by churches; now we cannot even build a Black business sector in 85% Black, Detroit! What happened?

Greed stepped in. Reticence and selling-out took their places. Self-aggrandizement got in the way. Mansions and Bentleys stepped into the pulpits. Apathy sat down in the pews. Ego set up residence in churches. When these influences creep into our "religion" we slowly but surely "<u>E</u>ase <u>G</u>od <u>O</u>ut" of the picture and start to think it's all about us.

If we need change on any level, we certainly and most urgently need change among those who call themselves "God-fearing. " We need to learn more about ourselves and how and why we came to practice our particular "religion." We need to study our history in this country, as it pertains to "church stuff," and raise our awareness of the fact that our "religion" did not start when we got off the boat on the shores of the Americas.

We need to realize that this country, although it casts itself as a nation founded on Godly principles, as it continued to enslave millions of Black people, used "religion" to control and to punish. This country only wants us to "come together" when there is a crisis. Is that Godly?

Most importantly, we need to understand that much of our "religion" and many of our "religious" practices hail from the very folks who desperately wanted to keep us "in our place." We need to know that some of our "religious" leaders are nothing more than gatekeepers and non-biblical overseers.

Finally, we must understand our individual responsibility to study and to seek the truth about "religion" and not allow the false prophets and charlatans to direct us down the wrong path. "There is a way that 'seems' right to a man, but in the end it leads to death." Proverbs 14:12

Brothers and sisters, we had better get the correct handle on our "Church Stuff" before it is too late.

Integration—Why did churches get a pass?
Dec. '04

IF INTEGRATION WAS SUCH A GREAT thing, if it was the "right thing to do," if it was good for the country, if it was such a Godly thing to do, why did we demand and fight for integration in every aspect of this society except within the Church? Why didn't we leave our churches, the way we left our businesses and schools, in favor of those established by white people? Considering that Sunday is the most segregated day in America, you would think those who believe that God wants us to be "one" would have fought for integration in the churches as well as restaurants, buses, restrooms, and water fountains.

I recall a quote by Dr. Walter Lomax, who said, "The only way integration can work is if it's an integration of equals... everybody brings something to the table; otherwise, in business terms, you don't have a merger [you have] an acquisition." That scenario could also be stated as a "hostile takeover," according to Brother Lomax. So it makes sense that if Black folks had matched white folks, church for church, integration may have resulted in more progress than it has.

The irony of integration, fought for by whites and Blacks, is the fact that most of those on the front lines were Bible-believing, church-oriented, Christians who loved their fellowman and wanted to do what was right in the sight of God. I am sure there were folks of other religious persuasions who marched for "equal access" right along with the Christians; they marched for equal access in everything except churches. Could this have been the epiphany that Malcolm X experienced when he visited Mecca? I don't know.

Could it be that church folks who pushed for integration were not willing to cross the religious line of demarcation? Could it be they ignored the "real" Lord's Prayer in John 17, especially the part where Jesus asks that we all may be "one"? Could it be that Black folks who pushed for integration wanted to hold on to their bastions of control and authority-and the currency that flowed through those entities? I don't know.

How could Black leaders stand by and watch as Black folks abandoned our economic resources for the right to support those owned by others? How could they have acquiesced to teachers who taught Black children to grow up and go to work for their children? How could our leaders have petitioned for integration in virtually every sector of society and missed the most important one, the one that could have caused us all to be more understanding, more compassionate, and more loving toward one another? I don't know.

By and large, the first opportunity for Africans in America to exert authority and have *titles*, other than "Overseer" or "House Negro," was in the church. As long as he could control it, *ole massa* "allowed" us to be preachers, deacons, and trustees. I suppose our status in the "Chuch" was something we were not willing to neither give up nor share when integration rolled around. Why didn't we demand equal access to all churches, white or Black? I don't know.

And what about white people? Were they culpable in the integration charade? Did they also draw the line at the front door of their churches? Did they not want Blacks to go to church with them? Or, did they see an opportunity to create their own integration monopoly game, as Dr. Claud Anderson calls it? Could they have known Blacks would not be an economic threat if all we owned were "nonperforming" assets financed by their banks? I don't know.

Did they know we would follow them from neighborhood to neighborhood and buy their old church buildings when they abandoned them? Did they know that each time we landed on one of their properties we would have to borrow money from their banks to purchase what they no longer wanted? Were whites unwilling to bring their church assets to the integration table? Were they only interested in acquisitions rather than mergers? I don't know.

Think about it. How many white ministers and congregants are under the authority of Black leadership? How many Black ministers and congregants are under the authority of white leadership? How many whites attend Black Christian schools versus the number of Blacks who attend white Christian schools? If any integration existed at all in church institutions, it was Black folks submitting to white religious authority and becoming members of their churches, rather than the reverse. Maybe that's one reason for the loss of Black owned and operated Christian schools and why those that still exist struggle so hard for financial stability.

If you're interested in reading about an exception to this rule, get a book titled, His Hand and Heart, *The wit and wisdom of Marshall Keeble*, by Willie Cato, a white minister, who sat under the authority and teaching of Marshall Keeble, a Black minister, during the height of racial animus and segregation in this country. Cato turned out just fine as a result of Keeble's teaching and authority.

We will explore this issue further in part two of this article. I don't know all the answers, but I sure can see the results of what has been, in my opinion, a terrible mistake by church-going whites and Blacks. Or, was it intentional? I don't know.

Integration—Why did churches get a pass? (Part Two)

IN PART ONE OF THIS ARTICLE, we posed some questions regarding integration in churches, both congregationally and administratively. As today's national political discussion centers on "Separation of Church and State," let's think about possible motivations for what has become the "separation of church and church."

The largest "mixed" congregations are led by white ministers. While you may see whites sitting in churches run by Black ministers, their numbers pale in comparison to those of Black people attending white-dominated churches. (As a matter of fact, there was one Black church that paid whites folks to come to its service!) So-called "mega churches," both Black and white, have multi-million dollar budgets, and have assets in the tens of millions, all controlled by one man, a man and his wife, or a small team of insiders who are not the least bit interested in integration, beyond that of everyone integrating their offerings in the same collection basket, of course.

Was integration planned so succinctly and in such great detail that Black folks fell for the biggest scam in American history? Were we so myopic about owning our church buildings and maintaining our church titles and status that we missed what was happening to our social, economic, political, and educational status? Could it have been, as the Church Lady used to say, "Satan"? Or was it, as I always say, "Money"? I think I have an answer to this one. It was both Satan and money. (Pardon the redundancy)

The "hostile takeover" called integration, to which we eventually succumbed, has put Black people in a very untenable position. Stable Black churches outnumber viable Black businesses, and Black churches control more unencumbered funds than Black businesses. While some churches are building businesses and creating employment, the majority of Black churches simply serve as transfer agents for Black dollars, moving billions from their coffers to those of non-Black businesses.

Many members of Black churches across this land only have the "pleasure" of seeing and sitting in an edifice built to celebrate a pastor. Many members who have their own businesses never receive business from the churches their dollars helped to build. History shows that as integration expanded and grew more acceptable, Black churches started landing on *Boardwalk* and *Park Place* with phenomenal regularity, and they didn't mind because they could pay the rent! Then they even started buying that exclusive and expensive real estate. Church integration? I don't think so. That was one place we had it going on, and we were not about to allow anyone to infringe on that sacred ground. Whites weren't either.

White folks sat back and watched as our churches grew in number and size, waiting for the calls that would inevitably come for them to sell us their land, construct our buildings, and then sell us everything we needed to furnish our churches. (After all, we had all but abandoned our furniture-making, printing, and robe-making businesses because integration gave us the right to use theirs.) Whites maintained control of their church resources, never having to share them with those "Integration now!" demonstrators, and they laughed on the way to their banks every Monday morning; they couldn't wait to see how much money Black churchgoers had dropped into their night deposit vaults.

The result of not integrating our churches along with everything else surely contributed to our economic demise and brought even more economic resources to white people. If churches had been included in the integration game, aside from the spiritual benefits that would have accrued, maybe Black construction companies would have won some of those white church-building contracts; maybe more Black banks would have stayed in business by financing some of those white churches; and maybe the Black economy would now be on firmer footing because of all the money harbored in Black and white churches. Maybe integration should have been an all-or-nothing agreement—a real merger, rather than an acquisition.

A final thought. Could the reluctance of many "religious" whites to stand up and speak out about blatant acts of discrimination and mistreatment against Blacks, something I see in my hometown everyday, be due to our not having integrated our churches? There was no outcry in Cincinnati from white churches when white cops beat Nathaniel Jones to death, or when they choked Roger Owensby to death, or when 500 Black families were put out of their homes under false pretenses. (Not a huge outcry from Black churches either) Is there an outcry from white churches in Columbus, Georgia about Kenneth Walker's death? Hey, no integration, no obligation. Right?

As I said several times in this article, I don't know all the answers to the questions posed herein. I reiterate, however, that I do see the results of our not having done some of the things noted in this piece. The point of this article is merely to get you to think and to rethink our integration strategy, if we still have one, because I agree with Dr. Lomax' assessment when he said, "Integration is slowly burying us as we become more politically and financially impotent."

I think it was a trick, a game that we lost. Maybe if Black folks had not been so enamored with mixing every resource except churches with those owned by white people, we could have played a few tricks of our own, and we could have won the game. What do you think?

The Power of the Collective and the Collection
June '06

FOR THE SECOND CONSECUTIVE YEAR I had the honor to speak at the Collective Banking Group's (CBG) Annual Conference on June 3-4, 2006. I also presented two workshops on "Building Collective Wealth." It was a privilege to be there among brothers and sisters who are striving to learn more and to do more to enhance the economic position of Black people in this country. It was also the "booster shot" that I need from time to time to maintain my equilibrium and to keep me on course, despite the hesitancy and uneasiness that often beset me. Sometimes it's quite difficult to work for the economic uplift of our people.

Rather than recount everything that happened, as I did last year in this column, I will highly recommend you get DVD's and tape recordings of the proceedings from the First Baptist Church of Glenarden. Just call 301 699 8449, and ask for the bookstore. You will be blessed by the speeches and the workshops that were presented. You can also go to www.collectivebankinggroup.org for more information on the event and the speakers.

The CBG continues to lead the way when it comes to doing what many Black folks just talk about in their dialogues and speeches. As I said to the conferees, the CBG is one of the best examples of collective economic activity in this country. I might add that it is amazing to me that we do not have chapters of the CBG across this country.

I am disturbed by the fact that our high-profile leaders and speakers are not promoting the CBG model as one of the solutions to our economic problems. Maybe it's because many of them get their sponsorships and speaking fees from banks and are afraid to speak out against the blatant discrimination that takes place everyday against Blacks by various banking institutions. Our collective activity as well as our collections can be used to put an end to such discrimination.

I often wonder why we do not understand that by working together and standing together against injustice and unfair treatment, regardless of the sponsors of our organizations and individuals, we could leverage fair treatment and still get our individual perks. Why? Because these banks, and others, would know that if they fail to treat us right hundreds of thousands of us would withdraw our funds from them.

The Collective Banking Group is a model that works; its President, Jonathan Weaver, is a visionary and activist. I ask again: Why are there not more CBG chapters across this country? Go figure.

I concluded my speech to the CBG by introducing a concept I have written about in this column and initially shared with me by L. Nathan Hare in Buffalo, New York: The Boycott Prisons Campaign. I held up the bumper stickers and campaign flyers to a rousing applause and a lot of Amens! As I took my seat, Pastor Weaver said, "It sure would be great if that slogan were put across the front of a T-Shirt; this will make a great national awareness/marketing campaign." I reached into my bag and pulled out my Boycott Prisons T-Shirt, and the campaign began, right there at the CBG conference.

Pastor Weaver held up the shirt and members of various churches immediately signed up for T-Shirt orders. Pastor Weaver and the CBG are determined to spread this message far and wide in an effort to turn our youth, and some our old folks, away from the criminal "injustice" system and toward positive alternatives like business ownership and higher education. I was literally overwhelmed by the show of support by the conferees.

I have written about the Collective Banking Group many times, including a chapter on the CBG in my last book. I have also written about the Boycott Prisons Campaign and introduced it to other organizations during my speeches. Now you are reading about them, either for the first time or once again. What are you going to do?

We must take economic models that work and replicate them. Forget who gets the credit; it's about who gets the benefit; and the beneficiaries of our work will be our children. Don't they deserve something more from us than rhetoric? I think so, and I know that by working collectively Black people can build an economic legacy and foundation on which our children can stand and prosper.

What better way and what greater leverage is there at the disposal of Black people—any people—than to utilize our largest "pool" of funds to obtain equity from banks in which we deposit our money? The same banks that will not give us business loans but will readily provide car loans, and the same banks that charge and overcharge us exorbitant and even usury interest rates, various add-on fees, and ridiculous ATM and "service" charges, those banks would not hesitate to compete for the business of a "collective" of churches. That's how the Collective Banking Group works.

I encourage you to contact the CBG and get a chapter started in your city. I encourage you to start a Boycott Prisons Campaign, and begin the deprogramming process among our youth. They are bombarded with negative self-defeating messages from media everyday; we can use the same strategy to reverse their downward spiral by creating our own messages, our own marketing campaigns.

The power of the collective and the collection is calling us. It beckons us to do more, for and among ourselves, to save ourselves and our children. Sure there are individuals among us who are doing quite well, but imagine the exponential power of their resources combined with many others. But you don't have to be affluent to be a part of an economic collective. The Blackonomics Million Dollar Club (BMDC) is an effort that anyone can join and, through our individual donations, some small and some large, we can make significant improvements in Black organizations and causes that need financial assistance.

There are many ways you can contribute to the power of the Black collective. I have given you three examples. Get busy.

God don't bless no mess, does He?
July '07

THE 2000 SELECTION OF GEORGE BUSH, Jr. opened the floodgates for several Black preachers and Black politicians to rally behind a person they believed was a "good" man. Bush quoted the Bible, went to church, visited Black churches, and always made a point to refer to some Christian principle in his early campaign speeches. Then he reeled us in by capturing our full attention with his Faith-Based Initiative.

Boy, were we hooked when he went in that direction. Old George was our friend; he was a Christian; he cared about the Church; he was a moral person; he was a principled person, he was being led by God, and he even told us that himself. Bush was a guy who could look into the soul of a man; he knew the hearts of men.

The mega-church preachers began pushing and shoving to get to the front of the Faith-Based handout line, and the smaller churches followed suit, of course, endorsing George Bush along the way. They genuflected their way into the White House for a meal or two with His Highness, got their check and came back to us bragging about Bush being such a "good man." They also bragged about being invited to the White House.

Bush was in the good "graces" of Black opinion leaders in the Christian community, which put him in position to do just about anything he wanted. He immediately went to the hot-button issues to divert us from the important things. He started talking about gay marriage and abortion, which really got our attention. We knew then that he was "filled with the Holy Ghost."

While he and his ilk railed against the "sins" of those two hot-button issues, Bush and company were busy committing other sins of their own. The same Black ministers who stood with Bush never said a *mumblin' word* about those sins.

The highlight of all of this, in my opinion, was displayed at Coretta Scott King's funeral. Of all people, Harry Belafonte was both dissed and "dis-invited" to speak, despite being one of the King family's closest friends and supporters. I understand it was because George Bush didn't feel comfortable being on stage with Harry and having him say a few words on behalf of Dr. King's wife. Who knows? Maybe Harry would have also said a few choice things about George Bush and company too.

My problem with the whole thing was that Black people went along with that level of disrespect for one of our strongest and most outspoken elders. Belafonte is one of our highly revered critical thinkers, unafraid to tell it like it is, and like it was. But Black folks, with Black preachers in agreement, settled and then settled in to hear George Bush speak rather than Harry Belafonte.

Much of the behavior we have seen and continue to see among our church leaders, both Black and White, is couched in the actual belief, albeit naïve, that Bush is being directed by God to govern the way he does, Bush's sins of war notwithstanding. Other reasons that Bush gets away with his antics are deeply embedded in self-delusion, greed, and self-aggrandizement among the Black Christian throng.

I wonder what God Himself thinks about this. Are His tenets of helping the poor and disenfranchised being followed? Do His precepts regarding "all sin" apply across the board in this case? Are we seeing the wholesale selling of souls in return for filthy lucre? Are we witnesses to the modern-day rich man who had so much material wealth he said he would simply build larger facilities to house all of his stuff? Have we disregarded the instruction that it is better to trust in God than in man?

Do you really think God is blessing this mess we have gotten ourselves into, mainly because of our attraction for the temporal rather than the eternal? Do you believe that you can do evil to obtain material possessions and always get away with it—forever? Sure, you may have it like that, "good measure, pressed down, shaken together, and running over," but if it did not come from God, what will it matter in the long run anyway?

While God can take our mess and make it our best, if we do our part, of course, I don't think He blesses our mess. We have free will to do whatever we want to do, the power of choice given to us by the One who created us; but there are consequences for the choices we make.

When we chose to do the things we exhibited during the early years of this new millennium, all under the guise of "Christian" principles and leadership, we became those children with "itching ears" the ones that are blown "to and fro" by any ill-wind, and the blind ones who followed the blind leader. "A simple man believes anything, but a prudent man gives thoughts to his steps." Proverbs 14:15

This mess we have created through our acceptance of actions that are completely contrary to what we say we believe will not be blessed. There are men and women out there who are totally committed to no one but themselves; you should "come out from among them." Early in the Church's existence there were folks who claimed to be something they were not; the warning was sent out, "Don't follow them!"

Our warning today is much the same, a big part of which can be found in political-religious circles. Be wary of politicians who try to legislate morality. Don't follow those who want to "amend" something that God has ordained. And please don't fall for the slick political campaign slogans in which the candidate professes to be spiritual; that will be self-evident in his or her actions.

On the religious side of things, study, listen, watch, and do what is right, not in the eyes of men but what is right in the eyes of God. Cause God don't bless no mess.

What does it profit a man...?
July '07

THE FAMILIAR SCRIPTURE THAT REFERS TO anyone who would sell his or her soul in exchange for earthly treasures or anything in this world, for that matter, reminds me of another familiar term: "Sell Out." Even in a Biblical context, as we also read about in Judas' betrayal, selling out yourself and/or your people is not a wise thing to do. That being the case, why do we see it in so many instances, especially within the ranks of our "spiritual leaders"?

The quick answer is simply, "Sin." We know that since the first sin was committed it's been downhill in terms of the things men will say and do. So it's no real surprise that we have folks standing in pulpits espousing "do as I say but not as I do" rhetoric, pretending in some cases to be for "the people" but really selling "the people" out to obtain personal riches.

It's not surprising but it sure is sad to know that some of our most revered and highly respected religious icons are nothing but money-grabbing and money–grubbing, self-absorbed, hypocrites. Even sadder is the point made by the scripture: "What does it profit a man to gain the whole world and lose his soul?"

The other pertinent question is, "What would a man give in exchange for his soul?" It seems that answer is also apparent in the devilish schemes and deals made by some of our church leaders. Take heart though; God forgives hypocrisy, lying, stealing, adultery, and all that other stuff we do in our walk through this life. But in return for His grace and mercy He expects us to do better.

In today's society, with all of its distractions and pitfalls, it is difficult to walk the straight and narrow all of the time. The temptations abound all around each of us on a daily basis. But since "selling out" obviously ranks high on the temptations list, we should be very careful not to tread on that ground.

I am appalled at some of the things I see being said and done by our spiritual leaders. And to think they have so many "followers" who buy-in to their mis-leadership is a sad commentary on where we are in our spiritual growth. I have seen preachers sell-out their brothers and sisters for the proverbial 30 pieces of silver; I have seen them deny their own people; and I have seen them demand money from the "flock," fleecing it rather than feeding it, so they can live the lavish lifestyle at the expense of those who can hardly afford to do the same for themselves. I see it all the time and I still can't believe it; at least I don't want to believe it.

What does it profit these folks when they devise worldly schemes, self-serving doctrines, and convenient accommodating "church practices" all in an effort to obtain more and more material possessions? It's heartbreaking to watch, but greed and selling out took place long ago, and they are still with us today.

I would hope and pray that those who are engaging in such practices will change before it's too late. I pray they will come to themselves, as the prodigal son "came to himself" and got up to go back to his father's house and ask his forgiveness, which he readily and immediately obtained.

While we can receive forgiveness if we seek it in the right way, the earthly consequences of our sins will still be around for us to endure. In the case of spiritual leaders selling their people out and storing up "earthly treasures" rather than "heavenly treasures," there will eventually be a backlash. As a matter of fact, we have seen the results of such behavior in several cases where ministers have gone to prison, suffered shame and embarrassment, and even death, either by their own hand or someone else's.

Look around today and see who has what and who is doing what, before you decide who you will follow. Don't follow "religious leaders" who display haughtiness over holiness, hierarchy over humility, havoc over hallowedness, and hypocrisy over heaven.

It is too easy to get sucked under by the same undertow that is dragging them down; so it's best to get away from them and pray for their enlightenment and a turnaround in their lives before it's too late.

If we would use the two questions posed in Matthew 16:26 to manage our day-to-day lives, we would see less and less selling out among our leaders. Unfortunately, many of them have been mesmerized by material things and are willing to sacrifice their own souls to possess them. There is nothing wrong with having "things;" that's why they were put here by God, for us to enjoy. But when we commit evil, corrupt, selfish, and sinful acts to obtain those things we are headed in the wrong direction. There will be consequences.

Black people, in my opinion, are paying some of those consequences right now; just take a look at the condition of our neighborhoods, despite a church on every corner, despite billions of dollars being donated and turned over to the "good stewardship" of church leaders, and despite the "good intentions" of those sitting in the pews. You know the saying "The road to hell is paved with good intentions." Keep these things in mind as you prepare yourself for what will surely come. Watch, and be prepared.

Finally, to all of you who are doing the right things for the right reasons, may God continue to bless you and your work. Many true spiritual leaders are doing exactly what God wants them to do. They are feeding and nourishing the flock by "rightly dividing" the word of truth; they are empowering the flock by teaching them how to fish; they are providing the proper example of what it means to practice the core values of religion; and they are edifying the flock by enriching their lives with the hope, faith, and encouragement necessary to wait for their true reward and to accept that in God's own time they will definitely receive it.

Of course, they too make mistakes, they too commit sin, and they too must fight against worldly desires; they are not exempt from those things. The key ingredient to winning that "crown" we sing and talk about, is getting back into the race as soon as possible, and that's what "true seekers" do. Selling out to the world is a very dangerous proposition.

James Clingman

There is no price that anyone should pay for a profit that comes by selling out. "What is your life but just a vapor? It appears for a little while and then it vanishes away." Eternity is a long, long, long time brothers and sisters.

Minority Stuff

"I've never accepted any inferior role because of my race or color. And, by God, I never will!"

— Paul Robeson

This subject really gets me angry! I cannot, for the life of me, understand why Black people continue to fall for the minority game. We have been relegated to a "less than" position in this country ever since we arrived, and now, sophisticated as it is, the minority game maintains the notion that we are, indeed, three-fifths of a person.

This is not so much about raw population numbers as it is about perception and how that perception is a disadvantage to Black people. We were the ones against whom the worst treatment was committed, and we were the ones for whom the laws were passed to ameliorate some of that treatment. But at the end of it all, we were not the ones who benefited from those laws, those Amendments, and those regulations.

Now we have so-called "race-neutral" programs in our various cities and counties that dictate small percentages of public business be given to "Small" (SBE) and "Disadvantaged" (DBE) Business Enterprises, of which <u>anyone</u> can own, "Minority" (MBE) Businesses, which include everyone except white males, and here's the kicker: "Women" (WBE) Owned Businesses, which do not include Black women or other so-called minorities.

I should not have to write anything else beyond the last paragraph for you to see the game being run on us. If "race-conscious" programs are prohibited by public entities, how can there be a separate category for WBE's, which is exclusively set aside for white females?

Can't you see how unfair this is? Can't you see why I am on the rampage about the minority game? It's a game in which Black people lose all the time. It's a game that keeps us fighting for crumbs, 20% and 30% of the spoils, while white folks make off with 70% or more—and they don't even have to be "certified."

The saddest part is that even when Black people are in the vast majority in cities like Detroit, Washington, DC, Baltimore, Atlanta, Gary, Indiana, and others, there are still "Minority" Programs set up for Black folks. That makes absolutely no sense at all. But we have been so well conditioned, as Carter G. Woodson said, "If you can control a man's thinking, you don't have to worry about his actions." Even when in the majority, even when in political control, even when there is no one in the room but Black folks, we end up adjusting, accommodating, and acquiescing to the white status quo.

This next series of articles speak to the ridiculous notion of Black people being relegated to subordinate status and the effects it has had—and continues to have—on our economic progress in this country.

They speak angrily, boisterously, and indignantly about our reluctance to stand up for ourselves against these "programs" that keep us on the bottom of the economic heap.

They speak seriously about the nature of our people to go along to get along, not make waves, not speak out, and continue to miss out on the economic benefits of our tax dollars.

Please think about the minority game being played in your town; critique it, analyze it, discuss it, and change it. One more thing: Don't accept being called a "minority."

Ban the M-Word
Jan. '07

NO, THAT'S NOT A TYPOGRAPHICAL ERROR. I mean the "M"-word. The M-word has the same effect as the other infamous word we are trying to eradicate and stop Black people from being called. So, as we work to wipe out the N-word, let's also refrain from referring to Black people, or allowing others to refer to us, as "minorities." Now before you go off, and start finding excuses for subjugating and subordinating your people, and before you start your search for other references to Black people, let's think about the M-word for a moment and see if it warrants banishment from our social and business lexicon.

Whoever defines you also has the power to control you. One of the best lessons we have on that was in the movie, <u>Roots</u>, when Kunta Kinte refused to be called Toby. The white man insisted, and went to extreme measures to break Kunta, because he knew that through the power of naming Kunta and determining who Kunta was, his control of Kunta Kinte would be much easier. Define and control. That's the name of the minority game.

So it is with the M-word. It has been used as a label to connote "less than" and has kept Black folks scrambling for and settling for less than our fair share of the very resources our forefathers and mothers worked and died for. In the business sector, both public and private, we have minority programs, minority affairs, and minority set asides. Despite meager attempts by the government to ameliorate the problems of discrimination against Black people with various Constitutional Amendments and such, "Black rights" soon became "minority rights" and everyone except white males became a minority.

Now it's even worse. After many cities completed their disparity studies in the late 1990's and found that Black people had been discriminated against, some of them, including my own city, moved from "minority" programs to race-neutral "Small Business Enterprise Programs." This program accommodates not just so-called minorities; it allows everyone, including white males, to participate. Once again, so much for helping Black people, the ones to whom the debt is owed.

Black rights have been watered down and are now recognized as "minority" rights because we have allowed someone else to define us as a people. Numerically we may be "in the minority" in this country, but we are not "a minority." To show you even further how silly this game is, in some cities the so-called minority groups collectively comprise the majority of the population, yet they allow themselves to be called and treated as a "minority." In other cities, where there is a majority of Black people, there are "minority" programs to which Blacks are subjected!

Look at towns like Gary, Indiana, Benton Harbor, Michigan, Detroit, Atlanta, or Washington, D.C., or many of the other small towns that are majority Black. Why would Black people take a back seat to anyone by settling for 20% or 30% of the contracts and other business, thus, allowing the other 70% to go to white males, without question or resistance?

The sad part is that we have been programmed so well to expect and accept being called "minority." What was supposed to positively respond to past discrimination and mistreatment has now put us at an even greater disadvantage in this country. So, I am saying we should ban the M-word, as well as terms like "people of color," when we are really referring to Black people. Let's not be afraid or ashamed to say who we are and let's not settle for less than that from anyone else.

Now, back to the objections we will surely receive about this. Blacks are engaged in an ongoing discussion about what we should call ourselves, that is, Africans, Afrikans, African-Americans, Afro-Americans, People of African Descent, etc. The context of my issue with the M-word lies with business, and the barriers to economic empowerment for our people due to our acceptance of a subordinate classification. I will defer to more learned brothers and sisters to determine what we should call ourselves in the context of nationhood, and I will accept what they recommend.

But for now, knowing how the game is played and how we are played when it comes to public assets bought by our tax dollars, and private sector contracts which are supported by our consumer dollars, I am advocating for the term, "Black." That's why we are saying Bring Back Black! We must define ourselves and take more control of our own destiny.

In his seminal work, The Destruction of Black Civilization, Chancellor Williams wrote, "The term 'Black' was given a rebirth by the Black youth revolt. As reborn, it does not refer to the particular color (or as one objector complained, the phenotype) of any particular person, but to the attitude of pride and devotion to the race whose homeland from times immemorial was called, 'The Land of the Blacks.' Almost overnight our youngsters made "Black" coequal with 'white' in respectability and challenged the anti-Black Negroes to decide on which side they stood. This was no problem for many who are light or even near white in complexion, for they themselves were among the first to proclaim with pride, 'Call me Black!'"

Williams went on to write, "In ancient times 'African' and 'Ethiopian' meant the same thing: A Black. This, of course, was before the Caucasians began to reorder the earth to suit themselves and found it necessary to stake their birthright over the Land of the Blacks also."

Today, in 2007, Blacks have reverted back to allowing whites to define us with words like "minority" and have thereby reordered this country to benefit themselves, as they did with the Kunta Kinte's. As for me, the disagreements among us notwithstanding, I am going with Dr. Chancellor Williams on this one. Down with the M-Word; Bring Back Black!

Minority Rules
Oct. '05

I KNOW YOU HAVE HEARD THE clamor about minority groups not getting their fair share of the reconstruction dollars being spent in New Orleans. Headline articles abound across this country disclosing the unfairness that is being perpetrated against minorities in New Orleans. Apparently white folks are taking over, giving no-bid contracts to their buddies. "Vice" president Cheney came in to survey the damage to see what he could channel to his company, Halliburton, and all of the other players are there already working and making millions while the newspaper headlines continue to say, "Minorities not getting in on the action in New Orleans."

Newsflash! I beg to differ. Minorities are, that's right, I said they "are" getting their fair share of the economic benefits from the reconstruction of The Big Easy. The newspapers, advocacy groups, television news shows and radio shows, politicians, and social activists are all wrong—dead wrong on this one.

As a matter of fact, in New Orleans the principle of majority rule has been surpassed by "Minority Rules, which has taken over and has assured that the minority will reap bountifully from the devastation of Black people in that city. How is that possible?

Here's how. The New Orleans Black population is 67%; at least it was before the hurricane. My math tells me that's a "majority." Thus, simply put, white folks are the minority in that city. White folks are getting more than their fair share of the contracts, business opportunities, and employment. In other words, the minority rules in New Orleans, brothers and sisters. But, don't feel like you're alone, New Orleans; minority rules are in full effect in Detroit too—and other cities.

What we see in New Orleans is exactly why I rail so much against this word, "minority." It is totally ridiculous for us to allow ourselves to be placed in that category under any circumstances, but even more so in this instance. We find ourselves giving in to being called minorities and complaining about not receiving equitable treatment in a city that has a majority Black population. Even though Black folks are the majority, they—and we—are acting like minorities. So stop complaining about the minorities not getting their share of the money in New Orleans. Believe me, they are getting their share, and most of your share too.

Let me be very frank by saying it is just plain stupid for Black people to continue to submit to such disparate treatment, all under the guise of minority programs, and accept being called minorities. It is even more stupid, insulting, and demeaning for Black people (or should I have used a small "b" there?) to use the term to describe themselves. We have blacks in my hometown who use the term all the time, but they are the gatekeepers and the Hayward Sheppard's of our town. They are always the ones who are "selected" and put in charge of the minority programs and the minority inclusion initiatives. But, as I said in my first book on economic empowerment, "We deserve what we accept."

Here we are in 2005 accepting some silly classification called "minority" and now are paying dearly for it in New Orleans as we subscribe to what the newspapers are printing: "Minorities not getting their fair share of construction contracts in New Orleans." If they mean Blacks are not getting their fair share, why don't they just say that? Is it because "minority" is less acerbic, less pointed, less threatening?

Do you see how messed up we are? We don't know whether we are pitching or catching sometimes. Although we are mostly catching, and you know what we are catching, we can begin throwing a few strikes of our own if we would simply name what we are and claim it. Talk about self-determination, this would be an excellent place to start. In cities where we dominate in population, please don't fall for the trick of being labeled minorities. And don't fall for it anywhere else; it's a losing game for Black people.

Here are a few "Minority Rules": Stop allowing yourself to be called minority. Stop using the term to refer to Black people. Stop accepting so-called black leaders who use the term to describe Black people. Stop participating in minority programs; start Black programs—just like other groups start and support their own programs throughout this country. Stop excepting the crumbs and work to bake your own loaf; you cannot do that by succumbing to the minority label.

Stop allowing gate-keeping blacks to slide in the back door and cut deals in the name of minorities. Stop accepting the usual chosen black suspects who always get the contracts, who always get the board seats, and who always get plaudits from the white establishment. Examine each one of them and jettison every one of them that is not working on behalf of the Black collective rather than for minorities.

Put an end, once and for all, to the games being played on us and sometimes by us, by greedy, conniving, slick-talking, self-serving, condescending, politicians, profiteers, and preachers. As we can plainly see in cities like New Orleans, Detroit, Washington, D.C., Atlanta, and others, unless Black people write our own "minority rules," the real minority will always rule us.

Who Speaks for Black People?
April '06

I POSED THIS QUESTION TO MY Black Entrepreneurship class at the University of Cincinnati, and much to my chagrin, after a long period of silence, only one young lady had an answer. Even sadder is the fact that I did not posit the question in the context of entrepreneurship; rather, it was just a general question. While I am not surprised at their lack of response, in the larger context of Black leadership, that response spoke volumes—their silence was deafening. So I ask you. Who does speak for Black people? Who stands up for Black people?

The one student who did have an answer, not surprisingly, named a national personality, which is where we usually gravitate when it comes to determining who our leaders are. But don't you think there should be folks who speak up and stand up for Black people on the local level? I am not talking about brothers and sisters who refer to themselves—and us—as "people of color" or "minorities" or any of those other namby-pamby words used to define who we are and, ultimately, what we deserve. I am referring to local leaders who are unwavering in their commitment to Black people and those who are not confused about their—and our—identity. So maybe a better question is: "Who defines Black people?"

I recently attended a workshop conducted by one of this nation's outstanding minister-scholars, Dr. Tony Roach, of Abilene, Texas. The five-day event titled, "You are God's Love Bank," was sponsored by our congregation, the Gray Road Church of Christ, here in Cincinnati, Ohio. During that workshop my eyes were opened to many things, but among all the outstanding strategies for living a spiritual life, presented by Dr. Roach, one thing he noted reminded me of our plight in this country. Roach kept emphasizing the fact that "He who defines you controls you." I probably could stop right here, couldn't I?

There is also a point to be made about "what" defines you as well. Roach's "New Self Love" versus "Old Self Love" segment helps us understand how incidents that took place in our lives long ago shape our personalities and determine to a large extent how we act and react as adults. He points to four conditions that have affected each of us in some way or another: Abandonment; Worthlessness; Abuse; and Rejection. These "Old Self" conditions have defined us for years, both individually and collectively. Thus, we should look at not only "who" but also "what" defines and controls us.

Before I continue, allow me to make a pitch for Dr. Tony Roach and his workshop curriculum. See: www.godslovebank.com. Dr. Roach's approach to spiritual growth is comprehensive and insightful. In addition to its application in our individual lives Roach's curriculum also applies to our collective status. Of course, Dr. Roach's teachings are applicable to all persons. But, relative to my message to Black people and our collective condition, his call for introspection and self-assessment, realization and love of self, and the powerful attributes of our spiritual heritage vis-à-vis what we are and who we really are, struck glorious chords with me. I am sure you will find something in the God's Love Bank Program that you can use to empower yourself, your children, and your entire family.

As for the collective Black family, it is obvious that we are allowing other people and past events to define us. Based upon that reality we find ourselves as a people who constantly look for a national leader to rescue us from local dangers. Because we have so few who are willing to speak for Black people alone, we succumb to being defined by folks who do not have our best collective interests in mind.

Because we fall prey to the "minority" game, being defined by a term that connotes deficiency, subjugation, and subordination, we collectively lose out on the benefits that accrue to those who proudly rally around their own heritage and culture, and stand together on issues of reciprocity and self-determination. Our collective acquiescence to the power plays by the "majority" and its overseers does not say very much about new self love, but it sure does speak volumes about our old self love.

A prime example is how Black people work tirelessly and dedicatedly on building minority inclusion programs and minority set-aside programs that provide, say, 25% to the entire "minority" group. In most cases, the programs never deliver even that meager portion of benefits, but even worse is the fact that 75% of the benefits go to white males, without question or contesting by Black people. Many of us are afraid to tread on that particular ground because of historical court rulings (Adarand and Croson) and due to the "threat" of being sued by white contractors who wave the "racial preferences" banner before the courts. But, who speaks for Black people? Who will stand up and use that same argument by asking, "Isn't giving white males 75% also a racial preference?"

As Dr. Roach says, "He who defines you also controls you." He also teaches the Seven Laws of Sowing and Reaping: "What you see is what you say; what you say is what you sow; what you sow is what you reap; what you reap is what you are; what you are is what you give; what you give is what you get; and what you get is what you deserve." Black people must start speaking up for who we are and what we are, positively and affirmatively, and change the way we think and act. Then, as we get what we deserve, we will be empowered.

Politics Stuff

"It is unfortunate, too, that such a large number of Negroes do not know any better than to stake their whole fortune on politics. History does not show that any race, especially a minority group, has ever solved an important problem by relying on one thing, certainly not by parking its political strength on one side of the fence because of empty promises."

—Carter G. Woodson

Much of the following probably could have been placed in the Dumb Stuff Section because most of what we see in the political arena is just plain, well, you know what I mean.

My disclaimer for including so many essays on politics is this: Black people have been enthralled by politics for the past several decades, especially since we began to get elected by the thousands all over this country. Our participation as Mayors of major cities and as U.S. Representatives seemed to give us the confidence and assurance that we had finally "arrived." Politics plays a huge and important role in our daily lives, no doubt about it, and to ignore that fact by failing to write about politics in an economic context would be disingenuous. Thus, we have included several pieces on the subject.

Don't get me wrong, I am in no way a "political animal," but most of my readers certainly know that already. Quite frankly, I really don't care what color a politician is, as long as that politician brings some bacon home to Black people. Politics is all about self-interest; it's a way to transfer public money into private hands, which we have seen in a large way with the Bush administration.

That being said, it is important that Black folks work to gain real political power in addition to political influence. We must have people in political office who are unafraid to do things specifically for Black people. White politicians do it all the time for their people by steering no-bid contracts, tax incentives, and business deals to them. They use politics to enrich themselves everyday, and the sad part about it is we know it and they don't care if we know it. So we had better wake up and start taking this game more seriously.

Since most of us know that economics runs the political game, it is no mystery why hundreds of millions of dollars are raised by candidates as an ante for them to sit at the table and play a few hands. First they count dollars, and then they count votes, all along crowning the most viable candidate because he or she has the most money in the bank.

Do you ever wonder why someone would spend, say, $50 million to vie for a position that pays $200,000 or even $400,000? Well, wonder no more. It's the power that comes with some (not all) political positions that causes the acceptance of such a skewed cost/benefit ratio.

Why would various people across this country give George W. Bush nearly $100 million for his 2000 campaign, and who knows how much for his second campaign? Surely it was not due to his political acumen, his business savvy, or his astuteness in and grasp of geopolitical and macroeconomic affairs. Do you think it was simply because he was "good guy," someone they'd "like to have a beer with," just a regular kind of guy, or was it his "plain-talk" they loved so much?

You got it. None of the above. The real power boys and girls knew they had a pigeon in G.W. and they could get him to do their bidding under the guise of "I'm the decider." They knew he was a childlike, *scaredy-cat,* silver-spoon fed, spoiled, shallow-minded, simpleton, who would be content to pretend he was large and in charge but would defer to the likes of Rumsfeld, Cheney, Wolfowitz, and Karl Rove.

Politics stinks, folks; it smells to high heaven, especially now in the new millennium. Corruption abounds. Deceitfulness and in-your-face disregard for the rule of law are the orders of the day. Politicians get elected and settle in for a multi-year stint of perks, favors, gifts, world travel, generous pensions, (even if they do get sent to prison for corruption in office) and one of the best deals ever: they don't have to participate in the ever-worsening Social Security Program, you know, the one they are all so concerned about and are trying to "fix." What a deal, huh?

Politicians have all of this, along with the power to bring their friends and relatives to the public feeding trough as well; nice work if you can get it. There is no color line where these acts are concerned, except that Black politicians have little or no real power and, for the most part, do not have authority over the real money. Yes, they do some of the same things, but $90,000 in a freezer pales in comparison to a few million in a foreign bank account.

A few thousand dollars or even a few hundred thousand funneled by Black politicians to their friends and family members is one thing; but where are the Black Halliburton no-bid contracts, the Black Bechtel deals, or the mysterious $9 billion in "missing" cash that went to Iraq? Did any Black folks get that money?

Black politicians are small-time players in a high-stakes game. The sad part about it is we think we are "all that" when we get elected, so much so that we forget about being Black and helping Black people.

Without an economic base the politicians we elect to work in our best interests will continue to immerse themselves in symbolic meaningless gestures and causes that take Black people into celebratory euphoria over empty victories like naming streets and erecting statues, getting folks to apologize to us, and a big party every year to cap it all off.

Black people, if we really want to be politically empowered, will have to be a lot more serious about playing politics. It is a money game, and a game of sheer numbers in voting strength. Since we can never win with sheer numbers alone, we must negotiate for our political rewards from an economic position.

Politics is not a popularity contest, as some of our people believe it is. It is a cut-throat, down and dirty, take-no-prisoners mud-wrestling match. Politicians are supposed to be about doing the right thing and protecting and serving "the people." Sadly, after being elected, many of them are reduced to a charade and a parade of incompetent, elitist, power-smitten, greedy, dishonest, prevaricating, "mannequins" as Dr. Rosie Milligan calls them.

Having seen the results Black people have gained playing by the rules, especially since 1970, we had better move quickly to rent, own, or even rent-to-own a few politicians that will help write some new rules and do our bidding for us, especially in the economic arena. Watch white politicians, the "masters of the game," and see who they are really helping. Without apology, they help their own, and it's all about money.

"The most important area for the exercise of independent effort is economics. After a people have established successfully a firm industrial foundation they naturally turn to politics and society, but not first to society and politics, because the two latter cannot exist without the former." **Marcus Garvey**

Are we getting the leadership we deserve?
Sept. '05

TAKE A CLOSE LOOK AT OUR situation in this country and think about the passage in the Bible in which Samuel warned the people about what would happen when they insisted on having a King. If you are not familiar with it, read First Samuel, Chapter 8, and see how similar that situation was to ours today. We have a leader who is doing the same things that Samuel told his people would happen if they rejected God's leadership for man's leadership. In other words, Samuel told the people they would get the leadership they deserved. Seems we are in that predicament today with George Bush and his buddies.

To begin with, when Bush was first discussed, at least in public, as a viable candidate for President, most of us thought, "What?" "Who?" Many of us wondered, "How in the world do the Republicans think this lightweight could be elected to the highest office in the land?" Talk about a long shot, at least that's what we thought; this guy was the most unlikely person to be nominated by the GOP. Boy, were we wrong!

Despite his shallow and shadowy reputation, his lack of management skills, his inability to lead, and his outright demonstration of a lack of concern and "compassion" for the James Byrd family, he "won" his party's nomination, beating out John McCain no less! Then we saw his debating skills, his communication skills, and his obvious lack of knowledge of world affairs. But still he moved up in the polls. And then the dénouement, contrary to what we always believed to be the standard procedure of the President selecting Supreme Court Justices, we saw a complete reversal when the Supreme Court Justices selected our President!

All of the indications leading up to Bush's "selection" point to the fact that we get the leadership we deserve. There is no way we should have the likes of George Bush as our President, but we do. To add insult to injury, we "elected" him again, for another four years, to continue his reign of economic terror on Black people, men and women in the armed services, the elderly, and poor people.

To prove my point even further, we see an intelligent person like Condoleezza Rice supporting and defending George Bush. She has to know how ignorant he is and how limited he is; she has to see the corruption in his administration, yet she stands at his side like one of Hitler's storm troopers, knowing that what he is doing is wrong but willing, nonetheless, to "follow orders." I wonder what she really thinks about her boss. Maybe one day she will write a tell-all book like Dick Morris did about the Clintons. There is no honor among those folks, you know.

There is more proof-positive that, despite what we thought, what we did, or how much we protested, Bush would be President. Think about the mind-boggling support he has from some of our most prominent Black ministers, and not just because of his "faith-based initiative" but because they say Bush is a Christian, he has high moral values, he is against abortion and gay marriage, two sins those ministers cannot tolerate in their President; but apparently they can tolerate lying, murder, stealing, and coveting another man's resources.

What we are seeing has to be prophecy; there is no rational way it could be happening otherwise. No way!

Now, at a time when Bush has the lowest ratings in history, having demonstrated a total disdain for some of the laws he swore to uphold, having shown the people of this country that he is obviously not equipped to be President, having taken the country from surpluses to deficits, increasing the debt exponentially, and presiding over a stupid war that virtually everyone knows should not have been started, even after all of that—and more—Bush has not been impeached nor has our vaunted Congressional Black Caucus drawn up papers calling for his impeachment. This simply has to be divine providence; we are truly getting the leadership we deserve.

I ran across a quote attributed to Thomas Sowell, which is very appropriate when you think about the leadership we have in George Bush: "It is hard to imagine a more stupid or more dangerous way of making decisions than by putting those decisions in the hands of people who pay no price for being wrong." That is exactly what we have done and we are paying dearly for having done so. Bush says, "Bring 'em on!" and a thousand Americans die. Bush is now saying, "The only way the terrorists can win is if 'we' lose 'our' nerve and abandon the mission." I wonder what he means by "we" and "our" nerve. Bush struts his stuff while others take the fall.

Despite the majority of the people telling him he is wrong on the war, wrong on the economy, and wrong on leadership, despite putting his cronies into positions they have absolutely no place being (Remember him saying, "Brownie, you're doing a heck of a job"?), despite his failure to come down hard on his family's buddies, the Saudis and Kuwaitis, after American lives were lost defending their oil, and despite his total incompetence, his constant deer-in-the-headlights stare and his "What, me worry?" Alfred P. Newman caricature, George Bush, is our leader. It just has to be the fulfillment of prophecy.

To give you some hope, I close with another quote. Also, as the following passage suggests, beware of the "hidden hand," and in this case, that hand is firmly implanted in George Bush's back as he sits on the knee of the puppet-master. "If you see the poor oppressed in a district, and justice and rights denied, do not be surprised at such things; for one official is eyed by a higher one, and over them both are others still." Ecclesiastes 5:8

Executive Privilege and Privileged Executives
Sept. '05

WE HAVE HEARD OF EXECUTIVE PRIVILEGE and have seen it in action several times, especially now that arrogance reigns in the White House. Our President exercises his executive privileges, and passes them on to his buddies in the private sector as well. The attitudes and actions of many privileged executives, as they peer down on the underlings, are *in-your-face, I-couldn't-care-less-about-you,* and *you-can-kiss-my-assets-and-go-to-hell*. Current political policies are a death sentence to Black and poor people in this country. The President travels across the country talking about why we should support the war in Iraq, all the while apparently not believing that the majority of the population is telling him what he can do with his war, as New Orleans, Biloxi, Gulfport, and Mobile drown. He finally "cuts his vacation short" to go to New Orleans and wants us to be impressed.

That's what Bush executive privilege is all about; and you thought it was simply about signing orders or withholding information from the public. This guy flies over the gulf coast and then holds a press briefing telling us what we already know, in addition to rattling off numbers of meals and other items he says will arrive in New Orleans, oh about four days too late. He has to read everything he says, even his regrets and sympathies to families that have lost loved ones. I suppose his executive privilege dictates his reaction to the recent hurricane devastation. Seems to me, as I recall, it was a bit different when hurricanes hit his brother's state of Florida.

Executive privilege by privileged executives like Bush, Ken Lay, Dick Cheney, Donald Rumsfeld, and others is both appalling and enlightening. People in this country are on the brink of starvation and epidemic, wandering through the streets like Darfurians, Rwandans, and Haitians

(Hmmm, I wonder why all of those groups happen to be Black), and Bush comes to the rescue four days late seeking credit for doing what we pay him to do. The hugging and kissing photo opportunities were great though.

Executive privilege supports lying, cheating, deceit, and arrogance of the highest degree. It allows the spending of a billion dollars per week on a dim-witted war, but not even a million per week on our own citizens who are stranded, stricken, and suffering from Hurricane Katrina. Water, so plentiful in this country is not even available to those who desperately need it; it took five days to get water to the people stranded at the New Orleans Convention Center! Food, in this land of bounty, is scarce and in short supply for the children caught in this quagmire. Executive privilege allows "fly-overs" and shallow speeches. Privileged executives continue to watch the big board at the New York Stock Exchange and applaud after the day's trading is over, especially the oil and drug execs.

The juxtaposition of the tragedy along the gulf coast against multi-million dollar earning CEO's, getting raises and making even more in Bush's compassionate economy, suggests a decadent and Nero-like society teetering on the edge of destruction. All the signs are there. How we treat the least among us is the determining factor in whether we will be treated kindly. But we get the leadership we deserve, don't we?

George Bush and his men of ill repute are now in their second term. They have lied to us and caused untold numbers of people to be killed in their war, yet they are still in charge. They have not been indicted; Bush has not been impeached, as Clinton was for lying about an affair; and now yet another Bush (Jeb) waits in the wings to be crowned leader of this country. We get the leadership we deserve.

Executive privilege among privileged executives will be the ultimate demise of this country because as it says in Ecclesiastes 5:10, "Whoever loves money, never has money enough, whoever loves wealth is never satisfied with his income" Many of our billionaire privileged executives will go to their graves thinking their money will be their salvation. They will continue to overcharge and rip people off in the midst of devastation. They will pass laws that negatively affect the poor and disenfranchised, while increasing their own assets. They will stand before us and lie to our faces, eat caviar and drink champagne, and watch thousands of their brothers and sisters wade through infested waters trying to survive. They will shake their heads and wag their fingers at poor people ripping off abandoned Walmart stores, while they rip off entire countries for their oil and other valuable resources.

Privileged executives, buoyed by executive privilege, are just plain greedy, aloof, and despicable. They do flyovers rather than parachute drops; they do press briefings instead of pressing into action; they read from teleprompters rather than speak from their hearts (If they have hearts); they are patronizing rather than patriotic; they are rhetorical instead of real; they are sarcastic rather than sacrificial; they are condescending rather than conscious; they are evil rather than good.

We had better awaken from our comatose state real soon, brothers and sisters. We may as well accept the fact that we are not high on the agenda of those who run this country. We must deal with the fact that some of our more prominent brothers and sisters have sold us out and continue to do so, as they follow and praise a guy like George Bush, despite all that he has done and now in the face of what he has not done. We may as well deal with the fact that some of our black preachers are closely tied to Bush and continue to support his sinfulness simply for money and the "privilege" of dining with him.

We must face these realities and move with whomever we have to assure that Black people in the U.S. do not become extinct. Look at New Orleans and ask yourself: "Do we have a choice?"

Bush-Leaguers and Minor Leaguers
Feb. '05

USED AS JARGON FOR THE MINOR leagues in baseball, the term, "Bush-League" has sunk to a new low. The term was originally used to point out unpolished manners, ignorance, and the lack of class. Interestingly, Bush-League is commonly used in baseball parlance, for negative actions on someone's part, and can also be used as a pun for President's actions. Further, George Bush once owned a professional baseball team, and now he "thinks" he owns this country and a major portion of the world. His actions as a baseball team owner, and as President, give credence and new meaning to the derogatory term, "Bush-League."

We can start with that Bush-League budget proposal sent to Congress? More money for the warmongers and profiteering corporate thieves like Halliburton, KBR, Custer Battles, and other shell companies formed by the Bushites, with less money going to the poor, disabled, and this country's veterans.

"Social Security is in a crisis," reminiscent of the WMD scare, is yet another Chicken Little Bush-League tactic. Two things could be done to assure Social Security's stability: Make members of Congress and the President enroll in the system and make their benefits dependent upon it. The crisis would be over in a heartbeat; they would make sure of that. Second, raise the cap on earnings from $90,000 to, let's say, $125,000. Oh yeah, now we're talking.

The lies and deceit just keep on coming, folks. Remember how quickly Bush did his best impersonation of the Apostle Peter when his buddy Armstrong Williams got his tail caught in the wringer? *It was Rod Paige's fault! I knew nothing about it!* Yeah, right, George.

Bernard Kerik. "We didn't know about his background," was the message sent out to the masses from the White House. Kerik is the same guy Bush put in charge of training police in Iraq; sure he didn't know about Kerik's background. What a joke! Has anyone heard from Kerik's mentor, Rudi Giuliani, lately?

Take Alberto "Speedy" Gonzales and Condoleezza Rice. Gonzales said Bush has the right to detain folks without due process and it's all right to torture them while they're in custody too. He'll make a good A.G. won't he? Condi, as she is affectionately called by her "husband" (she said it; I didn't), George W., just a few months ago, was soaring right up there with the rest of the hawks, like Rumsfeld and Cheney. She now has the interesting job of playing the dove, and making peace with those she denigrated, intimidated, and lied to. Some say she is well qualified for the job; she had better be.

Oh yeah, only now that Condi has been confirmed and the presidential "selection" has been made, do we find out about memos and strategies regarding Al Qaeda and its plans to fly airplanes into tall buildings. But didn't we already know they knew? Richard Clark told us.

What about that mysterious Energy Policy over which our "vice" President presided? As we now hear tapes of Enron executives laughing about ripping their customers off, we might have vague memories of Cheney saying he would not release the records of his meetings with his energy buddies.

As the definition of bush-league states, "unpolished manners, ignorance, and the lack of class" this Bush definitely meets the criteria. Manners? Why would any news reporter want to be in the White House Press Corps, (unless your name is Jeff Gannon, or Jim Guckert, or whatever his name is) and ask questions that are never answered, and be insulted and disrespected by Bush during his so-called press conferences? In his last one, Bush *allowed* one Black female, two white females, and about ten white males to ask questions he never answered. Bush's tone was arrogant and his responses were condescending; the reporters just sat there and took it. They should have walked out in protest, but that would take backbone, wouldn't it?

Ignorance? Well, if you heard Bush's definition of "tribal sovereignty," as he related it to a group of Journalists, you would know exactly what I mean. Say what? You have more evidence of his ignorance? You say he knew nothing about the extension of the Voting Rights Act that comes up in 2007? Noooo! Get outta here!

No-bid contracts, Ahmed Chalabi, Abu Ghraib, Jessica Lynch, illegal kickbacks, cost overruns, billions in cash unaccounted for, "bring 'em on," smart bombs and dumb children, denials, lies, deceit, Afghanistan heroin, gasoline price hikes, just say "No" to the Kyoto Protocols. What's left? Oh yeah, gay marriages and abortions. Okay, now we're bringing it home to Black folks.

Bush and his brain, Karl Rove, slicked Black preachers and some of their flock to fall for the morality charade; of course, a little money on the side, or under the table, made things easier, I'm sure. The election was all about sin. The crazy part is how they got us so caught-up in the two sins they were railing against, and how we completely forgot the sins Bush and his flock were committing and presiding over, sins such as lying, killing, and coveting. Sin is sin, isn't it? On those recently discovered tapes, Bush himself said, "…How can I differentiate sin?"

Now that I have thought about it, the President may be a Bush-Leaguer, but when it comes to Blacks playing on his team, we are strictly minor-leaguers.

Let's get rid of Congress
Jan. '06

WHY NOT? WHAT GOOD IS IT? What power does it have? For whom does it work? Considering the things that have taken place just over the past few months, it is obvious our Congress cannot do anything to stop the thievery, the cronyism, and the absolute power of King George and his band of miscreants, so we may as well call it day for Congress. We are just wasting our money paying their salaries; I'm sure Cheney and the gang can put it to better use. So let's try it, at least for a while, and maybe our Congress will finally realize they work for us—not George Bush and company.

Isn't Congress there for checking and balancing? Aren't they in Washington to legislate on behalf of "the people"? Didn't you elect them to protect your interests? Aren't they getting paid six figures, with the best retirement plans on earth to boot? Are they doing their jobs? The answers are obvious, so let's kick 'em out in November 2006.

Dubya recently called a meeting of political "O.G.s," which also included his two Black tokens, Condi and Colin; Bush did his fake mea culpa, we're-all-in-this-together charade, and his photo-op, to get us to believe he is sincerely interested in what we think. That was just after he went back into his bag of tricks and made another recess appointment of one of his gals, Julie Myers, a no-experience, neophyte who is now responsible for a $4 billion budget and 20,000 employees at the U.S. Immigration and Customs Enforcement Agency no less!. Bush is definitely a Playa! I might start calling him, "Goldie! Goldie!"

Congress meets and speaks and meets and speaks, ad nauseam, only to disappear when George starts to pimp "the people," which is virtually 24-7-365. You can't find them with a search warrant of the Capitol Building when you really need them to stand up for us. Are they afraid of the diabolical "Darth Vadar Cheney" and the evil villain "Simon LaGree Rumsfeld?"

Why do we need a Congress when we have a King and his court, or should I say court jesters? It looks like most of them will be busy for a while anyway, either in court or in prison, after taking bribes from Jack "Rip-'em-off" Abramoff. (Did Jack give any of his "jack" to CBC members? I didn't see any Black folks on his list.)

Congress doesn't have time to stop Bush's budget cuts in agencies that help poor people. They don't have time to look into what Bush knew prior to the mine tragedy in Tallmansville, West Virginia, just as they didn't have time to hold him accountable for the information he had before the levies broke in New Orleans. Should I also mention the information Bush had prior to the World Trade Center disappearing act? David Copperfield couldn't top that illusion.

I'm telling you, we don't need Congress. Those folks are doing a lot to us but very little for us? Are they really representin'? They voted for a bankruptcy bill that allows big corporations to continue to file but prevents poor people from doing so. They voted for a raid on Iraq's natural resources, disguised as a "war on terror," in which thousands have been slaughtered. They allow King George to lock-up U.S. citizens without due process, tap our phones, and check our records. What's next? Internment camps? Or worse? Watch out for those new televisions you are so eager to buy, especially you "gangstas" out there. As Jill Scott says, "Am I watching it or is it watching me?"

Let's throw the Congress out. Based on what it is doing now, we don't need it. Brothas, let's get out our platform goldfish-heeled shoes, our pink and mustard-colored crushed velvet, elephant-ear bellbottomed suits, and our wide-brimmed hats with the feathers on the sides, and let's kick it like George.

Sistahs, like Johnny Gill sang, "Put on your red dress"; break out your spiked heels, and maybe a feather boa to accent it all. Cowboy King George is comin' to a street near you looking to add to his stable. If you ain't quite up on your game, maybe he'll let Condi give you a refresher course on how to "get over."

Heck, we don't need no stinkin' Congress! We can get paid without them. George and his buddies are; let's see if they'll let us roll with them, 'cause George and his homies prove it really is all about the Benjamins. Aw-ight?

What good is Congress if it cannot or will not impeach this Commander-of-thieves? After all, they impeached the real Playa, the original Pimp, Bill Clinton, for gettin' it on with just one of his ladies. George Bush has been doin' it to most of the country and a brotha can't even get a hearing on Bush's high crimes and misdemeanors, John Conyers' efforts notwithstanding.

A long time ago, 56 men signed a document declaring they were not going to take it anymore. They told King George they were fed up. They put their lives, their families, and their fortunes on the line. I guess they were just tired of the nonsense, and they decided to at least <u>act</u> like a Congress and do something about their mistreatment by someone they called, "A Prince, whose character is thus marked by every act which may define a Tyrant…" They went on to say that this man "is unfit to be the ruler of a free people."

Hey Congress! Hello! Are you listening? Stop pimpin' us; and hollaatchaboy, George about pimpin' us too. If you ain't down for that and don't wanna represent for "yo peeps" then let the door knob hitcha where the good Lord splitcha! I'm out!

A Right Cross and a Left Hook
May '05

BLACK FOLKS NEED TO CHANGE OUR conversation. For the past forty years most of our conversation has been about politics. Most of our efforts have been centered on politics. Reminiscent of Reconstruction, when Blacks occupied political offices for the first time, many of our politicians are just figureheads, toothless tigers, and lackeys for the establishment. Many of them are simply "employed" and are only concerned about keeping their "jobs." Many Black politicians actually work harder on behalf of others than they do for their own brothers and sisters. I am suggesting that we change our conversation; change it from politics as usual to economics unusual.

Before you political hacks get angry, let me say that we must continue to be involved in politics. We must run for office and we must vote, by all means. But, we cannot afford to stop there. We saw what happened in Florida in 2000, and we saw what happened in Ohio in 2004, both times Black folks were told to "go out and vote." We were told we must vote in even greater numbers in 2004 than we did in 2000. We did it, and we still cannot even get a hearing on reparations. P Diddy told the young people to, "Vote or die." They voted, and when it comes to economic empowerment, they, and we, are nearly dead. Like I said in a previous article, where is the "Start a business or die" campaign, the "Pool our money or die" campaign?

In my neck of the woods, there are Black politicians who do absolutely nothing for Black folks, but they come out every year or two to tell us how good they have been and what they stand for on our behalf. What a load of fertilizer that is! Even stranger is the fact that Democrats and Republicans, Liberals and Conservatives do the same things. We may duck the "right" cross, but we will still get hit by the "left" hook. In other words, we have nothing coming from either political party, and they have proven that to us time and time again.

Our conversation must move away from the dead-end discussions on who is in and who is out this year, because if we don't get anything from the deal it makes no difference what candidate wins. Our practice of engaging in political discourse, ad nauseam, as if we control something up there on the hill, or down in city hall, is old and tired.

Black people must realize that while our relatives fought for and died for voting rights, those folks didn't die so we could spend the majority of our time "playing" politics. They wanted us to take our participation to the next level. What ever happened to that Black political party discussion from 1972? Black folks, your relatives and mine, also lost their lives because they chose to go into business; where is the rallying cry around that?

We must also come to the realization that if our vaunted voting "power" is so fearful to the two political parties, we should be using it in ways that support the most important political principle: *Quid pro quo*. Leveraging our votes to get something for our people is what we should be doing, otherwise, why participate at all? Just to be participating?

It really doesn't matter what color the politician is. What matters most is what Black folks are getting from the system and, believe me, Black folks are getting the shaft from many Black politicians. You know it, I know it, and they know it. It's bad enough that the leadership in the two major parties really doesn't care about us. One is throwing right crosses and the other is throwing left hooks at us, always causing us to be off-balance, out of sync, and off-kilter, as we try to avoid those haymakers.

The political "leaders" who continue to tell us that all we have to do is vote to change things should be voted out of office. The Black political "leaders" who always come calling for Black votes and votes for the party, Democrat or Republican, should be run out of town. This voting for all Democrats or all Republicans by Black folks is nothing short of political suicide because both parties have shown us they couldn't care less about what we think or what we do. Just look at the last presidential election.

The old game of Black folks being all or nothing to either party has proven to be our political demise. We give our all and get nothing in return. Seventy-five years ago nearly all Blacks voted Republican; now we have just the opposite. Neither scenario has worked, so why do we continue that insanity? Carter G. Woodson said, "Any people who would vote the same way for three generations without thereby obtaining results <u>ought</u> to be ignored and disenfranchised."

Black folks have been getting hit with right crosses and left hooks since we got into this political game, and now we need to start throwing some punches of our own.

The hardest punches Black people can throw are economic punches. Yes, we can start our own political party but that will not, in and of itself, solve our problems. We must be willing to take off the gloves and go with bare-knuckles into the marketplace and let our presence be known by withholding our dollars and redirecting our dollars. If we want to be players in the political game, we must put our money where our mouth is and give more to political campaigns. The only things that count with politicians are dollars and votes—in that order. We must leverage both to get what we need from either party, the Demopublicans or the Republicrats.

As the right crosses and left hooks continue to come from crooked, immoral, and unethical politicians, both white and Black, let's get busy economically and start punching back, before we get knocked out.

The Bushites–Sleaze with ease
Nov. '05

HAS THERE EVER BEEN A TIME in this country when the "ruling" administration has done so much dirt, right before our very eyes, with such arrogance, such disdain, and such outright disregard for "the people"? Think about it. For a guy who was appointed President by the Supreme Court after a crooked election process in his brother's state of Florida, and even after that debacle this same guy took his road show to Ohio for the next "selection" and did another in-your-face on "the people," your boy, George Bush, really has it goin' on. Can you believe some of the stuff he has gotten away with during the past five years, and the hits just keep on comin'.

Bush himself is bad enough, with his absolute dismal ratings among "the people" but to add insult to injury his boys and girls are worse than he is! Talk about sleaze with ease; they get the prize. Even before they joined the Bush, Jr. Camp, guys like Rumsfeld and Cheney were busy doing their dirt under the Great Communicator, Reagan. The lovely and talented "Condi" Rice was doing the bidding of George Bush, Sr. All the while, waiting in the wings (or was it a dugout, or maybe a bar) were George Jr., Karl Rove, Karen Hughes, Alberto "Speedy" Gonzales, and all the others who have participated in raping this country—and several others. And where did they find Scott McClellan?

A laundry list of shenanigans will only scratch the surface of what they have done. They came in with war on their minds. They entered the scene determined to commandeer the energy market. They lied, cheated, misled, pilfered, and smiled while they were doing their dirt. They continue to do the nastiest things to the neediest people of this country and we continue to allow it.

The Bushites are now mired in quagmires in Iraq and Afghanistan and trying desperately to get start wars in Iran and Syria. They face indictments, charges, trials, and convictions. They are Rovin' like a bunch of wild animals to see whom they can devour. They are Scootin" around, in attempts to employ "dirty tricks" to destroy those on their "enemies list." They are Delayin' justice and making every effort to change the laws to protect their comrades in crime. All of these acts are committed under their ring leader, the diabolical Dick "Spiro Agnew" Cheney, the head-sleaze-in-charge.

They have presided over a concocted and contrived war. They have directed billions of dollars to their friends at Halliburton and all the others, despite taxpayers being ripped off by these firms and their exorbitant prices. They cannot account for some $9 billion or so, in cash, that went "somewhere" to "someone" in Iraq. They watched while millions were being paid—in cash—to contractors in Iraq, while those who worked for those crooked contractors got kidnapped and beheaded as they tried to earn a living and take care of their families.

The Bushmen and Bushwomen have cut the benefits of those they say they love, respect, and revere. The soldiers fighting their war for them are facing a bankruptcy law that now makes it much more difficult to file. These revered soldiers must now pay for their food and other necessities and come home to live in conditions worse than those they had in Iraq. The Bushites wouldn't go to war, but they sure are great at using the sons and daughters of others to do their dirty work, and they mistreat them to boot! Sleaze with ease.

The top dog, or should I say, "The Top Gun," George Bush, has set himself up as an infallible, unapologetic, arrogant, capital spending ("I earned capital and I am going to spend it.") gunslinger from the wild, wild west. To really take the cake, he now thinks of himself as God. Did you hear him when he spoke of Russian leader, Vladimir Putin? Wasn't it something to the effect that he "looked into his eyes" and saw Putin's soul? And then his latest god-like announcement, as he spoke of his failed Supreme-to-be, Harriet Myers, "I know her heart." The last time I checked, knowing someone's heart was God's job. Oh well.

Black Empowerment with Attitude!

It would take a book, a series of books, to write about all the things these guys and girls have done to "the people," but let's just take a few more of Bush's words and let them suffice. Recently he responded to a question about his low ratings and the terrible job he is doing. He said, "There's some background noise here, a lot of chatter, a lot of speculation and opining, but the American people expect me to do my job and I'm going to do it." (When?) Hey George, the American people" as you call us, are the ones who rated your performance to a toilet-low in the first place.

Is this guy even awake when he makes those kinds of comments?

This makes me wonder if Bush rehearses the nonsense he espouses, or if it just comes naturally. If it were not so serious it would be funny, but this is far from funny. Our future hangs in the balance, and the best we can seem to do is have George Bush and his den of thieves in charge of our fate. Lord help us, because they have adopted a "Sleaze With Ease" campaign, and they are on the rampage. Why? The same answer Clinton gave when asked why he had his dalliance with Monica; they do it because they can.

Iran—Déjà vu all over again
Oct. '06

WELL, HERE WE GO AGAIN, FOLKS. George and his boys—and his lady friend—are about to drop a few smart bombs on another nation that Bush declared to be a member of the "Axis of Evil." The funny part about this latest act of world-policing is how dense much of the U.S. electorate is for believing the same lies that were told during the run-up to the Iraq invasion. Cheney and old Rummy must be cracking up in amazement at how easy it is to run their game on "the American people." And Yogi Berra must be saying, "I told you so."

Think about it. We have a dangerous "wounded duck" President and a do-nothing, virtually useless Republican controlled Congress that votes on horse meat and other silly issues. We have an Ambassador to the U.N., John Bolton, who despises the U.N. and can't wait for the bombs to start falling over Iran. We have this shady character, John Negroponte, head of "Bush intelligence" (Now there's an oxymoronic term), as if he didn't do enough damage in Central America under Reagan and Daddy Bush.

Afghanistan has a bumper crop of poppy plants now that we have "liberated" it from the Taliban, and the drugs are flowing faster than ever before, creating billions of dollars to fund the Taliban's resurgence. Iraq, the center stage of terrorism now that Bush "liberated" it from the Saddam Hussein regime, is literally imploding to the tune of 6,000 murders per month. It has become the hotbed of terror, according to Condi and George. But, who made it that way, guys? It wasn't that way before the invasion.

The dénouement of this comedy of errors was "vice" President Cheney saying, if he had it to do again, he would do everything exactly the same way. That's how sick these guys are. They rail against the sins of abortion and gay marriage, but they overlook their own sins of murder, torture, theft, and lying. Once again, the funny part is that we accept this crap. What hypocrites! How professed Christians, or anyone who believes that sin is sin, could support the Bush cabal is beyond my comprehension.

Iran's president has "dissed" George W. but is probably wondering when he should sound the air raid alarms. The Bushites are calling Mahmoud Ahmadinejad "Hitler" now; that's the death knell, the beginning of the end for him. I don't know how they are going to pull it off, but Bush, Cheney, Rumsfeld, and Rice are on the war path and things are about to get even hotter.

Who is he going to use for to fight Iran, his own family and friends? Lord knows he has enough cronies, and they owe him for all those cushy jobs he has given them. Maybe they should form an army and fight Iran. An even better idea is for Bush and Cheney to fight two individuals from Iran, and whoever wins is the victor of the impending war in Iran. Sure would save a lot of young lives. Ridiculous, you say? Not really, especially when you look at how many have already died by the actions of Spanky and the Little Rascals, or is it the Three Stooges?

There is so much we could recount as we look back at 2000, and even before that time, when it comes to the Bushes and their connections to evil, not the least of which was old Prescott Bush and his dealings with the Hitler regime (shhh, not so loud). But I have come to the conclusion that the electorate is simple and naïve, to put it mildly; we are afraid of the terrorists, and we are complacently willing to go through life just getting by and ignoring the geopolitical quagmire the Bushites have caused.

Why do I say that? Just look at the polls. Bumps and bounces every where for George, which means more of us are willing to support his rule over us and will vote for his supporters in November. Here is a guy who says something stupid like, literacy programs would prevent folks from being suicide bombers. He spews his venom at timid reporters, points his finger at them and says his point is the most important point in the room. Heck, he might as well have said, "In the world!" Why would anyone support this madness?

Bush presides over his own lies and the lies of his administration, but he would mitigate those lies by saying they had to protect us; after all, we would not be able to take the truth; the American people are too fragile and weak to hear the truth. He's the "Decider" and he will decide not only what the truth is but who hears it. Who in his or her right mind would want to elect anyone connected to such corruption, arrogance, incompetence, and hypocrisy?

Everything I have said, dating back to 2000, everything we have seen with our own eyes since then, and everything we know down deep in our souls points to the fact that we are on a path to destruction, maybe not physical destruction but destruction nonetheless. Now that gas prices have fallen, we are once again willing to accept Bush. How silly is that? Why do you think Cheney had those secret energy meetings? Talk about whimsical; we are the epitome of whimsical when it comes to politics.

So look out, Iran, Bush is coming to liberate you. Stay tuned Venezuela; you are next, because you have a fearless Black man, Hugo Chavez, in charge of all that oil.

Please, Don't Vote!
Oct. '06

ON NOVEMBER 7, 2006, WILL YOU fall for the politricksters' games again? Will you believe their hypocritical speeches and be lulled to sleep by their empty promises? Will you, once again, be tricked by the notion that all you have to do is vote and things will be all right for you and your people? Will you continue to be the fodder from which "politicians for life," political crooks and thieves, and political charlatans gain their wealth while ignoring you? Will you allow yourself to be played by the same old, worn-out refrain of, "Vote for me, and I'll set you free"? Will you be a "sucka" for the umpteenth time in this biennial, obligatory, political, mating dance? Will you buy-in to the tired, played-out, electoral bait-and-switch charade?

I truly hope and pray you won't. And the best way to assure the politricksters will not trick you again is by not voting for them. So don't vote on November 7th and show these "smiling faces that tell lies" you will not take their shenanigans any longer. Show these disingenuous, pandering, condescending baby-kissers that you are an intelligent, informed, and rational person who has decided not to vote for them.

Don't get hung-up on the fact that you are a "life-long" Democrat or a Republican. Don't be led by a false sense of loyalty to any party. Don't feel guilty for not voting for party favorites. After all, who made them the favorites anyway? It certainly wasn't you. We only vote on choices that have already been made; we vote for folks who have already been selected by others. Take Bush, for instance, (to borrow a line from Henny Youngman, "Please take him."). He was selected as the party favorite and you had to vote for him or one of the other guys.

In local races we are "allowed" to vote for politicians who are selected by party bosses. Why are they selected? It could be to return a favor; it could be patronage; it could be cronyism, it could be nepotism; it could be collusion; it could be corruption. Whatever the reason is, we get to vote on somebody else's choice rather than someone who will do our bidding, someone who will finally get something done for Black people.

By and large, Black people play the political game just to play, not to win. We just love to feel like we have some political juice. But we always lose in this cut-throat game of chance. If we played to win, by leveraging our so-called voting power, a voting bloc that everyone says can determine the outcome of an election, we might have some juice. Our children's future might be considered in those secret caucuses held by politricksters. We don't count because all we do is vote. So, this time, don't vote.

To show how politically weak we are, in the 2000 Presidential election, one black (small "b" intended) man had more power than all of the Black people who voted. That black man was Clarence Thomas. Although his wife was said to be collecting applications from perspective Bush employees, Thomas failed to recuse himself, as did his god, Anton Scalia, who supposedly had two sons working as lawyers for Bush. The final 5 to 4 "selection" by the Supremes meant that Clarence Thomas had the power to determine who the next President would be; he picked George Bush. Who did the vast majority of Black voters pick? Remember: "It's not the people who cast the votes that count; it's the people who count the votes that are cast."

Because the political game is obviously too sophisticated for the Black electorate, because we just can't seem to understand that politics is about self-interest, and because we don't seem to get it when it comes to our allegiance to the Dems or the Repubs, let's not vote. We are sworn to the Democratic Party, just like we were loyal to the Republican Party 80 years ago; what have they delivered to us?

So, once again, I say, "Don't vote!" Don't vote for crooks. Don't vote for liars. Don't vote for cheaters. Don't vote for smiling faces. Don't vote for candidates who have shown their lack of regard for you by their past actions. Don't vote for incompetent sweet-talkers. Don't vote for

Black Empowerment with Attitude!

Black-skinned people who are not also Black-minded people. Don't vote for popular people who are not interested in the Black populous. Don't vote for every-now-and-then politicians, both Black and white, who come around every now and then but mostly during election time.

Don't vote for promises made but never kept. Don't vote for weak-kneed hypocrites. Don't vote for sellouts. Don't vote for dunces. Don't vote for lapdogs. Don't vote for smoke and mirror solutions. Don't vote for issues that are not in your best interests. Don't vote for nonsense. Don't vote for arrogance. Don't vote for elitists. Don't vote for racists. Don't vote for movie stars and ex-football players—at least not this year. Don't vote just to make history. Don't vote for empty suits. Don't vote for religious zealots. Don't vote for dreams rather than realities. Don't vote for hopes rather than substance. Don't vote for speeches. Don't vote for the dumb stuff.

Now that you have a long list of what not to vote for, your checklist of what to vote for should be short enough to make your voting decisions much easier. Of course you have to do some work, be informed, do some research, and watch the count on election night (they cheat, you know). But if you are not willing to think independently and put in a little work before and after you exercise your precious franchise, "Please, don't vote."

Note: This article, written with a lot of "Attitude," caused a lot of Black folks to be uneasy. I was treading on sacred ground with this voting thing; their responses supported what I was saying even more. I received e-mails asking how I could say such a thing, how I could tell folks not to vote. Talk about upset; they really were. My point was to shake-up our people, sometimes by shocking us into reality. This piece certainly accomplished that end for those who wrote or called me on the carpet for writing such an irreverent piece about the precious act of voting. Let's hope it causes them-and you-to change the way we participate in local and national elections. Heaven knows we need to change the way we play that game.

Government–All Checks with No Balance
Nov. '06

BY THE TIME YOU READ THIS article the election of 2006 will be over. I wanted to write it anyway in anticipation of the change I hope and pray will take place in the Congress. I am trusting that we will kick those good-for-nothing perpetrators (or is it just "traitors"?) out of office and finally let the world know that the "American people" are not as stupid as we appear to be, having selected and supposedly elected a dunce for our President and a Congress that rubber stamps everything he proposes—even if it's illegal.

I was taught in my early years in school that the three branches of government were instituted to assure a system of checks and balances. In our current administration the only checks are those being handed to Halliburton and Kellogg, Brown, and Root, and all the other war profiteers, such as Exxon Oil receiving tax incentives despite profiting to the tune of $10 billion per quarter.

Billions of dollars in checks are being passed among the corporate insiders that Bush has brought in to perform jobs for which they have no experience. In Iraq, where they are building the largest U.S. Embassy in the world, at least $9 billion is still unaccounted for, and Congress is not checking on it.

Checks and balances? I think not. What we have gotten from this corrupt government we live under is in direct contradiction of the principles upon which the U.S. was founded. Read the Declaration of Independence's list of complaints against King George and you will find an eerie similarity to our complaints about our "King" George. This administration is all about the money and power, and they will do anything to get it and keep it.

Heaven only knows what awaits us after the election, depending upon which way it goes. I know change in the make- up and control of Congress is not a done deal yet; Deibold will work hard to maintain status quo with its corrupt and corruptible voting machines. So, don't be surprised if your vote does not count. Don't be surprised if the exit polls say one thing and the results say the opposite. And don't be surprised if those candidates who were behind by double digits win their contests. Computers can work wonders, you know.

The way to check this gang of thieves is to kick them out of office, if we can figure out how to get a fair election on November 7, 2006, and then again in 2008. I don't know if that is possible, but I am not giving up on those of us who want to bring back the original system of checks and balances. I pray we will follow through, because right now the only checks we have are those flowing through world banks, and the only balances that count are found in those huge bank accounts of corrupt politicians and corporations.

That said, I trust we are angry enough to turn out in droves and change this system. We talk a good game; will we follow it up with the necessary action? By the time you read this, we will all know, that is, unless Marshall Law is declared or something else drastic takes place. One never knows with the gang we have in charge now. Power corrupts absolutely, right?

Tricky Dick Cheney and his wife are ranting and raving about how great things are, and actually lying about things she has written. The level of their temerity is mind-boggling. Condi is who knows where, suddenly quiet and out of the picture as the election draws near. "Rum-filled" is still interviewing himself, asking and answering his own questions before an embarrassing press corps that cannot get a word in edgewise.

And then we have the "Decider" and his henchmen, Karl Rove, Speedy Gonzalez, and Michael Chertoff (does his Russian surname really mean "son of the devil"?). These guys and their cohorts around the country, some of whom have already been convicted and sentenced for corruption, some of whom are awaiting sentencing, some of whom are perverts of the highest order, and some of whom are wealthier beyond their wildest dreams because Bush is President, they have given us the worst corruption in history. (Is Ken Lay still dead? Did he really die?)

I trust we have the will to change this government before it's too late. Too many lies have been told, too many lives have been lost, and too much money is missing. I trust our votes will reflect those realities.

Let's get back to real checks and balances. And may we never again get ourselves into a situation like the one we are in now. We must have a Congress that really does check the President when he or she is out of order; and we can only have that kind of system through a balanced approach to how we vote and for whom we vote. All the negative advertisements we saw were a stark indication of how low some of these candidates would stoop to get elected. They also illustrated how stupid they think we are. Doesn't that just make you sick?

I am writing this on November 3, 2006. I look forward to November 8, 2006 with optimism, expecting a majority of voters, fed up with the lies and corruption, to have cast their votes to check the madman we currently have in office, and bring some balance back to this government of ours. And while we painfully endure the final two years of George Bush, let's start now and draft Keith Olbermann for President!

Republican Debate—A Reagan Séance
May '07

DID YOU SEE THE REPUBLICAN PRESIDENTIAL Candidate debate? I found it to be even more ridiculous than the Democrat's debate, not that either of them meant anything serious when it comes to the 2008 election. While I am not on either side at this point, I thought the Repubs were simply pitiful. There are also three or four other white male candidates, which seem to be the only gender and race the Repubs can find in the 21st Century, who are waiting to get into the fray. I can't wait to see which Black Republican will come out publicly and endorse one of those white guys, especially one of those who participated in the "debate."

The Republican "debate," or so it was deemed, was more like a séance for Ronald Reagan. They were trying to raise him from the dead! Who won the debate? It was Reagan, hands down. Held in the Reagan Library, with not a Black person in camera-shot, in none other than Simi Valley, California, where the cops who beat Rodney King were acquitted, the séance was an exercise in hero-worship and groveling at the feet of Nancy Reagan, whose greatest contribution to Black people was her admonishment to "Just say no."

If they wanted to remember Reagan instead of having a real debate, maybe they should have held the event in Philadelphia, Mississippi where Reagan kicked off his campaign for President. Oh yeah, that's also the city where Goodman, Cheney, and Schwerner were murdered.

The Reagan Love Fest was something to behold, and now that the upcoming Republican campaign has been relegated to a remembrance of the "good old days" of Ronald Reagan, I can only imagine a handful of Black folks voting for a Republican candidate in 2008. For the most part, Black people suffered under the Reagan administration; why go back and suffer again? Therefore, the next election should be even more polarizing than the previous two, because a vote for the Republican will be a vote for Reagan. I don't know about you, but I couldn't take another four years of the guy Gil Scott-Heron called, "Hollywierd."

I have thought for a while now that if Giuliani and McCain are the best the Repubs could offer they would be in deep trouble in 2008. Now they have Mitt Romney, the one who invoked Reagan's name the most during the debate, and they are recruiting Fred Thompson who, they say, "looks and sounds" presidential, has the same characteristics as Reagan, and is a staunch Conservative that can lead the Repubs back from the abyss. Now I get it; all it takes are "looks" to be President. Andre Agassi was right; "Image is everything," especially in politics. That's why George Bush rolls up his sleeves when he visits a disaster site, as if he's really going to do some work.

Considering the Repubs' Presidential candidates, if they should win again, Black folks will be the ones in deep trouble. White guys all around? Where are Michael Steele, Ken Blackwell, J.C. Watts, and the other two or three Black Republicans? It would seem that at least one of them would be in the race—for show if for nothing else. Instead they are recycling the likes of Newt Gingrich, who is now waiting to make his dramatic entrance into this race. But whoever is in the race, it won't matter to Black folks. We definitely will not have a dog in the Republican hunt.

You know, by now one would think Black people understood national "politricks." After all, we have been here since the country started; we have fought and died to play in the game; and our group has suffered the most under the U.S. political system, which has been dominated by white men since its inception. One would think that we would always be on top of our game, not allowing the crooks, liars, and baby-kissers to lull us to sleep every four years with dumb answers to dumb questions. But noooo; we continue to go along to get along; we continue to "play" politics, never to win, just simply to play.

What we witnessed in both debates was a mating dance that we have seen over and over again. It was a ritual performed to keep the lemmings in line and to make us believe something serious is going on in the political arena, something different, and maybe even something—this time—that will benefit Black people.

The Democrats held a love fest and the Republicans held a Ronald Reagan séance; we were hit with a left hook followed by a right cross, in the first round of this fight. I am sure those early blows were delivered to keep our attention diverted from more pressing issues. There can be no other reason for such "theater," such pretentiousness, such phoniness, and such condescension by ten white guys on the Repub side and a "We are the world" cavalcade of stars on the Dem side.

Were you persuaded by anyone? Have you made up your mind yet? Do you think Black folks will benefit no matter who gets elected? My cynicism as well as my historical perspective tell me "No." Also, I am reminded that if we continue to do the same thing, we will continue to get the same results.

It's pretty much cut and dried who the Black Dems will support; they have safe bets all around. But I can't wait to see who the Black Republicans endorse from their gang of ten white guys. Or is it fourteen now?

I hope the 2012 Republican debate will not be held at the George W. Bush "Library." What an oxymoronic setting that would be. Meanwhile, back at the Reagan Ranch, there have been Ronnie sightings.

Vote for me and I'll set you free!
Oct. '04

"Nobody frees a slave; a slave must free himself."

— Marcus Garvey

AS WE CELEBRATE MARCUS GARVEY'S BIRTHDAY, August 17th, we should all take a moment to reflect on his writings as well as his accomplishments despite the tremendous adversity he faced. In addition to the above statement, Garvey admonished Black people to build and maintain a strong economic base and harness true economic power, without which there would be no reason for us to think we will ever have any real political power. Unfortunately, many of our people know very little about this giant of a Black man, and some of us fail to heed the lessons Garvey taught us.

Every four years Black folks get so fired up about the Presidential election that it consumes us and takes up every ounce of our energy. It holds our attention and captures our wildest imaginations; it makes us long for the day when we will finally be free; and it entices us into believing that there really is a political white knight on a white horse (or should I say, a donkey?) that will ride into our lives and make it all better. Newsflash!! He ain't comin' y'all. And, even if he (or she) does come, it won't be to free Black people. Aren't 139 years long enough to wait?

Have you ever wondered where the statement, "… and I'll set you free" came from anyway? Well, who has been enslaved in this country? Bingo! It's a statement often used in a comical context and has survived so long because Black folks really think our salvation will someday be gained because we vote for a particular presidential candidate. Maybe that's why it's so funny; it's a joke.

This year's political election is very important, we all know that. But so was the election of 2000. Now we are "really" mad and we plan to "really" get our people to the polls this time—just like we did in 2000. The pundits are fired up; the preachers are getting "all souls to the polls"; the Hip Hop folks are rocking the vote—once again; and the talking heads are poll-watching and prognosticating on who will be our leader in 2005. Don't you just love it?

Brother Sharpton told Bush the Black vote is not for sale. I don't know, Al. You could be wrong on that one. I think many of our votes are for sale, and I think many of those who say they operate in our interests are selling their vote and ours too. They are the ones who maintain that all we have to do is vote for a certain one and we will be free.

Will Black people ever learn that our redemption is not in the hands of Bush, Kerry, or any other President? Sure, it makes us feel good to fantasize about our role in determining the outcome of the Presidential election, but all we are really doing is choosing between two decisions that were made without our input. We choose; they decide. But you already know that.

What is more important is what Garvey tried to make us see. We will have to free ourselves, thus, we cannot and never should have bought into that promise of "vote for me and I'll set you free." Neither this upcoming election nor any other election will set us free. Our freedom will come by building our own economic foundation, from which we can reward our friends and punish our enemies.

Like most of you, God willing, I will cast my vote in November too, but it will not be accompanied by an orchestra playing the William Tell Overture or someone singing, "Happy Days Are Here Again." I will do it because it is my duty and my right, and I will do it because it's better to have the lesser of two evils in office than it is to have the greater of two evils there.

Yes, I am concerned about who picks the next two or three members of the *Supremes*, and I would like to see someone else in charge of those important Congressional committees, but in the long run, I know that no matter who occupies those seats, economic freedom will only come to us, as Martin Delany said, "…by the work of our own hands."

Barack Obama, the new fair-haired child, has recently been crowned as the probable first Black President. (Whatever happened to Harold Ford? Wasn't he the latest to be crowned?) But Obama may turn out to be the Tiger Woods of politics; we will have to wait and see. Some say Obama "transcends race" because he is not the "stereotypical Black man" (that's what they said about O.J.); one commentator said, "…he is not black in the usual way." What in the world does that mean? (Rhetorical question, folks.) Does it mean that he is light-skinned and doesn't seem too threatening? Harold Ford is light-skinned; does he not fit the mold? Maybe he just doesn't say the right things.

Obama is certainly an excellent candidate for the Senate, but let's not fall for the game, brothers and sisters. If he is deemed "safe" then what label will be put on the rest of our Black politicians? Besides, even Obama will not set us free. That's our job.

A New Iraq or a New Orleans?
Dec. '05

WHY HAVE WE SPENT AS MUCH as $1 billion per week to build a "New Iraq," and yet our compassionate government, headed by George Bush and his boys and girls, cannot find a billion a week to spend on New Orleans and those wiped out by Hurricane Katrina? What kind of a country is this anyway? What kinds of people are running this show? Immediate expenditures totaling billions of taxpayer dollars to rebuild a country we intentionally destroyed, but four months after the worst catastrophe in this country our government has hardly moved to take care of its own.

Yes, our eyes have been opened to several realities since the hurricanes hit the gulf coast, most of which we knew all along but were afraid or ashamed to admit, but this is ridiculous. Now we must face our deepest fears; Black and poor people must look at this country in a different light now; and we must respond, because we cannot like what we see. We cannot turn deaf ears to what is being screamed at us: "You don't count!"

Yes, it took a hurricane, but as Eric Benet says on his latest CD, "Hurricane" released, by the way, prior to Katrina, "Sometimes what you fear the most is what you need, to find that road, right around that curve a lesson learned, now that I have the eyes to see. A hurricane—sometimes the only way to wash away the pain." How prophetic!

The President is touting his "plan" for victory in Iraq, now that the oil wells are secured and the petro-dollar is back in full swing in that country. He is spending our money like a drunken sailor, urinating on us and telling us it's a spring rain. His attention is always on the New Iraq and seldom on a New Orleans. Victims of Katrina are testifying at congressional hearings, while Bush is busy justifying a war that he started under false pretenses.

Bush and his ilk try to instill guilt in those who want to withdraw from Iraq by saying if we leave the 2000+ who have died, they will have died in vain. Two questions: Have not those killed in Iraq, no matter when the war ends or how it ends, already died in vain, since they were only there because of lies and deceit?

What about the folks in New Orleans who died as a result of mismanagement by FEMA's "Brownie," the guy George Bush said was doing a "heck of a job," and the disconnected Director of Homeland Security, Michael Chertoff? Did those citizens die in vain? Did the 911 victims die in vain, since we have not caught Osama Bin Laden and ignored information that he would attack us via airplanes flying into tall buildings?

We cut and ran from New Orleans, but in New Iraq we will stay until the people "put their lives back together," "…until they are back on their feet," "…until they have a stable government." We can't have a timetable for leaving Iraq, but we certainly came up with a timetable for putting New Orleans evacuees out of their hotel room shelters. George Bush says, "We have $62 billion on the table" for New Orleans (that's the problem, George; it's "on the table"); but, we have about $250 billion "on the ground" (And in the pockets of corporate raiders) in New Iraq.

What hypocrisy! What disdain is being shown for the people of New Orleans by Mr. Compassion himself! Why so much concern for the New Iraq and little or no concern for New Orleans. Could it be economics?

In an interview, Bush said, "Call me anything, but don't call me a racist." Well, here goes, George. You are arrogant, vindictive, egomaniacal, and aloof; you are disconnected, discombobulated, befuddled, entrenched, recalcitrant, obstinate; you are corny, spoiled, ignorant, scornful, disrespectful, phony, condescending, and just plain weird. Maybe it would be better if you <u>were</u> just a racist.

I am sure there is some good stuff somewhere inside this guy; I just haven't seen it.

Black Empowerment with Attitude!

Bush spends billions for the New Iraq, while he emphatically brags about asking congress to allocate a measly $1.2 billion to stockpile bird flu vaccine, which by the way will only buy enough to vaccinate 20 million citizens. I wonder which 20 million they will be.

Bush's Secretary of Defense should be happy with that decision; according to an article I read, Rumsfeld stands to make "a fortune on royalties as a panicked world population scrambles to buy a drug worthless in curing the effects of alleged Avian Flu." Another article stated, "Among the beneficiaries of the run on Tamiflu is Secretary of Defense Donald Rumsfeld, who was chairman of Gilead [Sciences] and owns at least $5 million of the stock, which has jumped from $35 in April [2005] to $47." Why should Dick Cheney and Halliburton have all the fun, right?

Finally, Bush says the New Iraq is comparable to the nascent years of the United States. Oh, really? What if a "coalition of the willing" had come to this country during the Revolutionary War to liberate enslaved Black people from the tyranny under which they suffered? Too bad there was no coalition back then—with cowboy George W. leading the charge.

Instead, George W. is leading the charge to build a New Iraq but has little time for and will not allocate adequate resources to build a New Orleans. Hey George! Be sure to close the door to the bank vault when you and the guys finally get as much money as you can carry, O.K.?

Note: On the second anniversary of Hurricane Katrina's onslaught through New Orleans, a massive protest is being planned to bring attention to the fact that the people of that city are still in the same relative shape they were in just days after the hurricane. Called "A Day of Presence," hundreds are expected to participate. It is a shame and a disgrace that two years after the fact, we are still making attempts to "show" the world what it already knows: The people in New Orleans are in desperate need of assistance, both from the government and from their brothers and sisters across this country. Sadly, many are subscribing to the words of Barbara Bush, who said, "And so many of the people in the arena here [in Houston], you know, were underprivileged anyway, so this (she chuckles slightly) is working very well for them."

"At the Bottom of Politics ... Lies Economics"
Sept. '04

BOOKER T. WASHINGTON SPOKE THOSE WORDS as he did his best to show us what is really happening in this country, as he tried to convince us to stay focused on the money-side of things, and as he admonished us not to immerse ourselves in the political whirlpool, thereby abandoning our economic resources. Well, as I look at the upcoming election, and as I have written during the past four years since the Florida election debacle, all I can now sadly say is, "Sorry, Brother Booker; we did not listen to you."

Once again, this is the "most important election of our time," and we are geared up for the fight—this time. We must register to vote-once again-because our people died for the right to do so. We must come out as we have never come out before, you know, like we did in 2000, because 2004 is the "most critical election of our lifetime"—again. Black folks are so hyped about this election that we can hardly hear our leaders, and the man for whom they suggest we vote, say anything about how Black people will be positively affected by the outcome. We definitely hear the negatives, but where are the positives?

Our leaders tell us—once again—that Black folks have the "power" to sway the election in either direction. The question is: If we have that kind of power, why aren't we using it to get a few concessions for ourselves? Why aren't we forming an independent political party and leveraging our "power" for a *quid pro quo*? While some say Black people, collectively, have the power to swing the vote, according to the latest polls, it doesn't seem to matter. I suppose a better way to say it is that Democrats need the power of the collective Black vote to win, because all the Republicans needed was one Black vote in 2000 to win; it was cast by Clarence Thomas.

Black Empowerment with Attitude!

Who are we kidding, folks? This political game, at least the way we are playing it, is one that keeps our attention on the surface and away from what's beneath it all. We have had four years to do many of things we are so feverishly doing now. Didn't we see what happened in 2000? Why did our political leaders go back to sleep after they yelled, screamed, and ranted about the Presidential Selection? What were the folks doing in Florida after their rights were destroyed by Hurricane Katherine (Harris)? Oh, that's right, they sent her to Congress.

What have we been doing to avoid a repeat of the same thing we so vehemently complained about four years ago? Most would say in answer to that question: "We have been registering new voters." Well here is what the other folks have been doing. They have been building voting machines to sell to various states for billions of dollars. Private companies have used the past four years to figure out how to make more money from the political chicanery that takes place in this country. Private companies have been wooing our Secretaries of State, hawking their wares across this nation, and licking their greedy chops at the thought of raking even more filthy lucre into their coffers.

A couple of companies, the main ones now receiving the contracts to install computerized voting machines, have even offered to open new offices in counties where their systems are purchased and have offered backroom deals such as discounts on software upgrades and who knows what else to the purchasing agents and decision-makers. Lawsuits have already been filed against some of these folks and their E-voting machines.

What has been the response from Black political leaders, other than hand wringing and catchy voting slogans, regarding the irregularities that have cropped up thus far? Have any of them endorsed and pushed for Brother Athan Gibbs' TruVote System, which has <u>real</u> built-in protection against voter fraud and tampering, and provides a paper receipt for auditing purposes?

Before his untimely death, Athan traipsed across this country trying to get his system endorsed and ultimately utilized in the national election;

his system was successfully tested by organizations and other verifiable sources, but we did not hear our Black political leaders cry out in support a Black man's invention that would prevent the disenfranchisement of Black and other voters. As I recall, registering and voting were not the biggest problems the last time; it was votes not being counted, votes being thrown out, and eligible voters being denied the right to vote.

Now, in 2004, just prior to the election, we are probably looking at the same kind of scenario, and this time it will be easier because of corrupt voting machines sold by corrupt companies to corrupt election officials. We failed to listen to Booker T. when he told us what politics was all about back at the turn of the last century. We also failed to listen to Brother Athan Gibbs when he told us how to overcome the political shenanigans of 2000. Moreover, had we supported TruVote, millions of dollars could have flowed into a Black owned company for many years to come.

Maybe by the time 2008 gets here we will have learned once and for all that politics is all about money, power, and maintaining status quo. I sure hope so, because right now Black people are losing on all three fronts.

Prison Stuff

"The criminal justice system is sick. It will only incarcerate and kill African American males. The only way we can beat this system is not to be a part of its wickedness."

— Efrem B. Martin, It's Time to Come Correct

*D*oes *the African American community, by continuing to permit itself to be "legitimately" exploited by non-African American communities, thereby de-legitimize itself and permit itself to be criminalized while de-criminalizing its exploiters? Has the African American community-addicted to wasteful and nonsensical consumerism, with its unwillingness to invest its wealth in human resources in itself, in America, and uncommitted to controlling its own internal markets—contributed in no small way to the criminalization of its sons, to the increasing impoverishment of its children, to the violence which prevails in its households and neighborhoods?*

When the Black community squanders the economic inheritance of its children, while it fills to overflowing the coffers of the children of other communities, when it does not regulate its consumption behavior in terms of its long-term interests—it gets the crime it deserves. Dr. Amos Wilson, Black-on-Black Violence

Dr. Wilson also taught us that just as power corrupts, so also does powerlessness corrupt; and he said, "The violently oppressed react violently to their oppression."

What lessons can we, should we, must we learn from our experiences in the criminal "injustice" system in which Black men and women are disproportionately represented? Upon our release from enslavement the U.S. penal system responded to America's need for free labor by writing laws that would surely entrap the newly "freed" Black people. Regulations were written to allow the prisons to "lease" their prisoners out to work on the farms. Remember Mose Allison's song, Parchman Farm?

As time went by, the prison system morphed into a money-making machine, a veritable Wall Street juggernaut that could not be stopped. Now that system, while earning billions for its owners, and that includes everyone from the beat cops to the Chiefs-of-Police, to the Prosecutors, to the Judges, to the prison-builders, suppliers, and owners, has achieved critical mass with the help of some of our people who are still too stupid to stay out of harm's way, some who are still mentally captured and captivated by a society that exploits their desires to possess things, and some who have done little or nothing to deserve incarceration.

But $30,000 per year per Black man in jail is more attractive than a Black man earning $30,000 per year on a job, or a Black child costing $3,000 per year in Head Start, or a Black teenager being allocated $13,000 per year for his education in a public school system, or a Black entrepreneur with $300,000 in annual revenues.

The criminal injustice system was invented to play and prey on Black folks, and it has been exponentially successful, both in its economic mission and its genocidal mission—in many cases with our assistance, of course.

These next articles speak to this issue, sometimes in a harsh way, but always out of love and deep concern for our brothers and sisters who are either incarcerated or "willingly" on their way to being incarcerated—or even worse, shot down on the street like a rabid dog.

It is enough that many of our people are in jails and prisons unjustifiably; it is yet another thing for us to ignore the fact that we are the economic fodder for the U.S. prison industrial complex and some of our people continue to "volunteer" to occupy every new cell that's built.

As Dr. Wilson noted, much of the crime we see committed against one another is directly related to economics, on both sides of the supply and demand equation. We need to wise-up and stay as far away from the corrupt criminal "injustice" system as we can.

Let's Boycott Prisons!
Jan. '06

JEROME AND JENNIFER WILLIAMS CHOSE ME to speak on Ujamaa—Cooperative Economics, during the 2005 Kwanzaa Celebration in Buffalo, New York. I take this opportunity to thank my newfound brother and sister. While there I met several others with whom I am sure I will have long lasting relationships, people like Sam Radford, Dr. Florence Flakes-Rozier, and L. Nathan Hare. I was especially excited about a conversation I had with Brother Hare; he suggested that Black folks boycott prisons. Wow! What an idea!

Do I need to reiterate the bare facts concerning how the prison industrial complex is raking in billions in profits, mainly because so many Black folks are incarcerated? Must I recite the words of the 13th Amendment of the Constitution, "Neither slavery nor involuntary servitude, 'except' as a punishment for crime whereof the party shall have been duly convicted, shall exist within the United States…"?

Do we need to revisit the 1990's during which time Bush Senior and Bill Clinton went on a spending spree to build prisons? Is it necessary for us to check out the stock market and see how much money is being made by private prisons? How about reemphasizing what Brother Amos Wilson said in his book, Black on Black Violence? He wrote, "Five years after the Civil War, the Black percentage of the prison population went from close to 0% to 33%."

I think most of us know the stats, the history, and the outcomes of such realities vis-à-vis the U.S. prison system, so the only question we should be dealing with is: Why are we allowing ourselves to be the sacrificial lambs for the establishment's prison profiteering? A recent article I wrote asked, "Why are Black folks so dominant in the cells but absent in the sales when it comes to prisons?" To further solidify that point, I repeat: We must move away from being the labor pool for the prison industrial complex. Back during the post-civil war period, former enslaved Blacks were imprisoned and then "leased" to landowners to provide free labor, essentially profit without investment.

So, understanding as we do the real motive behind this "criminal injustice system" and the reality of the prison system, a boycott of prisons is an appropriate and sensible response to many of the problems we face. In addition, a boycott of prisons would by its very nature, also obviously be a boycott of stealing, murdering, drug-dealing, gang-banging, and all the other activities in which some of our brothers and sisters are involved.

Since we have boycotted prisons on the supply side of the economic spectrum, that is, building them, owning them, and supplying their business needs, boycotting prisons on the demand side is a logical next step. Knowing that we cannot tell folks what <u>not</u> to do without also telling them what <u>to</u> do, how can we accomplish this reasonable, sensible, practical strategy, which will keep more of us out of prison and, at the same time, provide positive alternatives? Here's my plan.

I have already had bumper stickers printed, by a Black owned company, of course. We are working with a group of young men who will establish their own business entity and sell the bumper stickers as well as T-shirts, buttons, and other "Boycott Prisons" paraphernalia. We will also create flyers to be distributed throughout the city, especially to the brothers on the streets. The flyers will have information relating to the history of the prison system, its social repercussions, and its economic benefits. Additionally, we will stress the importance of the legal side of business, employment, and ownership of income-producing assets.

If we can get Black people to boycott prisons for just one year, as Brother L. Nathan Hare suggested, we would make a tremendous economic statement, and maybe put a few brothers and sisters on a diversionary track, away from crime and prisons and toward positive activities for wealth-building. Are you willing to start a Boycott Prisons Campaign in your city? If so, get started right now.

It is up to us to free ourselves; no one else is going to do that for us. Can't you see by looking back in history that this country never intended for us to be free from creating profits for those who control the country? Is it so difficult to face the words of the 13th Amendment? If slavery has not been completely and forever abolished, why would we continue to place ourselves in a position to be slaves again?

Did you see George Bush, as he went to "view" the Emancipation Proclamation on MLK Day? The subliminal suggestion and Bush's outright statement that this document actually freed an enslaved people are totally ridiculous. If that document freed us, why was a 13th Amendment necessary? It surely set the stage for further action on our behalf, but it did not free the so-called slaves. All you have to do is read it!

So how about it, brothers and sisters? Are you ready to start a Boycott Prisons Campaign in your city? No, it's not a panacea, but it can help in our efforts to curtail crime and to lower the horrific numbers of Black men—and women, working in the prison industrial complex, making 50 cents an hour while corporations make billions in profits from their labor.

Boycott Prisons, for one year, and let's see what happens. Don't worry; prisons will always be there, just in case some of us want to become residents again. But, for now, let's stay out of the cells and get into sales-legitimate sales that is.

Note: Please take some time to read the Emancipation Proclamation to your children. Show them a copy of the 13th Amendment to the Constitution and talk to them about what it really says. Don't allow them to grow up believing something that is not true. They are being taught these untruths in school everyday and, for the most part, we parents allow them to remain stuck in and stymied by their ignorance. Parents are the primary educators of their children; let's act like it! Do your job!

Stupid Black Men (and women)
Aug. '06

YEAH, I KNEW THAT WOULD GET your attention. We all chuckled when Michael Moore wrote his book titled, "Stupid White Men." It was cute, made some people think, and he made a ton of money from it. I wonder how many of those stupid white men have changed anything in their lives when it comes to politics, education, injustice, or their economic status. Was Moore really serious about them being stupid, or was it all said tongue-in-cheek? I don't know what his motivation was, whether it was sincere or whimsical; what I do know is that he made money and he received tremendous notoriety for his rant.

Now, let's talk about stupid Black men and the rising number of stupid Black women too, and see if we can generate some money from a change in our actions. The stupid ones I am talking about are those brothers and sisters who expose themselves to the criminal "injustice" system, the ones who are out there committing crimes only to end up at the "mercy" of a system that hates them; those who think they are slick and will never get caught; and those who literally have no understanding of this prison industrial complex and the economic role they play as prisoners or even as accused perpetrators.

There is one word that describes a Black person who knowingly puts himself in criminal jeopardy, especially in a nation that can't wait to imprison him. There is one word for a Black person who complains about how he or she is treated by "the man" and then commits acts that will ultimately subject him or her to the prejudices of "the man." There is one word that aptly describes the Black person who would volunteer to be a slave in jail, creating wealth for a slave master, while sentencing himself to a life of poverty. There is one word for the Black person who associates with folks who are doing things that may lead to contact with police officers, many of who are just itching to do bodily harm to a Black person. One word: Stupid.

I understand that every Black man or woman in jail should not be there. Some of them did nothing to deserve being incarcerated, and they should be set free. I still lament William Mayo's situation, as he literally rots away in a Georgia prison for a crime he did not commit. I went to one of his hearings down in Georgia and watched that white racist judge dismiss the whole situation like it was an annoyance rather than a criminal justice proceeding. I understand, as I watch brothers like Michael Austin in Baltimore, Maryland, walk out of prison after serving decades for crimes they did not commit.

I definitely understand, and I am not talking about those who get profiled and wrongly accused simply because they are Black. Stupid are the ones who actually commit the crimes, thus, volunteering to be used in a corrupt, greedy, and hateful system that has profit as its only motive. Why would anyone volunteer for that? Are material items that important that we would risk our lives for them? The answer is an obvious and resounding "yes."

If you know the history of this country you probably know why we commit some of the crimes we see so often, even the murder of our own brothers and sisters. If you know history, you know, as Amos Wilson says, that much of the violence we see today is "The psychodynamics of Black self-annihilation in service of white domination." But many of our young people don't know history; they don't know who they are; they don't know about the legality of slavery in the prison system; and they don't know about the economic role they play in that system. I still say it's stupid to voluntarily do anything that you know will result in being locked down for years under a hateful slave master.

It's time we stop citing the numbers of Black men and women in jail. It's time we start educating ourselves about this latest way to eliminate Black people, or at least to use us economically. It's time we start to change our thinking and really get serious about the problem we face—

not just the symptoms. It's time we stop being stuck on stupid. Why rail against the issue if you are unwilling to address it with action?

So here's the deal. Let's stop being stupid. No, I don't want to hear the excuses on why you "have to do whatever it takes" to get yours. No more excuses about being poor and deprived. No more excuses about "the man" not giving you a break (What kind of a break do you think you are going to get in jail, and then after you are released?) No more self-hating, self-deprecating responses to your unfortunate situation in life. This stupidity of filling up the jails and maintaining an economic windfall for white folks is, as Mike Tyson would say, "Ludicrous." Yeah, Mike was stupid too.

Aren't you sick and tired of knowing that in addition to Black folks being the number one consumers of goods made by everyone else in this world, we are also volunteering in many cases to do even more to enrich other folks? I implore you; don't be stupid. Stay out of the line of fire; stay out of harm's way. It's easy enough to get picked up for not having committed a crime. Why volunteer for it? The only thing Black folks have coming from this criminal injustice system is time. Don't do anything that will cause you to be imprisoned. Get involved in the Boycott Prisons and Jails Campaign, and let's put a big dent in the number of brothers and sisters languishing in prisons throughout this country.

Do we really care about our children?
March '07

IS IT ANY WONDER THAT BLACK children are angry at Black adults? Is it any wonder that Black youth feel unprotected by Black adults? Is it any wonder that Black youth are out there "getting theirs" and doing anything else they want to do? Is it any wonder that as Black adults complain about the behavior of Black youth, our behavior toward them and toward ourselves is equally despicable?

There have been others, but the case of Shaquanda Cotton, the 14 year-old girl in Paris, Texas, who was sentenced to 7 years in jail for shoving a hall monitor in school, should be the final straw for Black people all over this country. This case is especially troubling because the punishment definitely does not fit the crime, and the judge in this case also sentenced a white 14 year-old girl to probation after she was convicted of arson!

This is not an isolated incident of miscarriage of justice by any means, but more and more we are seeing Black children being mistreated by authorities across this country, younger and younger, while we adults simply talk about it and wring our hands about it. There have been at least three cases of 5 year-old Blacks being handcuffed, disciplined, and threatened by the police—one of which occurred right here in Cincinnati, a city in which a law exists that allows 7 year-olds to be electrocuted with 50,000 volt Tasers.

How much abuse are we willing to have heaped upon our children before we really get serious about stopping it? When people begin to allow the abuse of their children it is the death knell of their society. I was one of the few in Cincinnati to speak before city council in opposition to the 7 year-old Taser law. It did not matter; it passed, and even one Black councilman voted to pass the motion. He is the same councilman who, as he was beating his own child said, "I'll beat the Black off you," and he was arrested for it. Maybe his vote had a lot to do with self-hate.

What has happened to us? We have turned our children over to someone else to be educated, and they have come back to us totally messed up. We have taken away the discipline necessary to keep our children on the right track, and they are in the streets doing whatever they want to do. We have turned our heads when our children have been abused and mistreated, and now they are being sent to prison for 7 years for shoving someone, while white children get probation for committing arson.

The recent 50-shot barrage that killed Sean Bell in New York City and the 14 year old sister who was killed in L.A. were, I thought, the very last straws. But I also thought that about the brutal police killings of Kenneth Walker in Columbus, Georgia and Nathaniel Jones in Cincinnati. How could Black people sit idly by and allow these things to occur without shutting some cities down, the way the illegal immigrants did? How could Black men, especially, be so accepting of these and other atrocities against us?

Maybe now, because of our docility and complacency, we have arrived at a place where we can be treated in any manner by just about anyone, and the only reprisal they can expect is a two-hour demonstration. Are we really in such a disadvantaged position in this country that we are unable to prevent our daughters from suffering at the hands of racists?

What can we do? In addition to the Free Shaquanda Cotton Petition being circulated and signed on the Internet, Black folks should be so outraged with righteous indignation—all across this country, not just in Paris, Texas, and demand Sister Cotton be released from prison. If she is not released we must not only hit the streets but also use our dollars to obtain the victory. If we seriously withdraw our dollars from various businesses and events in this country we will not continue to be taken for granted.

When people know they can do anything to you, anything they want, without a serious response, they will likely continue in that vein. How sad it is that now we have moved from abuse of our adults to abuse of our children with no serious response. We could name other young Blacks, boys and girls, who have been killed or otherwise abused, with impunity; it is occurring more and more each year. What are we going to do about it?

There are two areas of consideration here. First, we Black adults, must admit our own faults and our own neglect of our own children. Having exposed them to the horrors of dependence on and vulnerability to a society that only sees them as an object from which to create more wealth, by way of mis-education and prison occupancy, our youth are running wild and doing all sorts of outlandish things to one another. That is our fault, and we must rectify that.

Then we must let our children know and let this society know that our children are off limits, that there is a line that cannot be crossed without a fight. We should make one collective statement in support of our children, letting this society know that we love them so much that we really would die to protect them. Are we men and women enough to do that? If your answer is "Yes," you can start by contacting the brothers and sisters in Paris, Texas, and join them in their struggle for justice, and help Shaquanda Cotton get out of prison.

Note: Shaquanda Cotton was released from prison on March 31, 2007, after a huge public outcry, this article included. It demonstrates what we can do when we work collectively with resolve and determination. Now, let's get Genarlow Wilson and William Mayo released from those Georgia prisons.

Prisons and Blacks: Occupancy, High; Development Opportunities, Low.
Dec. '05

AN ARTICLE ON CHARLOTTE.COM BY LIZ Chandler, titled <u>Black Contractors Used as Fronts?</u> reminded me of an economic incongruity: Black people occupy most of the cells in the U.S. prison system but have very little participation in prison development, construction, and long-term contracts for vending, i.e., supplies, food, equipment, etc. Another in a long line of expose´ articles on minority programs, the latest uncovering of the prison-building money-pit discloses several issues relevant to the economic disempowerment of Black people.

As usual, a history lesson is in order here. Amos Wilson, in his book, <u>Black on Black Violence</u>, wrote, "Within five years after the Civil War, the Black percentage of the prison population went from close to zero to 33%. Then, as now, the Black prison population performed an economic and political function for the benefit of Whites." (Featured in the City Sun, July 18-24, 1990, and written by Clinton Cox, *Racism: The Hole in America's Heart.)*

Another tidbit of prison history is found in the 13th Amendment of the U.S. Constitution, which says, "Neither slavery nor involuntary servitude, except as a punishment for crime whereof the party shall have been duly convicted, shall exist within the United States..." We should pay special attention to the words, "except as a punishment for crime whereof the party shall have been duly convicted." Need I say more?

It is obvious that Black people have been and continue to be the profit margins, first for the agricultural industry of the 19th century, and now for the prison industrial complex of the New Millennium. As I read the article I thought about our history, and I thought about how we continue to contribute to our own economic demise by serving the new master as front companies, even in the prison-building industry, of all places.

What a shame that some of us would do that, as if Black people don't have the capability to stand on our own, collectively, and secure more than front money from prison-building, convention centers, waterfront developments, museums, and stadiums, where there is another economic "Blackout" brewing in Dallas, Texas with the construction of their new sports facility. Being out front is one thing; being a "front" is an entirely different animal.

I am pleased to report that the two Black firms that were offered "deals" as front companies in North Carolina turned them down and then turned in the companies making the offers.

The article questions whether there are Black (or is it minority?) contractors who are being used as front companies, conduits through which a miniscule amount of money flows to the Black company for doing little or no work. These Faustian deals also carry the added benefit of the prime contractor "doing business" with a "minority" firm.

The first problem I saw was the ridiculous notion that women are "minorities." Oh yeah; since when? The U.S. Census says women comprise the majority population. Thus, when women are declared minorities by "minority programs" they must be referring to white women, right? That's part of the game. In the Charlotte case, "women-owned" businesses received more contracts than Black owned businesses—Black men and Black women combined!

The article stated, "…nearly 21 percent of the prison work will go to minority firms, primarily those owned by women. African American firms, one of the most underused groups in state construction, are to get 3 percent to 4 percent of the prison work, obtained only after complaining to the state." According to the 2000 census, Charlotte is 33% Black.

The other problem is something I harp on all the time: Black people referring to ourselves as "minorities" in the first place. I have said it as plainly as I can say it. It's a game, folks. It's a game that we can never win. No one should ever be confused about who we are. The organization fighting against the economic injustice in the Charlotte case is the Carolinas Associated Minority Contractors. Unless this organization comprises Asian, Hispanic, and Indian members, it is a Black association, not a "minority" association.

The construction shell game is controlled by whites, and Black people will remain on the margins as long as we settle for the crumbs thrown at us. Prime contractors will rationalize about why they continue to get the vast majority of the deals. The Charlotte article stated, "It's not what the courts call overt discrimination," says Steve Humphrey, whose Florida research firm, MGT of America, conducted the [2003] study. "It's what's called passive discrimination ... where general contractors call up people they know, and most of them are white." That should make Black contractors feel better, shouldn't it?

Bottom-line: The onus is on us. If we can occupy the prisons to such a high degree, why are we not also represented in building them, in maintaining them , in supplying their needs, and in selling them equipment, food, and other necessities? Can a brother get some Black-made (and distributed) hair grease and some Shea butter soap and lotion up in here?

We must be more assertive, more aggressive, more determined, and we must build more capacity to take on larger projects. We must also have the backbone of Tommy Vaughn, who was offered $18,000 to be a front company by "supply[ing] materials -- even though he says most of the arrangements had already been made," and Bobby Nichols, who was offered $20,000 "for going six times to the Eastern North Carolina prison to observe painting practices." Hats off to these two brothers! They did their part; now Black folks in Charlotte should commend and support them by insisting they get contracts, not bribes.

Georgia on my mind
May '07

Unfortunately, thousands of African-American people have been wrongly incarcerated over the years because of rogue cops, shabby lab work, and overzealous prosecutors. Being Black in Americas is a constant fight for justice." **John V. Elmore, Esq. <u>Fighting for your Life</u>**

WILLIAM MAYO HAS BEEN WRONGFULLY imprisoned in Georgia for 15 years now, having received two life sentences plus forty years (I guess that was just in case he is reincarnated) for a crime he did not commit, a crime committed by two young men who have since told the courts that William had nothing to do with the crime. One of the two has been released, having done the "short" time he was given for committing the crime of, hold on to your hat, ROBBERY! That's right, robbery. No one was hurt, stolen articles were recovered, and William, implicated by intimidation of the two young men by the prosecutor, is paying dearly for it, by serving double-life! As Ray Charles said, "Georgia, Oh Georgia!"

It didn't matter that Mayo had never been in trouble before; it didn't matter that he was just a few hours from getting his degree from Morehouse; it didn't matter that William Mayo was a positive role model and mentor for young men, in the act of helping the two young men who did the crime; and it didn't matter that he was a church-going, law-abiding citizen prior to being dragged into the abyss in which he now finds himself.

In June 2005 I attended Mayo's court hearing (at least that's what they called it) and wrote an article titled, New Jack Slavery, after watching a racist judge make very short work of Mayo's attempt to present evidence to prove his innocence (he was not even allowed to speak at his own hearing). Talk about a travesty of justice, that Georgia Judge displayed it that day.

So Georgia has been on my mind lately, not only because of William Mayo, but also because of other cases such as Genarlow Wilson, the young man in prison for consensual sex, and Jade Sanders and Lamont Thomas, Vegans, whose child died of malnutrition; they received life sentences for murder. LIFE? C'mon, Georgia. Sure, they should be punished for child neglect; but LIFE? What kind of State do you Georgians live in? Or is this the kind of punishment reserved strictly for Black folks, like the seven years given to Shaquanda Cotton in Paris, Texas, for shoving a hall monitor?

Georgia is on my mind because of its lack of fairness and its blatant disregard for even a modicum of compassion for Mayo, Wilson, Sanders, Thomas, and others I am sure. Even if William did commit robbery, don't you think the fifteen years he has already done are enough? He can't even get a fair hearing to review his case. Sanders and Thomas loved their child, I am sure, and although they were misguided and uninformed in the diet they fed the child, I don't believe they intended to "murder" the baby. Their sentence should be reduced.

Is there no common sense in Georgia courtrooms?

The state that boasts the likes of MLK, Maynard Jackson, Cynthia McKinney, John Lewis, Joseph Lowery, and many more strong Black folks cannot seem to get it right and fair when it comes to its Black population, which is the first or second largest Black population of all the states. Two life sentences for robbery, and life for the unintentional death of a baby by his parents. That's why Georgia is on my mind.

Here are the questions: If a Black man can get double-life plus 40 years for robbery and a couple can get life for the unintentional death of their baby, what is the penalty for premeditated murder? What's the penalty for shooting a 92 year-old Black woman? What's the penalty for the cop who murdered Kenneth Walker? What's the penalty for beating Paul Johnson to death in a police holding cell? What is the penalty for mass murder in Georgia? Triple-life plus fifty years?

Yes, Georgia is definitely on my mind; so much so that I would love to find out why a state with so many Black political figures and influential "leaders" such as Andrew Young, who defends Paul Wolfowitz but utters not a word on behalf of William Mayo, cannot effect change in Georgia's ridiculous criminal "injustice system."

What good does it do for Black folks to occupy high political offices in Georgia, especially in its Capital, Atlanta, and have such glowing historical claim to being "civil rights" fighters and change agents? What good is it if these folks do not assert themselves to bring justice and fairness to a court system under which they and their children must live?

There is no way anyone can look objectively at the Georgia system of punishment and say it is equitable. That's not to say the same issues do not exist in most other cities across this country, but right now, I have Georgia on my mind.

About forty-five years ago, Georgia was a place where only those Blacks who were from there would travel. I didn't make my first trip to Georgia until 1970, scared of what I would encounter as I stopped at a gas station on the outskirts of town. It was the only time in my entire life that I carried a firearm (borrowed) with me on a trip—or anywhere else for that matter. I was pleasantly surprised when I pulled up to the gas pump and the white attendant said, "My I help you, sir?" I exhaled at that point and have been to Georgia too many times to count since then.

But even today, despite some Black people referring to Atlanta as the Black "Mecca" and despite the positive changes in other parts of the state, the criminal justice system imposed in Georgia is straight out of the Dark Age, and Black folks must stand up against it and demand real justice—for the innocent as well as for the guilty. Meanwhile, I pray I never get accused of anything in Georgia. With my editorial reputation, they would probably give me quadruple-life for speeding.

Free William Mayo, Georgia; somebody do something to help this young man, please!

The Right Stuff

"How can we expect to hear the words, 'Well done,' if we haven't done anything?"
"Well done beats well said every time."
"There's a big difference between feeling good and doing good."
It's not how much or little you have;
it's how much you do with how much or how little you have."

— **Jim Clingman**

If you have read most of the preceding pages you probably have an attitude by now. You are probably so "righteously" angry and so fired up that you just want to DO something to help rectify our situation. I know the feeling, believe me.

I told you at the beginning of this book that anger and righteous indignation are not bad emotions, but we have to direct our anger toward positive outcomes.

It makes absolutely no sense for us to recant all the problems we have, all the negative aspects of our lives, and all the bad stuff, unless we offer some good stuff to replace it.

In all of the writing I have done, all of the speeches I have made, and all of the initiatives I have participated in, my main objective has always been to cause our people to take action, positive action to empower ourselves and build an economic foundation for our children.

Thus, I have not written yet another book on economic empowerment merely to display my anger and frustration, lay it all on you, the reader, and then move on to the next book. I guess I am a different kind of author, because my main objective is not to sell books; it is to help our people. Of course, I hope to sell thousands of books (I still have to send my daughter college, y'all), but I will always keep my priorities straight. When it comes to economic empowerment, follow-up action is vital; it's all about the "doing." You know what they say about words without action, and symbolism without substance.

So now we will get into a few essays that speak to action. We cannot go back to sleep; we cannot sit back down; and we cannot continue to be quiet. It's time to get busy; it's time to get empowered; and it's time to have a real attitude about doing so.

We seem to be the only group of people that is afraid to disturb the status quo, reluctant to make waves, and downright timid when it comes to standing up for ourselves and speaking on behalf of Black people only. We are the only group that goes along, accommodates, and acquiesces to our own mistreatment.

Many of our "leaders" fail to speak up for us for fear of losing what they gained by selling us out. Some of them, and some of us, are too busy trying to be accepted and validated by white people that we have completely lost sight of who we are and what our obligation is to one another. We opt to give our business to others rather than to our own brothers and sisters, as in the cases of the National MLK Monument and the NAACP Black Authors' Pavilion, which makes absolutely no sense at all, unless that kind of action is the result of a psychological dysfunction. It still makes no sense, but at least there are mitigating circumstances.

We must reverse our headlong rush toward economic suicide by rallying around one another and getting real serious about our future and that of our children. We must take the helm of our Black ship of state and concentrate on the fact that we are all we have. No one else out there is trying to assist, support, uplift, or rescue Black folks. Besides, that's our job anyway.

It's a matter of being an Assimilationist or a Nationalist. In a nation within a nation, just as other groups demonstrate everyday, nationalism is the key to progress, both political and economic. Assimilation by a smaller group into larger group causes the eventual disappearance, the extinction, of the smaller group's heritage, culture, and self-interest. Do you want that?

Please do not fall for the guilt trip that some will try to put on you. They will accuse you of disliking white folks and other groups of people. Let them know this is not about anyone else; it's about us. It's not about disliking anyone else; it's about loving yourself and your people.

Let them know by your attitude that you are willing to take action on behalf of your children's future, and if they have a problem with that, so be it.

Don't live in the past; learn from it.
Oct. '04

WE SPEND A LOT OF TIME reminiscing about the past. We devote some of our time remembering and revering those who have gone before us, and we commemorate the accomplishments of past generations. In addition, we commiserate about the treatment and mistreatment of Black people in this country ever since we were brought here. Personally, I often ponder and write about the past 40 years of Black American history. Now that 2003 has passed, and in some cases, passed us by, what do we have to look forward to in 2004? Will we relax in the *easy chair* of the past, or will we get up and start running down the road of new possibilities?

The first thing we do each year is celebrate Martin Luther King, Jr. In my hometown, they will get together, hold hands and march, sing and pray, render sermon-like speeches, make political pontifications, and quote "I have a dream" so many times it will almost trivialize the point King was making on August 28, 1963. They will tell us what Dr. King wanted and what he meant and what he would be doing if he were alive today. They will co-opt his "dream" and use it as a balm to soothe Black folks who are fighting for justice—fighting for the very things King was fighting for when he shared his "dream" with us.

What they will not do in my hometown, where the King Day March has been going on for many years now, is deal with anything that has to do with economic empowerment, like starting an investment fund by collecting a few dollars from the thousands who attend the memorial celebration. (MLK Black Business Investment Fund. Now there's a thought. It sure beats naming streets after him.) They will not discuss what Dr. King said during the end of his final speech in Memphis, Tennessee, in 1968. They will genuflect at Dr. King's ideals but will not implement his instructions. When it comes to Dr. King, it's much easier to relive and celebrate the past than it is to do the work of realizing the "dream."

After King Day we will move into Black History Month. McDonald's will roll out their Black Inventors Campaign, once again for the *umpteenth* time, and tell us how smart our people were, that is, if you buy a Big Mac. Other corporations will mesmerize us with Black History Month sales and promotions. We will esteem the pyramid builders and celebrate our great heritage, all while we continue our *conspicuous consumption*, as described by economist, Thorstein Veblen, and we will stay in our mode of "verbal recalcitrance" when it comes to obtaining true economic freedom.

As this year goes by, and we get caught up in our celebrations and holidays, some of us will face another New Year's Eve and make resolutions for 2005, having been lulled to sleep once again by the "dreams" of Unity, Self-Determination, and other Kwanzaa Principles we celebrate rather than practice each year. The powers-that-be will exhale, having realized the benefit of another year of high retail sales and billions in revenues from our $700 billion in "Black Buying Power." Let the party begin -- again!

The past is a great teacher but a poor landlord. As long as we keep reliving the past we will never get to preparing for our future. And we can only prepare for our future by using the present to do all we can while we are alive. Unfortunately we fall prey, sometimes willingly, to the hoopla of celebratory gestures and empty rhetoric from politicians and business owners who really have no interest in our future; they are quite willing to hold hands when it comes to our past but you can't find them with search party when it comes to supporting the economic future of Black folks. But that's all right; we can do that for ourselves.

We must get busy building some pyramids of our own, in addition to celebrating the ones our ancestors built. Since it would defy all logic for greedy, corrupt, and evil men to teach and promote the economic advancement of those outside their group, Black people had better get out of the past and get on with our future—for ourselves and among ourselves. Other groups are doing just that, and we had better get with the program.

Here's an interesting thought to support my contention. Each year we get a mega-dose of Black history from corporate marketers and politicians, telling us how great we "were." Why then do many of those same folks tell us to forget about the past when it comes to things like reparations, slavery, and lynching? They say, "That was in the distant past;" "Let's move on;" "All of the slaves and slave masters are dead." In one breath, they tell us to remember our history, but in the next breath they tell us to forget about it.

We must remember our past; we must teach it to our children and not allow others to do that in our stead. We must not, however, live in the past. It is there for our learning; it is there for the benefit of our collective future. Reflect on last year, and then get busy "doing" this year.

Taking Action
Aug. '05

TOO OFTEN I SEE BLACK PEOPLE lying down and allowing others to walk on them. In many instances we simply accept whatever is doled out from so-called powers-that-be, and end up only complaining about it when it's all said and done. We have proof positive that we are discriminated against and mistreated in other ways, but we only talk about it, march about it, or ask folks to apologize for their transgressions.

We participate in and even promote and perpetuate ridiculously flawed "economic inclusion" programs, succumbing to the notion that we are "minorities" and therefore, in order to be treated fairly we must subject ourselves to being "certified" and validated before we can obtain work paid for by our own tax dollars. Why won't we take action commensurate to the problems we face?

I read an article that described how 300 Black contractors in St. Louis, Missouri, who were literally fed up with how they were being treated, protested by blocking Interstate 70. While 100 of them were arrested, their actions spoke so loudly and clearly that positive change began to take place. A similar incident took place across the river from St. Louis, in East St. Louis, when a group of angry contractors threatened to block an interstate highway there. Their threat was all it took to get things moving in their direction and brought instant concessions from the so-called powers-that-be.

In Nigeria, protesters, angry at the way Chevron and Shell are treating them and Nigeria's oil resources, are taking matters in their own hands by putting their bodies in the way of oil production. The locals say the big oil companies and other multinational organizations are "colluding to keep the spoils for themselves," according to a report on National Public Radio. Apparently actions taken by the Nigerians have certainly gotten the attention of a lot big wigs. One Nigerian told a Chevron official that the crude oil belonged to Nigeria and the primary benefits from that oil should go to Nigerians. As I often point out, not only ownership but also control of income-producing assets are vital to our success.

Everyday in this country, Black people are mistreated in some form or fashion by the establishment. We see it; we feel it; and we know it happens. Sadly, in most cases we merely talk about it; we seldom really do anything about it. We refuse to take matters into our own hands by risking something to secure our demands. We love to talk about Dr. King and what he stood for, but we are not willing to do what he did to achieve the ideals he espoused. Yes, he was non-violent, but his resolve to make change subjected him to violence from violent people. Nonetheless, he took action.

Are we just too afraid to do what must be done for our survival in this country? Are we satisfied with our condition? Are we unwilling to place ourselves in the line of fire in order to gain the rights and privileges of a people who helped build this country and create the wealth it now enjoys from our labor? Will we go down in history as a people that gave in to discrimination, abuse, mistreatment, and unfairness, unwilling to fight for what is rightfully ours? Thus far, it looks that way.

Look around and see how we remove ourselves from the fight for justice for our brothers and sisters. Observe how we cower in the presence of white folks. Watch as our so-called leaders smile and acquiesce to wrongdoing by this country's political establishment. Monitor the results we get versus the results others get from legislation and programs put forth to help "minorities."

You will see, if you are willing to look, an array of disparities, a veritable laundry list of inequities that occur each day against Black people, with impunity I might add; all while we just look on and wonder when things will change. The bad news is they won't change just because they ought to. The good news is they can be changed if are willing to resort to tactics such as those used by the groups I mentioned.

Nonviolent but radical action must be taken by Black people in this country in order to effect change. That means we must put ourselves back on the front lines for justice. We must physically stop construction projects if we are not included in their planning and their resulting benefits. We must use our collective economic strength against companies that do not have our best interests in mind by withholding our dollars from them. When we put someone out of business or at least cause a severe slump in the profits they earn from our dollars, we will signal a new era in our determination to gain fair treatment. More importantly, we will demonstrate to ourselves where our real power lies—in our economics.

Taking action, appropriate action, when it comes to our complaints is the logical and rational thing to do. We can't just rail against everyone else and never assume the responsibility of doing for our people what must be done in order to make change.

And please, don't fall for the notion that we must wait for the next election to make change. Can't you see by now that most elected officials are not concerned with our progress and are working against it on a daily basis?

Those politicians who do work on our behalf are too few and cannot do it by themselves. They need our help, and that help must come in the form of action-oriented solutions, some of which include civil disobedience, disruption, and refusal to go along with the status quo. Take action!

Organized and United Resources for Self-Sufficiency
May '05

IN 1995, AFTER THE MILLION MAN March (MMM), hundreds of brothers and sisters in Cincinnati started meeting every Saturday morning to work on the things we knew were necessary to uplift our people. We developed social, economic, political, educational, and legal strategies that would help us manifest the pledges and commitments we made during the MMM event. We also formed several committees to work on these initiatives. Of course, I chose to work on the Economic Development Committee, during which time I offered a concept called O.U.R.S., which is an acronym for Organized and United Resources for Self-Sufficiency. Ten years later, I offered to set it up again, as a commemoration of the tenth anniversary of the MMM; I now offer it to you.

As I travel around the country speaking to different groups, inevitably I am asked what local groups can do to change the economic condition of their people. Understanding that all cities have unique challenges and opportunities, one thing we all have in common is the need for money in order to implement our initiatives. My intention back in 1995 was to create a fund that we could use to assist with the myriad of concepts our group devised, knowing that anything we decided upon would require money. Likewise, no matter where you live, and no matter what your particular challenges are, you are going to need some money to meet them.

O.U.R.S. is a way not only to establish a Black-operated funding base for initiatives, it also is way to instill in our people the principle of doing more for ourselves with our own resources, paying our own way without having to ask and beg someone else, to form a habit in us to help our own people, and to make the necessary sacrifices for our collective uplift. As I often say, the concepts I write about are not mine; I place no proprietary claim on them. These things have been done by our relatives since the 1700's. Numerous business cooperatives were developed and managed by Black folks, two of the most famous of which were the Colored Merchants Association and the Cooperative Consumers of New Haven, Inc.

Pooling money and resources is nothing new; many groups in this country do it and use their collective resources to start new businesses, get lower prices in the marketplace, and to build an economic foundation for their children. Why are we so reluctant to do it? In every city there should be at least one O.U.R.S. fund. Deposits to the fund could be made whenever we get paid, just a few dollars per person, and would soon be built up to a level at which we could do some very positive things. Each person can decide what he or she would put into the fund from time to time, and an accounting of the fund could be published and sent out to all who participate. You make your own rules on the use of the funds and how they would be disbursed.

There have been national movements to start such funds, but I am convinced that they must be started locally and managed locally, and then maybe we could leverage a national movement from several local funds. With all of the challenges and opportunities I see in various cities around this country, if we would do the simple things, like starting an O.U.R.S. fund, and supporting the Blackonomics Million Dollar Club (BMDC), our time would be well spent and the results would be most beneficial.

O.U.R.S. funds could be used to assist our people with day-to-day issues that arise; they could be used to invest in or make loans to Black businesses; they could be used to bring events to our cities; they could be used to set up food co-ops and business associations; they could be used fund our think-tanks and pay for our meetings; and they could be used to purchase venues for our Juneteenth Celebrations, our Kwanzaa Celebrations, and other events that we like but now, in many cases, have to run to someone else to foot the bill or use their facility.

Think seriously about what an O.U.R.S. fund can do for you in your particular city. In addition to the tangible things I mentioned, it will also demonstrate how serious you are about freedom. The revolution may not be televised, but it sure will have to be financed. O.U.R.S. funds all over this country will make our revolution much easier to manage.

It is reasonable to believe that we have the resources to achieve this simple task without a lot of hoopla, meetings, analysis, and all the other diversions that keep us from doing the things we should for ourselves. It is reasonable for us to want to engage in some kind of collective activity that will uplift our people. It is reasonable to assume that if Black people are at the bottom of every economic category in this country that we must create and execute economic strategies to get us out of this mess. Therefore, O.U.R.S. makes sense, doesn't it?

All right, here's the charge. Go out and get some brothers and sisters of like mind and start an O.U.R.S. fund. Name it something else if you like, but start a fund in your local community through which you can begin to move toward a modicum of self-sufficiency. We owe it to ourselves and our children to have some kind of economic tool that we have built and over which we have control.

Don't wait. Don't put this article down and say you will get around to it. Don't procrastinate. Do it right now. Make a phone call to someone else and make a commitment to get it started right away. Solomon, the wisest man ever, said, "Money is the answer for all things." Even with all of his smarts, he knew that, at least on this earthly plane, we could solve a lot of problems by having and controlling money. O.U.R.S., and other economic initiatives, will create the opportunity for us to do just that. Our dollars must start making some sense, y'all.

O.U.R.S. is now YOURS. Use it.

A Case for Dieting and Plastic Surgery
Aug. '05

IN CASE YOU HAVE NOT BEEN watching the economic trends, you might want to know that things are about to get nasty. No need to cite the exorbitant price of gasoline; I am sure you feel the impact of what is swiftly becoming one of the biggest heists in human history. Is Enron's Ken Lay in jail yet? Did Halliburton ever get sanctioned for stealing all that money and cheating on the price it charged for gasoline? Did "vice" President Cheney ever reveal what really took place in his secret energy meetings? But I digress.

This country is going down the tubes fast, at least for those of us who cannot keep up with sinful prescription drugs costs, out of sight medical insurance payments, usury fuel costs for transportation and heating our homes, and decreasing real wages for ordinary workers. The warning signs are there, for all who care to look, of an impending economic crisis within the so-called middle class and below.

Bankruptcy will no longer be an option after October 17, 2005, but not so for the corporations and affluent. Additionally, since we will not be able to file bankruptcy I am sure the credit card companies will tinker with their "minimum payments" and come up with even more ways to steal from their customers. In case you didn't know, credit card companies were the biggest lobbyists for the new bankruptcy law, which by the way was supported by members of your Black Caucus and your beloved Democrats. Of course, we know where the Republicans stand on it.

With billions, maybe a trillion dollars in credit card debt among those who really cannot afford it, and in light of the restraints being placed on those who need to file bankruptcy, a reasonable person would ask, "Where is that compassionate conservative we elected? Where does he stand on this?" But we already know, don't we? Apparently this guy is very conservative when it comes to demonstrating his compassion for those who need it most.

As we face this economic meltdown, Black people should act upon the principle of self-preservation. We are in a country ruled by folks who don't care one iota about us; economically we are at the bottom; we own very little of this country's assets and control a miniscule portion of its wealth; we are openly and blatantly mistreated, physically abused and assaulted by police officers, discriminated against by banks and real estate companies, and we have the highest number of persons trapped in a corrupt criminal justice system.

We live in major cities across this country but have no real economic enclaves to support and sustain our children; we purchase everything someone else makes including the biggest cars and trucks, and now have to fill them up with $3.00 per gallon gasoline; we just love to be displayed on television by BET and VH1 acting the fool or just singing and dancing; our young men have fallen prey to the foolish thought that performing on the basketball court will keep them out of the criminal court, thus much of what we see them doing is showing how high they can jump on their way to some overplayed slam-dunk.

All of these things and many more suggest quite vividly that Black folks are in deep trouble. Of course the country is in trouble too, but we will be the first to feel the effects of its economic decline. We are the expendable ones, the obsolete workers, the unwanted residents of this country. I know this will alarm and embarrass some Black people who read this, but even you, at some point will have to come to grips with the fact that you are not what you have been made to believe you are. You may be earning millions, but think a moment about how much money you are earning for your bosses.

So, it's time for dieting and plastic surgery. We must curtail our insatiable appetite for trinkets, cut our credit cards in two, and refuse to use them again. Credit cards are driving the ravenous, greedy, evil society of moneychangers, and we must no longer play into their hands by falling for their offers of financial freedom y going into more debt. Or, you may need to file bankruptcy prior to the new law coming into effect.

Another thing we must do is stop falling for the hype of the SUV. The latest news reports say buyers are still purchasing these monstrosities despite the hike in gas prices. They also say consumers are not cutting back on gas purchases despite the skyrocketing prices. Are we in a coma or what? Have we simply succumbed to the madness of economic suicide? I guess the brothers can sit in their trucks on the streets and play their loud stereos and move their furniture into them as well when things worsen. Hummer anyone? How stupid is that?

This is real. You can turn away if you want, but sooner or later it's going to hit most of us. And those of you in the "protected class," if things get bad enough you will be the first to go too, the first to be jettisoned from the spaceship of state, because whether you accept it or not, you were only "chosen" to create more profit for someone else.

Please find ways to build economic empowerment for our collective survival in this country. Pooling our funds, buying co-ops, collective farming, manufacturing, ownership and control of more income-producing assets, and looking at opportunities and industries in which we have a competitive advantage as consumers, are just a few of things we must do. Let's get busy!

Civil Rights Symbolism and Economic Substance
Dec. '05

I ALMOST USED "OR" INSTEAD OF "and" in the title of this article because it seems we have settled for symbolism over substance when it comes to our economic freedom, but I know this is not an "either or" argument. We need symbolism; issues, causes, and tangible objects that make us proud, celebrate our history and culture, and keep us positively motivated, are very much needed among Black people. But our tendency to settle for symbolism while ignoring, in many cases, the need for substantive, concrete, economic initiatives is slowly but surely dragging us down to a point of no return.

How long will we allow our sensibilities and our senses to fall prey to and be held hostage by symbolism without substance, especially when that symbolism lies in our civil rights? Take, for example, the recent celebration of Mother Rosa Parks. On the national level we saw George Bush co-opting our dear elder and the occasion of her defiant refusal to give up her seat on the bus, by signing a bill urging Congress to support the voting rights extension bill. Mind you, less than a year prior to signing the declaration Bush said he didn't even know what the 1965 Voting Rights Extension was!

CNN described the occasion of the signing as a "surprise" to many civil rights leaders and said, "The Rev. Jesse Jackson lavishly praised Bush for committing to seeing the expiring portions of the Voting Rights Act extended. He called the President's public urging 'a significant breakthrough' since he had previously declined even in private to support the renewal."

Jesse Jr. also gave praise to Bush for agreeing to commission a statue of Rosa Parks and place it in Statuary Hall. Jesse, Jr. then continued on his quest for a "more perfect union." I wonder what that really means. I always thought perfect was absolute, the highest, the best. More perfect? What is that? If this "union" of ours is perfect, how can it become "more perfect"? If our "union" were perfect Bush would have supported the extension without the grandstanding and without having to be cajoled into it. You gotta admit though, it sounds good, it feels good, makes for good theater, and it's great symbolism.

On the local level, Black councilpersons in Cincinnati presented a last-minute motion to get three blocks of a street named after Rosa Parks. Talk about symbolism! Rosa Parks is now deserving of street names and statues, but while she was alive she had no opportunity to see a Black owned bus company named after her, a Black owned hotel named after her, or a Black owned restaurant named after her in Cincinnati. Before you ask, in 2001 a Black development group proposed such a hotel and restaurant, named for Rosa Parks, but was refused by the Port Authority to even submit a bid for the $800 million project.

As a matter of fact, Black people own nothing on those three blocks named after Parks, nor do we own anything on the way the to National Underground Railroad Freedom Center, where Parks' three blocks will lead. If those in charge of the riverfront development project continue in the same mode as the Port Authority, and if Black folks in Cincy keep falling for symbolism only, never demanding more than symbolic gestures, we will continue to be left out of ownership opportunities that accrue to these symbolic sites of freedom and civil rights.

We have Martin Luther King, Jr. streets all over this country, many of which have no Black owned businesses on either side of them. Do you think MLK would trade his name on a street sign for the economic empowerment of his people? How about Sister Rosa? They did not fight to get <u>their</u> names on things; they fought to get <u>our</u> names on things, to get our names on things like deeds, mortgages, businesses, and development contracts.

Again, this is not an either/or scenario; it is a both/and scenario. We abandoned our own economic base in the 1960's and chose to pursue political offices; we cannot afford in the 2000's to abdicate our quest for substantive economic accomplishments and be content with symbolic, feel good, warm and fuzzy gestures that are grounded in civil rights only.

The best tribute to Rosa, Martin, Marcus, and other brothers and sisters that taught us the value of economic empowerment is to take what they did to a higher level. They did their parts, but I am sad to say, we are not doing ours. We have resigned ourselves to soft and cushy Kum-ba-ya celebrations; and we have shied away from pragmatic, sacrificial, and vital initiatives that will most assuredly lead us to collective economic empowerment. We have accepted and settled for symbolism over substance.

The good news is that we can have both. In order to win economic freedom and be inspired to look back and celebrate our proud history of civil rights victories, we must have healthy doses of both symbolism and substance. Currently, we are overdosing on symbolism and have a substance deficiency. We must change that.

We cannot allow the likes of George Bush to co-opt our past in order to move his economic and political agenda forward. Haven't you had enough yet? We cannot allow our local and national leaders, and our politicians, to continuously put forth initiatives that only make us feel good, but seldom bring initiatives that make us do "good" and do well at the same time.

Enough of the symbolism; bring on some substance!

The Eagle Flies on Frida
Sept. '06

THIS FAMILIAR LINE SHOULD BE THE mantra of Black people when it comes to recycling our dollars among ourselves. Why? Well, we always talk about recycling our dollars and spending our money in our neighborhoods, with our own business, to the extent they are available, and considering the fact that the eagle does indeed fly on Friday, we should employ a related economic strategy. Maybe we should use the theme Brother Ashiki Taylor, of Atlanta, Georgia, uses: "Freedom Friday."

Ironically, the term, "The Eagle Flies on Friday" comes from a familiar song, "Stormy Monday," which goes on to say, "…and Saturday I go out to play…Sunday I go to church, and I kneel down on my knees and pray: Lord have mercy, have mercy on me." I say it's ironic because this is exactly what many Black people do on the weekend.

We get paid, and the eagle starts to fly; and sadly, it flies away rather than around. Our money leaves us so fast that even a real eagle couldn't keep up with it. Then on Saturday we go out to play; it seems that's the top priority for us these days—playing or watching someone else play. If it's not games, it's parties, all night long. Nothing wrong with a little entertainment every now and then, but let's not be lulled to sleep by it.

After the party is over, yes we have to get our "praise on" as some call it. We "go" to church (forgetting of course that we are the church) and start praying and asking God to have mercy on us. We spent all our money and must face a stormy Monday all over gain, trying to regain the money we threw away over the weekend, and we want God to have mercy. He's probably saying, "Give me a break!"

I can imagine all the groups with which we spend our money saying, "Thank you, Lord, for Black consumers." Their eagle will fly around their communities many times before leaving, if it ever leaves at all, and they look forward to Mondays because theirs are far from stormy.

Have you ever considered that our Mondays are stormy because our eagle flies on Friday? If we approach our spending with that in mind our Sundays would be filled with more "Thank you's" rather than "Have mercies." I pray we will get this through our heads some day soon and stop this economic death spiral we continue to follow by allowing our eagles to fly away rather than around, making stops at several of our own businesses instead of everyone else's.

So what will it be, Black folks? How about a Freedom Friday? Do you think we could designate every Friday, just one day per week, as the day we make a concerted conscious effort to buy something from a brother or sister? At the same time, do you think we could cut back on spending our dollars at the businesses owned by others? I know it will be hard; but you only have to do it on Fridays.

Freedom Fridays could prove to be the genesis of an economic revolution for Black people in this country. C'mon, y'all. A little self-discipline is all it takes; it would certainly be well worth it. We cannot have anything of substance without sacrifice. Start your personal Freedom Friday Campaign this week, and let others know what you are doing. Let them know that you are raising your consciousness by taking more control of your dollars and making sure that you spend more with your people.

If we fail to implement economic strategies of some kind, both personal and collective, we are literally doomed in this country. And as the song goes, Tuesdays will be "just as bad," Wednesdays will be "worse," and Thursdays will be "oh so sad." I suggest Freedom Fridays, but you can call it whatever you want; it's the action that counts. We can come up with all sorts of cute sayings and slogans, but if we don't put the appropriate action behind them, we will have accomplished nothing.

We can turn that song into a joyous refrain if our eagles start flying around our neighborhoods, in and out of Black owned businesses, into the pockets of Black employees who work for those businesses, and even making a few stops at Black investment funds.

I travel across this country speaking at conferences, doing workshops, and lecturing students and church members; I have been writing this column for more than 12 years now; I am on radio talk shows all over this country; and I have come in contact with thousands of brothers and sisters who say they want to do something about our economic situation. They call talk shows decrying our economic position and the lack of ownership and control of resources where they live and the fact that someone else owns all the stores, the gas stations, the restaurants, the grocery stores, and other vital retail outlets in their neighborhoods.

After all I have said, written, and, more importantly, demonstrated by personal action and commitment to the principle of economic empowerment for Black people, I truly wonder if it is a lost cause. I wonder if we really want to be free, if we are serious about our consciousness, the same kind of consciousness and nationalistic thinking employed by the very groups about which we complain.

Despite my deep frustration, I will continue to write, speak, initiate and participate in economic strategies that will move our people forward because it is part of my purpose, my mission, my work. I am very concerned about our eagles flying, but I am more concerned about our eagles dying.

Common Sense Leads to Common Cents
Nov. '06

SOME PEOPLE SAY "COMMON SENSE IS not common," which may be the main reason Black people are not as far up the economic ladder as we should be. Having been in this country since it started, having provided the free labor that led to the creation of much of the wealth now enjoyed by those in charge, and having established a history of self-help and entrepreneurial initiative since our enslavement, Black people have the strongest case for and the greatest need to exercise a little common sense when it comes to working collectively to improve our current position in the U.S.

If we use our common sense, we will definitely have common cents. Common sense suggests that we do as other groups are doing, and as our ancestors did in this country: pool our resources and support one another.

Common sense tells us to look around and see the dire straits our children are facing in this country and start compiling some common cents to help them meet and overcome their current and future economic challenges.

Common sense teaches us that we must not do anything that will subject us to the misery of incarceration and the profiteering of this nation's prison industrial complex; we must institute a national Boycott Prisons campaign and work to give our youth alternatives, especially economic alternatives, to their negative behaviors.

Common sense should have taught us that banks and other financial institutions still discriminate against us, and by using our common cents we can overcome much of that discrimination by collectively leveraging our resources and creating and maintaining our own financial institutions. (Before anyone gets scared or asks why we need Black owned banks and credit unions, think about the Korean banks, the Cuban banks, the Polish banks, the Chinese banks, and all the others that exist in this country.)

Common sense dictates that we utilize our common cents to fund our own initiatives, first, and then look to others to support them—support them, not control them. Having common cents would also increase our ability to defend ourselves against local political issues that are not in our best interests; our common cents can be used to fund ballot initiatives, finance the campaigns of candidates who will work on our behalf, and pay for research, analyses, and recommendations that can be used to make informed voting decisions.

Common sense instructs us to pursue our self-interest in a society that is rapidly becoming more polarized. Common sense tells us that Black people do not control the major political and economic games, but to assure our participation in the game and our being in a position to win every now and then we must use our common cents. Economics runs this country; common sense should tell us that.

If we use our common sense we will also use our common cents to create and sustain an economic foundation from which to operate and on which to build even more common cents initiatives. We must use our common sense the way our ancestors did, as they quickly caught on to the system they faced and immediately went to work building their economic resources to purchase their freedom and that of their relatives and friends. Freedom still ain't free, y'all.

As we look back on our progress for the past 45 years, common sense shows us how far we have come relative to the strategies we chose to pursue and the leadership we decided to follow. Common sense says several of our leaders have done marvelously well, but as a whole Black people are still stuck at the bottom of the economic ladder, a ladder with rungs that begin at the halfway point. It is up to us to figure out how to get to the halfway point; common sense suggests we must add our own rungs to that economic ladder.

Utilizing our common sense would lead us to the accumulation of common cents and we would be well on our way to developing the resources we need to survive and thrive in this nation. Currently we are too individualistic in our thinking and our actions to create common cents strategies. We must change our minds, raise our level of consciousness, and put positive action behind our rhetoric.

We must be willing to use our individual God-given gifts, to contribute to the uplift of a people who have suffered more horrendous treatment, both physical and psychological, than any people in this country. Common sense tells us that. How else are we going to prosper? How else will we achieve economic empowerment? How else will we ever be able to positively impact the futures of our children?

Many of us have heard that common sense is not common. If that is true, then I guess I can understand the paucity, or lack of common cents initiatives among Black people. But I don't believe Black people are short on common sense. How did we survive in this country? How did we progress in the face of adversity and at the risk of even death? Why are we still here? How have we retained our sanity? How could there have been a Greenwood District in Tulsa, Oklahoma—and all the other Black economic enclaves across this country?

Our great-grandparents could not have done all they did without possessing a tremendous amount of common sense that, in turn, directed them to accumulate a great deal of common cents with which to take care of their business? What's up with us?

It's tax filing time. What should we do?
Dec. '06

ONCE AGAIN WE HAVE THE OPPORTUNITY to support a Black owned and operated business by seeking out and using Black tax preparers. Once again many of us will also have the opportunity to support one of this nation's best tax preparation companies, Compro Tax. Celebrating its 25th anniversary in 2007, Compro Tax was founded by Brother Jackie Mayfield, originally from Louisiana, but who now resides in Orange, Texas, just a stone's throw from the main Compro Tax offices in Beaumont, Texas.

Every year I write an article about this company because I want you to know about it and support it. I want Compro Tax to grow beyond the wildest dreams of Brother Mayfield. I want this Black business to thrive as it moves to building a convention center in Beaumont and opens new tax preparation, mortgage, and insurance offices across this country. I want it to continue to create new entrepreneurs, of which there are already more than 2000 in some 125 offices across the United States.

Compro Tax is a company we all can be very proud of, and Jackie Mayfield and his staff are brothers and sisters we can hold up as role models for our children to emulate. There is no reason, other than inaccessibility, not to use this company, should you require assistance with your financial and tax situations. Of course there are other Black owned tax preparers available. Use them as well. Imagine the money we could circulate just by doing that, and imagine how these businesses would grow.

Every year the vultures come out and invent even more ways to take that tax refund from the impatient, unsuspecting, "I gotta have it now" taxpayer. You will start hearing the commercials in December, the enticing repartee, the great deals, and the "buy now—pay with your refund check" proposals that seem to penetrate Black neighborhoods and Black radio and Black media so easily and so heavily. Don't fall for the hype. Support a Black owned tax preparation company and do your part to build a Black economy.

That giant screen plasma television can wait; that new or used car will be around; they will continue to make those play stations; and Lord knows we can do without those clothes, furniture, and other "stuff" long enough to get our maximum refund rather than give most of it to rip-off businesses offering you instant credit but with a sky-high interest rate.

Talk to the folks at Compro Tax. They will teach you ways to save more of your return and they won't rip you off with exorbitant fees either. In fact, if you want to be trained to become a Compro Tax representative, or if you want to own a Compro Tax Franchise, they will help you with that too. There is no other company I am aware of that provides so much training, technical assistance, and equipment to its franchise businesses for so little in return. But that's the kind of company Compro Tax is; it's the kind of person Mayfield is: a conscious and conscientious Black man using his intellectual and financial resources to help himself and his family as well as his people.

There are Compro tax offices available to serve you from coast to coast. Just look on their website, comprotax.com, for the office nearest you. The more business we give them and the greater our demand for their services, the wider their reach will be. Check out Compro Tax this year, that is, if you are using those "other guys." If there is no Compro Tax office near you, find another Black owned tax preparation firm and support it—or start one yourself! It makes dollars and sense.

There are many multi-billion businesses in this country, and expenditures by Black consumers contribute greatly, and in some cases disproportionately, to their profit margins. Tax preparation is just one of them. Others include tourism, food, entertainment, clothing, automobiles, and electronics. If Black people would spend our dollars as informed consumers rather than whimsical consumers we could capture more of those billion dollar businesses. We would be able to reclaim those industries in which we have predominance. Can you say, Black Hair Care? How about Black Book Publishing, just to name a couple.

Let's wise up, brothers and sisters, especially now that we are in the "taxing" time of the year. We are tempted to buy everything in sight, in many cases, simply because we are in line to get a big refund sometime early next year. Think about this before you make your purchasing decisions, especially if you plan to make them with a tax refund you plan to get a couple of months from now. Don't spend that refund before you get it, and please don't sign most of it away in interest and fees to some company that promises you a few new trinkets.

Sit down with the folks at Compro Tax and let them help you with your taxes. You will not only be doing yourself a favor, you will also be doing your part to economically empower our people.

Tiny men growing into big babies
Dec. '07

WE HAVE ALL PROBABLY HEARD OF the singing group, Boyz to Men, right? Sounds like a logical sequence of growth, don't you agree? Well, it seems we have another trend going for our Black males today, and that is growing from "men" back into "babies." While they physically grow in stature, instead of growing mentally as well, many Black men are regressing into children even as they reach physical maturity.

Physically grown men, especially fathers, who dress, talk, and act like teenagers and even younger boys, are misguided at best. Check them out as they walk alongside their sons; both have their caps turned to the side, both are wearing those short pants, which remind me of the little boy with the snotty nose that Martin Lawrence used to portray, and they wear the obligatory basketball or football jersey. If it were not for their physical size, you wouldn't be able to tell father from son.

Of course, we know that many of today's parents are really children themselves, not having shaken off the "street" mentality. They are still ensconced in partying and hangin' out. They have not yet "put away childish things." In addition, a trend that has, in my opinion, done more harm than good to our Black men is the power of words. Historically, Black men have been called "boys" by white folks, which in the 1960's was like whites signing their own beat-down warrant, at least in my neck of the woods.

I remember the first day I reported for duty in the Navy. I walked out on deck for morning muster and the Boatswain Mate said, "Where you been, boy?" I was already 21 years old; it was 1966; he was a southern racist; and I was already angry about being there anyway. Not a great way to have started my career in the U.S. Navy. I was immediately put on report because I responded by saying, "Who are you calling a 'boy'? I am a grown man." From that day forward, for the next two years I spent on that ship, all the white guys knew the boundaries they could not cross when it came to the words they used to address me.

Out of 750 men on that ship, there were only about 50 Blacks. We knew we had to stand up for ourselves, especially in the mid-sixties when many of the men in the Navy were really white "boys" themselves, most of who came from the southern states and had no respect for Black people and the skills we brought to the table. During that period the Navy was not many years removed from Blacks only being allowed to work as Cooks and Stewards.

The main thing was our willingness to stand up for ourselves and be men rather than boys, even in the face of sure and swift punishment from the Captain of the ship, who was just below God in status. We were willing to fight against the odds when someone said the "magic word" we now call the "n-word." We were unwilling to be defined by someone else, especially a bunch of rednecks who found pleasure in ordering us around like we were still enslaved to their fathers.

Today, as I have stated many times, we allow others to define us, and as grown men, many of us have become nothing more than little boys, in our dress, our language, and in our demeanor. I assert that some of what we see is the long-term result of our parents, especially our mothers, referring to their baby boy as "my little man." We dress them in adult clothing, and when they hurt we tell them to "take it like a man."

In the later years, when a boy is supposed to put away childish things and start acting like a man, the mothers start calling him "my baby." The girlfriends and the wives refer to their mates as "baby." When grown men hurt, they are held and hugged by their ladies and mothers who comfort them by saying such things as, "It will be all right, baby," or "I know, baby," or "What's wrong with my baby?"

Grown men being called "baby" may seem innocent enough, and you may be asking, "What's the big deal?" But I think we are seeing the negative results of the misuse of a word, just like the other words we have been called and have called ourselves, to the degree that a whole generation of parents and children are really confused about who they are and what their proper roles are.

That confusion has turned us around, put us in reverse, and caused many of our Black males to end up as boys rather than men. Rather than going from "Boyz to Men," they have gone from "Little men" to "Big Baby Boyz."

So what, you say? Words create imagery followed by action. We must teach our male children who and what they are as early in life as possible, so that as they physically grow into "men" they will also grow mentally. They will no longer speak, act, and think "as a child." They will define themselves and speak up for themselves and their children.

Let's start calling our children, especially male children, "babies" rather than "men." And ladies, stop referring to your grown men as "babies." Maybe they will stop spending their money on all of the ridiculous things other folks are selling, turn their caps from sideways, stop wearing those droopy short pants that resemble knickers, make better choices, be real Black men, conscious Black men, proud of who they are and not intimidated by others, and stop committing acts of violence against one another.

"Long after our eyes glaze over and our ears grow numb watching and listening to the TV roundtable discussions that seek to address our fate, we can still keep our sons awake and perhaps alive if we teach them that the first line of defense against racism is to mold themselves into disciplined, self-respecting refutations of its ability to destroy our souls and ourselves.

Marita Golden, <u>Saving Our Sons</u>

Listen Up! Turn Off Channel Zero!
Mar. '07

HAVING HAD THE RECENT EXPERIENCE Of seeing the new documentary film, <u>Turn Off Channel Zero</u>, I was encouraged to see young brothers and sisters speaking out and standing up against the negative Black images being portrayed on VH1, MTV, and BET, all owned and operated by Viacom. Let me say right now that every Black family should have a copy of this film. Not only is it uplifting, educational, and inspirational, it is also anathema to the status quo as it uncovers the real truth behind media that would keep Black folks in check and mentally enslaved.

What I like about <u>Turn Off Channel Zero</u> most is its emphasis on the economic aspects of all the Black negativity that abounds in the media, much of which is perpetrated by our own people, and all of which is accepted by many Black people. The film comes straight at us with a message of self-love rather than self-hate, self-reliance rather than self-oppression, self-determination rather than self-exploitation, self-confidence rather than self-aggrandizement, self-acknowledgment rather than self-denial, self-consciousness rather than self-oppression, and self-pride rather than self-flagellation.

The film is produced and directed by Brother Opio Lumumba Sokoni and featuring Abiodum Oyewole (The Last Poets), Davey D, Professor Griff (Public Enemy), Afrika Bambataa, Dr. Ray Winbush, and one of my favorite "little sisters," Kenya James (Black Girl Magazine), along with many other young, conscious, proud brothers and sisters from across the country.

Readers of this column will remember my article titled, Buffoonery, Exploitation, and Taboo, in which I railed against the content aired on BET. <u>Turn Off Channel Zero</u> goes beyond that by allowing young people to voice their concerns not only about BET, but also about the trash that appears on the VH1 and MTV, especially the likes of "Flavor of Love" and the latest insult, this misguided sister named New York, her "strange" mother, and the men who participate in the show.

It's one thing for an "older" brother like me to write about the negativity of these media outlets; after all, as we grow older most of us finally come to the realization that what we used to do and accept was wrong. It's one thing for me to give advice to our young people and try to guide them in the right way; after all, I am beyond the stage of placing more value on entertainment than I do on education. But it is an entirely different thing for young folks themselves to come out and make decisive, direct, and lucid statements and take in-your-face action against the perpetrators of degradation and derisive portrayals of Black folks. (But that's what we did in the 1960's, wasn't it? I guess what goes around does come around)

I like the question Brother Afrika Bambataa posed: "What's so good about the hood? We love the hood but it does not love us. Why do we love the hood? We don't own the hood. We rent the hood." He also spoke about getting rid of the dope dealers and other negative influences in the hood. That struck me in a positive way because we must own where we live, control the environment where we live, build businesses where we live, and do business where we live.

Professor Griff reminds us that it only takes one person to do great things, one person to make a significant difference, and one person to start a revolution. The young sisters in the film reminded me of the strength among our women and the legacy of Ida B. Wells, Fannie Lou Hamer, and Harriet Tubman. Watching this film was a much-needed confirmation for me, a confirmation that says our young people do "get it," a confirmation that lets me know they are not afraid, and a confirmation that instilled in me a refreshing outlook on their future. I am proud of those who appeared in the film and those who had a hand in making it.

I strongly urge you not only to watch the film when it becomes available via various media outlets but also to purchase a copy of it. More information on Turn Off Channel Zero can be found on the following websites: www.poli-tainment.com and www.luv4selfpublishing.com.

Taking control of the media images of Black people is a laudable and very necessary goal. We can start by following the lead of our young lions, the ones that our BringBackBlack.org movement is seeking. These young folks have stepped up and taken the lead; we must follow and we must help them.

It was great to see the young folks in the film sitting with Brother Oyewole, listening to his historical perspective and taking in his wisdom. That's what our survival is all about. A collective consciousness among the generations, and a cooperative spirit between young and old, will surely lead us to victory.

This is not about anyone else but us. It's about the action we take to stop the exploitation of our people; it's about our resolve to resist selling out; and it's about our strength, resiliency, and raw determination to hang in there no matter what, to get up no matter how many times we fall, and to prevail no matter the odds. As the commercial once said, "Image is everything." Do not allow our image to be portrayed in a negative manner without speaking out and taking action against it. He who defines you controls you.

We must take control of our own story and rebuff anyone, Viacom included, that disrespects us in their media, as we move to widen our ownership and control of media. We do not have to watch their negative media, and we do not have to purchase the products they advertise. Start by Turning Off Channel Zero.

A Reconsideration of Black History Month
Feb. '07

CARTER G. WOODSON BEGAN NEGRO HISTORY Week in 1926, designating it to take place during the second week of February to coincide with the birthdays of Frederick Douglass and Abraham Lincoln. That second week in February eventually became the entire month of February, and is now called Black History Month. We cannot discredit in any way the efforts of Dr. Woodson's initiative, his Black consciousness, and his resolve to strengthen our people through history and education. His effort to establish what is now an entire month of celebrations and remembrances of our people is laudable. But I have a bone to pick with Black History Month.

In 1926, things were very different. Personal transportation was scarce among Black people; very few Blacks even wanted to fly, and many could not afford the price of an airline ticket anyway. Blacks pretty much stayed in the areas of the country where they lived, especially during Negro History Week in February. They celebrated in their homes, churches, and schools for the most part. Besides, as it is now in 2007, it was flat-out cold in February 1926, and you know how much Black folks dislike cold weather.

Today we celebrate Black History Month across the country, and we often travel to different cities to participate in celebrations as well. In addition, Black people organize events during Black History Month and invite out-of-towners to speak and to participate in other ways. This is a real problem in eastern and northern cities, and even in some of the near western cities like Denver, Kansas City, and Oklahoma City. Why? Because it's cold, and most of the time it snows in February!

I recently read where Chicago had to cancel one of its events again this year because of the cold weather, and I am sure that happens in many other cities. Yes, this is personal with me because I love to drive to most places when I speak, and February driving is not my idea of a fun time.

"So what," you ask? Well here is the plan. Let's change Black History Month from February to June. The obvious reason is the weather but we could also fold in our Juneteenth Celebrations with Black History Month activities and not have to worry about the cold, snow, and ice of February canceling our events or making it difficult for us to participate. Hey, we can pick up two more days in the process too!

It may appear that I am joking around, but I am dead serious brothers and sisters. I understand the deference to Carter G. Woodson, and his reason for assigning Black History Week in February, and I am grateful to him for doing so. But we do not have to continue to conduct our celebration of what he started in what probably is the coldest month of the year.

We need to be traveling and mingling with one another during the celebration of Black History. We need to be visiting relatives and celebrating the fact they we are still on this earth; we need to see one another, be able to eat outside, play outside, and remember our ancestors when the leaves are on the trees, when the sun is shining, as we watch our children playing. February is just not the month for that. As my man, Gil Scott-Heron said in his "vibration" on the Ghetto Code, "There is something wrong with February."

I would venture to guess that our ancestors didn't like February too much either. There were no leaves on the trees for cover at night and very little visible black and brown soil for camouflage; instead, in some cases, they had only a backdrop of white snow and a trail of footprints, which were not conducive to escaping. They endured bitter cold, day and night, with few clothes to warm their bodies and thin blankets to warm their children. No, I don't imagine our ancestors liked February very much at all.

This year during Black History Month, I was honored to be invited to speak at Pittsburgh's Carnegie Mellon University, Youngstown (Ohio)

State University, and the Northeast Church of Christ in Oklahoma City, cities that are known for unpredictable winter weather in February. I am sure many of you had places to go during Black History Month as well; I pray you were not stranded or delayed because of the miserable weather we had during the first three weeks of February. I don't know about you, but I certainly enjoy traveling more in June than in February.

Yes, this may be a little selfish, but I think it's a reasonable task for us to undertake. We don't have to ask anyone; the corporations and mass media will go along with whatever we say in this case; so don't worry about your annual donations. They will adjust their sales and their commercials to whatever month we decide we want to celebrate OUR Black History. So before you get cold feet, just remember the real reason for our celebrating Black History, and remember who owns it. Black History is definitely a "Black Thang," y'all.

So, what do you think? Can we start a campaign right now, and change our month from February to June (or maybe you have a better month to suggest)? This time next year we can just sit at home, stay warm, and look forward to Black History Month in June, when the sun will refresh our bodies and remind us of the natural habitat of our ancestors.

Should Black People Leave America?
Nov. '05

EVER SINCE WE ARRIVED IN THIS country there have been conversations about our leaving. Movements, threats, bribes, cajoling, incentives, and every manner of effort by Blacks and whites alike, from Paul Cuffee to Marcus Garvey, and from James Monroe to Abe Lincoln, have been discussed and, in some cases, implemented to get Black people out of this country. While there have been several prominent Black people who have left, there has been no mass exodus by Black people since Liberia, the 1967 move to Africa by the African Hebrew Israelites notwithstanding.

In light of all that has happened to Black people in this country, in addition to what is occurring now in the new millennium, should Black people seriously consider leaving America? We have been here since the beginning, contributed more than anyone else to the foundational wealth of this country, sacrificed more than anyone else for this country, and yet we are still treated like the "three-fifths" they called us when they wrote their Constitution. Should we now walk away?

There comes a time in the lives of most people when they can no longer take seeing their people being left out, marginalized, mistreated, abused, and murdered. They simply throw their hands up, pack up, and leave. Although many have followed the examples of Black musicians and artists, and other brothers and sisters who simply yearned to "breathe free," as the inscription on the Statue of Liberty says, let's look at two Black men who left. Those men are W.E.B. DuBois and Randall Robinson.

"After ninety-five years of the most courageous unflagging devotion to Black freedom witnessed in the 20th century, W.E.B. DuBois not only left America for Africa but concluded: 'I cannot take anymore of this country's treatment. We leave for Ghana October 5th and I set no date for return…Chin up, and fight on, but realize that American Negroes can't win.'" <u>The Future of the Race</u>, Louis Gates and Cornell West.

In Amitabh Pal's recent interview of Randall Robinson, an eerie similarity to DuBois' words and thoughts came forth from Robinson as he explained his reasons for "Quitting America," also the title of his latest book.

"I was really worn down by an American society that is racist, smugly blind to it, and hugely self-satisfied. I wanted to live in a place where that wasn't always a distorting weight. Black people in America have to, for their own protection, develop a defense mechanism, and I just grew terribly tired of it. When you sustain that kind of affront, and sustain it and sustain it and sustain it, something happens to you. You try to steer a course in American society that's not self-destructive. But America is a country that inflicts injury. It does not like to see anything that comes in response, and accuses one of anger as if it were an unnatural response. For anyone who is not white in America, the affronts are virtually across the board."

Looks like these two brothers just got fed up with the nonsense and the "struggle" as we love to call it. Looks like they just made up their minds to pursue something better than the American status quo. Looks like they decided that life was too precious to spend any more time waiting for white folks to change this corrupt, disparate, one-sided system in which we live. Looks like these brothers finally got the message. Have we gotten the message?

Before you ascribe this article as a call for Black people to move out of the U.S., let me make it clear that I am not advocating such an action, but I certainly understand why it occurs. One day I may leave this country for good, but I am not saying all Black people should do so, nor am I saying we should stay here. I just want to use history, both old and recent, to stimulate thinking around what is happening to Black people in this country.

It's not so much that DuBois left for Ghana; it's what he said when he departed. It's not so important that Robinson quit this country; it's what caused him to quit. The rest of us who remain in this country must, first, see what is happening to our people, and then make up our minds, both individually and collectively, to do something about it. Those who choose to do nothing must keep in mind that acquiescing to mistreatment is really doing something.

The latest cuts in initiatives that assist poor people, the elderly, veterans, and college students, juxtaposed against continued tax cuts for millionaires, should serve as a very clear indication of how the majority of Black people are viewed. While we play the political game, and that's exactly what it is, others run off with the economic spoils. By the way, don't be surprised if there is another catastrophe in this country soon. If you know the history of America you know that's the best way to get "the people" back on the President's bandwagon.

So what's it going to be, Black folks? Fight or flight? Right now it looks like we are unwilling to do either, which is unconscionable when you consider our collective condition and the continuous assault on our people by our local, state, and federal government. Was DuBois correct? Is Robinson's life, and his family's, far better off now?

If you choose to leave, no one can blame you. If you choose to stay, you had better prepare yourself for battle. The battlefield is the marketplace; the weapons are our pockets and purses; and the bullets are our dollars. Fire at will! That is, if you have the will.

The Key to our Consciousness
Nov. '06

I REMEMBER BACK IN THE 1960'S when I was an angry, militant, rebellious young man, repulsed at the discrimination and prejudice I had seen and experienced, especially during my two years (1960-1962) of high school in Winston-Salem, North Carolina. While those two years of living "down south" were the absolute best of my youth, looking back, they were also the most illuminating for me when it comes to the birth of my Black consciousness. For the first time in my life I had Black teachers. Billie Matthews, Walter Farabee, Florence Creque, Bernard Foy, Eleanor Ballard, and others who genuinely cared about their students' progress; they taught us how to work individually for the benefit of our group.

By 1965, my enlightenment grew and during the remaining five years of that decade I tried to learn as much as I could about Black History and Black Culture, which led me to a place in Chicago, called the Topographical Library. Talk about eyes being opened and mind being freed, I was on my way to Black consciousness. Then a Professor named Paul Smith at the University of Cincinnati began to pour more consciousness into my brain and into my soul. I was growing into what I am today because brothers and sisters cared enough to share their knowledge with me—knowledge that did not come from the school's core curriculum.

I was blessed to have those teachers, and looking back down my road to Black consciousness and where I stand right now, I know they were right, and I know I am right in my support of and advocacy for Black people. And it all came from Black people who were willing to deviate from the norm, to buck the system, and provide the proper and appropriate education to Black youth.

What about the youth of today? Where will they get their push to Black consciousness? Who will give them the jumpstart they need to continue in the footsteps of Marcus Garvey and Carter G. Woodson? How will we replicate modern-day Marcus Garvey's like Keidi Awadu, Rosie Milligan, and John Brown in Los Angeles, Kwame Kenyatta, Theo Broughton, and Joann Watson in Detroit, Ashiki Taylor, Joe Seyoum Lewis, and Saadiq Mance in Atlanta, Dr. Ed Robinson, Anthony Phillips, and April Bridges in Philadelphia, Jackie Mayfield, Yusef Muhammad, and Fred Zeno in Beaumont, Texas, Curmilus Dancy, Paul Scott, and John Raye in North Carolina, and my brother right here in Cincinnati, Kenneth Price? Who will step into their shoes and what will it take to assure that?

Those I named are just a short list of the many brothers and sisters across this country that are not only conscious but are also demonstrating their Black consciousness through their actions, their sacrifices, and their commitments to Black people. How do we create more of them? Education, that's how. We must take more control of our children's education, and guess what, we have the folks to do just that.

When it comes to group progress, when it comes to group support, when it comes to individual sacrifice for the group, when it comes to work over words, when it comes to Black people living up to the legacy left by our ancestors, Black consciousness is the key. And the key to Black consciousness is education.

Among those coming to our Bring Back Black Leadership meeting on December 9, 2006, in Cincinnati, Ohio, are Chike Akua from Atlanta, Kwa David Whitaker from Cleveland, Haki Madubuti from Chicago, Kweku Akan from Ft. Wayne, Amefika Geuka from West Palm Beach, Kimya Moyo and Eric Abercrumbie from Cincinnati, Taki Raton from Milwaukee, Freya Rivers from Detroit, and Ali Salahuddin from Philadelphia.

All of these brothers and sisters have been actively involved in educating Black children. They have the expertise, dedication, and the knowledge necessary to "draw out" the Black consciousness that lies dormant in our youth. These experts also possess a boundless love for our youth, which drives them and assures quality in their work. If we are going to Bring Back Black we must begin with consciousness; and the key to consciousness is education—not mis-education.

Although there are many Black people who have tremendous wealth, there are few who use their resources to empower the "masses" of Black people, as Jackie Robinson suggested they should. I contend that most of our brothers and sisters, somewhere along their journey to affluence, lost, traded, sold, or willingly surrendered their Black consciousness, their birthright, in exchange for assimilation, acceptance, and/or validation by the larger society.

But thank God for the few Black folks who have both consciousness and capital, a willingness to serve, a collective mindset, and a sharing spirit. We revere them and we thank them.

Just as we will deal with education during our meeting, we will also deal with economic empowerment, political empowerment, communications, technology, health, and we will explore ways to get connected and stay connected on a national level. Finally, but certainly very important, we will devise ways and means to support the local initiatives we are all working on in our various cities, because at the end of the day, that's where our first priority lies.

Let's work on our Black consciousness; it's inside of all of us. Let's teach our children who they are and what their obligation is to their people and to the world. And understand that Black consciousness does not mean the absence of math and science skills. Just think, if our children knew that Black people invented math, don't you think they would have a greater appreciation for it?

Raise your level of Black consciousness by reading the right things, watching the right things, and doing the right things. The key to our empowerment is consciousness—the key to consciousness is education, the right kind of education.

Buying Black—It just feels good.
Jan. '06

OF COURSE, AS I ALWAYS SAY, it's not just about feeling good; it's about doing good too. It's true that we get so strung out on things that make us feel good and neglect the doing good part, but for now I just want to sit back and think about how good it feels to buy Black.

Understanding that Black people in the U.S. could not, even if we tried, spend all of our money with Black owned businesses, that fact alone should make us feel good when we spend some money with our brothers an sisters. In light of the fact that we spend a miniscule percentage of our disposable income with Black folks, we should rejoice when we are able to find just one with whom we can do business.

We brag about our so-called $750 million spending power and stick out our chests about being one of the world's largest economies—if, we were a nation. That "if" is so big that it almost makes no sense to discuss our aggregate income, because we spend most of it in non-Black owned businesses. Such an anomaly defies the logic of "nation-building." Nevertheless, I am happy and it makes me feel so good to spend whatever I can with Black businesses.

The opportunity to buy Black is always present; sometimes it takes a little sacrifice, a little inconvenience, and maybe even some perseverance, but in the long run, and toward collective economic empowerment, if more of us participated on a regular basis, we would make significant economic strides.

Last summer (2005) I finally needed to buy a new car. (Notice I said "needed" not wanted.) I looked in my Black Enterprise Magazine for Black car dealers. I found one 250 miles from Cincinnati, in Akron, Ohio, that sold the kind of van we preferred. There are several dealers in my town that had the same van, but I wanted to buy ours from a Black owned company, or at least from a Black salesperson.

I called Greg Edwards, a dear friend and President of the Akron Black Chamber of Commerce, and asked him if he knew the owner of the dealership, Mike Pruitt. He made a call and the next thing I knew, Mike Pruitt himself was calling me back. I told him how I found his name and what I wanted to purchase; he put Marcus Morris, one of his salesmen, on it right away.

Yes, I live in Cincinnati, but I bought the van from a Black dealer in Akron. Of course, had I wanted a different kind of automobile and could have gotten it from one of the Black dealers in my area, I would have done that. I remember buying a car for my sister at Mel Farr Ford, here in Cincy, about six years ago, and financed it through a Black owned credit union. Both transactions made me feel real good.

That's just one example of what we can do, even if it is a little nontraditional, even if it is logistically cumbersome, even if it takes a little longer. Try it; it will make you feel good too. The next time you need to make a major purchase, look around and see if it is possible to make that purchase from a Black company.

It's tax time. As I say every year, check out Compro Tax. If there is no Compro Tax office near you, there is probably a Black tax preparer somewhere close-by. Let the brother or sister prepare your tax forms. I get sick every time I hear these other companies pitching their business to Black folks. They insult us with their goofy commercials that always feature some Black person who is in a hurry to get his or her refund. "I can't wait; I need my money now." And, they will give it to you now—at a huge interest rate.

Hey, even if you can't wait, you don't have to be insulted by some company that does not care about you, a company that is not interested in building businesses in your community. Compro Tax is just the opposite of the tax preparation companies that portray you as some buffoon who will pay any amount of interest to get his refund. Compro Tax is a company with a conscience and a consciousness; and Compro Tax loves and respects its customers. You should support this company and other Black owned tax firms.

Yes, it feels good to buy Black. Why? I know that by spending whatever I can with other Black folks I am helping to empower them; I am helping their business grow. How can we continue to say that economic empowerment is the primary issue for our people and not do the very minimum and obvious thing that leads to economic empowerment?

By empowering our businesses we empower ourselves, not by being customers alone, but by giving feedback to business owners, letting them know when they are doing a good job and when they have missed the mark.

Please don't insert your Black business horror stories here. Don't start searching for excuses not to support them. Don't send me e-mails decrying all of the negatives. I already know about them; I teach entrepreneurship and, believe me, I stress the positive aspects of business owners taking care of their businesses and doing right by their customers. But for now, I just want to feel good about Black business; I want to rejoice in them; I want to honor them; and I will continue to support them. You should too.

The Million Dollar Club
July '07

NO, THIS IS NOT ABOUT THOSE individuals among us who have been blessed to be millionaires. This is not about creating new millionaires. This is not even about celebrating millionaires. This is about a national collective of Black folks who have the ability to give a million dollars, over and over again, to Black organizations, Black schools, Black museums, and Black causes. This is about an effort by dedicated Black folks who believe in self-help and are willing to sacrifice just a little so that more of us can have a lot. This is about the Blackonomics Million Dollar Club (BMDC).

Since 2005, we have pressed forward with the call for 200,000 persons to sign up as members of the BMDC simply by adding their e-mail addresses to the BMDC Mail List on the homepage of Blackonomics.com. Then, no more than five times per year, they are asked to submit recommendations to which we can each send $5.00 or more to a selected recipient. It's just that simple. No middleman, no administrative costs, no fuss no muss. Just a postage stamp and a check.

All funds-let me say that again for all of you doubters and for those who are still fighting against the power of that "Willie Chip,"-<u>all funds</u> are sent directly to the recipient. One of our members has even set up an online channel for making BMDC donations. What could be simpler and easier for those who are serious about supporting our own organizations and initiatives?

Most of the members of the BMDC send far more, but all we ask is a minimum of $5.00 be sent. That's $25.00 or more per year, brothers and sisters. How can we allow those "other" organizations to take money out of our checks even before we see it and yet refuse to support our own organizations via the BMDC?

Thus far the BMDC has assisted several African-centered schools across the country, and even one in Africa. We have donated to the Haitian Relief Fund, the William Mayo Defense Fund, the D'zert Club, and various Black museums such as the Black Holocaust Museum in Milwaukee and the Harriet Tubman Museum and Home in Cambridge, Maryland and Auburn, New York, respectively.

It all started after I visited Piney Woods School in Mississippi. After organizing a national campaign to raise funds for that school, we expanded the concept and started on a mission to help other Black organizations. We have been successful but not as successful as we can be if more would sign up and follow through on sending in their donations.

Yes, that's bad news, but we can change it to good news in a heartbeat. We are nowhere near 200,000 members yet, which really boggles my mind because I know at least that many read my column every week, have e-mail addresses, and can certainly afford to part with $5.00 or more to help our brothers and sisters. I often wonder why it's so difficult to get folks to do this simple task, why it's such a chore for us to do more for ourselves rather than relying on the largess of folks who really couldn't care less if our organizations survive or die off tomorrow. They are too busy taking care of their own to get involved with ours, and when the budget cuts come, and they will come, we go into our panic mode and start begging.

We don't have to beg; we have the resources to take care of our own stuff. Yes, other folks' money spends too, and they should contribute to our causes; we certainly support theirs. But isn't the primary responsibility for supporting Black causes, Black schools, Black museums, and Black efforts that of Black people first? With all of the income we generate annually, and all of the intelligence we have accumulated over the years, I know we can do much better.

Look at the NAACP having to lay off staff, folks who need their jobs. While we should be creating and "owning" jobs, the most famous, the oldest, and the largest Black Civil Rights organization has to lay off

Black folks because it is broke, but that's another article for another time. The point is we can and must do better. We must find more ways to pool our resources and leverage more benefits from those resources. But, of course, our organizations also have a responsibility to be good stewards of their funds, and to work for their constituents, not just hobnob around the country, camping out in plush hotel suites, playing golf, and eating and drinking like there is no tomorrow.

In spite of that being the case for a relative few of our Black organizations, we must still find ways to support the ones that are doing good things for Black people. They are the little known ones, the small ones, the unsung organizations that are out there everyday educating our children, keeping our history alive and well, fighting for justice, and maintaining venues across this country that are uniquely Black.

Won't you sign up for the Blackonomics Million Dollar Club? And then won't you follow through by sending in your donation when the call goes out? I know you believe it is well worth it for Black people to be in control of our destiny, for us to be self-determined with our own money. I know we can get 200,000 members, one at a time, if *you* will just do our part by signing up today.

As I said, this is not about millionaires, although they are more than welcome to join the BMDC; we'd love to have them, but there are no big I's and little you's in the BMDC. As a matter of fact, most of us have very little knowledge of who else is in the club. That's the beauty of it though; besides, aren't we taught that we should do our alms without shouting it from the rooftops? Aren't we taught that it's better to get rewarded from God for our charitable acts rather than from men?

Go to www.blackonomics.com and sign up for the BMDC today! And thanks so much to those who have already done so.

10-11—Another Date We Must Never Forget
Sept. '06

HAVING MOURNFULLY PUT ANOTHER SEPTEMBER 11th anniversary behind us and as we move closer to October 11th, I urge you to stop for a moment on that day and remember the life and death of a brother who was just as significant as each one of those who perished on 9-11. Although he died alone, from an assassin's bullet; although the nation does not pause for a moment of silence; although no bells ring in his memory; although his name is not called from a roll; and although there are no marches held in his name, we must never forget our dear Brother, Kenneth H. Bridges.

Ken was a family man just like many of those we mourn in the World Trade Center, in the Pentagon, and in Shanksville. Ken was also at work when he was killed. Ken is just as much a hero as those who died trying to help others on 9-11 because he died in the act of helping others. Ken sacrificed his life, before he was killed, by giving so much of his time to the cause of economic empowerment for Black people and taking so much valuable time away from his beloved wife and his six adorable children.

On 10-11, at nearly the same time the first tower fell in New York, and after making his last cell phone call to his wife, Ken Bridges lie on the ground dying, a bullet having ripped throw his body, thinking the same things I am sure those who died in on 9-11 were thinking just before they transitioned. Knowing him the way I did, I feel confident in saying Ken was thinking about his family, his work, his brothers and sisters, and the quest he had been on since 1997: The MATAH Network.

Ken Bridges was a man among men and we should never forget him and that infamous date, October 11, 2002. Just as we commemorate others who worked and sacrificed for our people and who loved us more than they loved themselves, we must do the same in memory of Ken Bridges. He deserves no less from those for whom he fought so valiantly, so eloquently, and so tirelessly.

Each one of the persons lost on 9-11 left loved ones behind, mourners who still love them and will never forget that tragic day. There can be no less from us for Ken Bridges, who touched thousands of individuals with his engaging smile, his bear-hugs, and his infectious and indefatigable enthusiasm for true economic freedom for Black people. Had he been on one of the upper floors of either of those towers, or on one of those planes that crashed into the Pentagon or in Shanksville, Pennsylvania, we would owe him the same homage, not because he happened to be there at the wrong time, but because no matter where he was when he met his demise, we know he would have been working for us.

As Ken's long-time partner and friend, Al Wellington, said in his remembrance of his fallen confidant, "The world doesn't know it yet, but Ken Bridges was the most significant Black leader since Martin Luther King." How right Al was in his assessment. Ken Bridges "died on his way to freedom," never lagging back, afraid to be out front, but as authentic leaders do, he led the way; he showed us how it was done; he lived what he taught.

In so doing, Ken found himself in the right place at the wrong time, just as those who lost their lives on 9-11 did. They were where they were supposed to be that day, and so was Ken. He just stopped to get gas, as he was making his way back to his family after a marathon "freedom session" that could have catapulted Black people to new heights in economic freedom.

Ken was in the right place, doing the right thing, for the all the right reasons, but just not at the right time. Those in the World Trade Centers were doing much the same. In both incidents there have been rumors of conspiracy and intentional targeting by someone other than the ones accused and/or convicted of these crimes. Parallels abound between these two occurrences, but the parallels cease when it comes to how we treat the memory of Kenneth Bridges and how we treat the 9-11 tragedy. Yes, there were 2900 lives lost that day, but to their families each person lost was a single horrendous act just as Ken's death was to his family and friends.

I think about Ken quite often, like nearly everyday, as I see his portrait in my office, his "If I Should Die on My Way to Freedom" poster in my basement, the African doll he gave my daughter, and the MATAH jacket he gave me the first day we met, which I still wear. I remember him as I listen to the tapes and watch the videos on which he speaks so passionately about the importance of Black economic freedom.

I remember him through his wife and children whom I speak to and see from time to time. I remember him through our mutual friends and associates, and I remember Ken Bridges because he actually brought to fruition an institution, an entity through which Black people could circulate our dollars among ourselves. He was an "authentic" leader who paid the ultimate price for his leadership and concern for his people.

It's so nice when my daughter remembers something about Ken and mentions it to me. I am so glad she had the opportunity to meet him. It's good to know that she will never forget 10-11. Will you? Go to www.kenbridges.org and get to know him. Rest peacefully, my brother.

An Open Letter to Black Americans, written by Bob Law and Jim Clingman:
It Is Time to Bring Black Back
Nov. '06

IN RECENT YEARS SOME NATIONALLY PROMINENT Black leaders have complained that they resent being known as Black leaders, they say they want the world to know they are capable of leading anybody. Rather than demonstrate that leadership by leading their own people to the necessary levels of self- sufficiency and competitiveness, these leaders have abandoned the critical issues facing Black people and have begun to chase an ambiguous romanticized notion of alliances with other groups without any demonstration or even an explanation as to how these alliances will actually empower Black people.

For decades these leaders have stood on the shoulders of the Black community to challenge and threaten corporate America in what we were told was a struggle for economic justice, and while the Black community is still being exploited by corporate America these nationally prominent Black leaders acknowledge that their operating budgets are now sustained by their corporate sponsors. It appears as though these leaders, a small cluster of their friends and, in some instances, members of their own families are the only ones to have received concessions from the nation's major corporations. This mis-leadership is precisely what noted sociologist Max Weber warned against when he made the distinction between living off politics and living for politics, Weber contends, "He who strives to make politics a permanent source off income lives off politics as a vocation, whereas he who does not do this lives for politics."

Leaders not only examine issues and point out inherent problems; they also craft solutions and lead by example. These nationally prominent Black leaders and organizations have actually abandoned the specific needs of Black people, Case in point: Black Americans have never received proportional benefits for the time, energy, and resources that they have devoted to voting. No major party or candidate has delivered benefits to Black people in return for their votes. Still these nationally prominent Black leaders tell Blacks simply to vote, while politicians hide behind mythical concepts and broad groupings, like people of color, minorities, poor people, multi-culture, and diversity in order to justify doing nothing specifically for Blacks in return for their votes. Unless the politician or political party is committed to repairing the damage done to Blacks by centuries of historical inequities, telling Blacks to just vote is to engage Blacks in nothing more than a keep busy activity. Too often these nationally prominent leaders have engaged in a flawed analysis of the problems confronting Blacks, and as a result have offered inadequate solutions.

Black people are offered a meaningless covenant with America that leaves all the power and resources firmly in the hands of white power brokers. These leaders have cooperated with major white developers in securing huge development contracts to build anything they please from Stadiums in downtown Brooklyn to an entire urban riverfront in Cincinnati, Ohio. Rather than secure the development project itself for a consortium of Black developers they, on behalf of the white developers, urge Black people to accept temporary dead end jobs as the Black benefits, jobs they would never allow their own children to accept.

These prominent leaders argue that unemployment is so high among Blacks that any job is of value. When you consider that unemployment among Asians is 0%, among Arabs 0%, Hispanics 4.6%, with Hispanics receiving 41% of all new jobs since 2004, and among whites unemployment is 4.5%, it is clear that other groups have an economic plan working in and for their communities. With unemployment at 48 to 50% in Black urban centers throughout the country and thereby making any job acceptable, the real question becomes, how is it that under their watch unemployment among Blacks remains twice the national rate that it was for all Americans during the Great Depression of the 1930's. Black leaders, where is your economic strategy to empower Black America?

Black Empowerment with Attitude!

While ignoring the work being done to revitalize Black communities by lesser known Blacks in various cities, and in some instances even moving to block and discourage those efforts, these prominent Black leaders have agreed to become the mouthpiece for other groups in order to make the agendas of those groups sound like an extension of the civil rights movement. Black leaders should be taking Black people to the next level, addressing the unfinished business of our civil rights movement, which will then make our people politically and economically competitive and self-sufficient.

Allowing any and all groups to use broad terms like diversity, people of color, and minorities is a ploy to avoid addressing the specific needs of Blacks, and to equate the grievances of these groups to the historical suffering of Black people does Blacks and history a great disservice. For over a century and a half, Blacks in America have marched and protested against every perceived affront. Blacks have marched and sued for equal rights, minority rights, women's rights, poor people's rights, gay rights, workers rights, voting rights, and now immigrant rights. Blacks have held hands, sung songs, prayed and swayed with everyone, yet have barely moved an inch economically and politically in terms of real power and influence.

Blacks have the strongest legal and moral grounds for justice due than any other group, but have not enjoyed the full support of any of these other groups. Given our history of struggle we are offended by these national Black leaders and organizations that scold and chastise us for not embracing their newest gimmick to impress white power brokers, that of immigrant rights. They don't seem to understand that there are still critical issues unresolved that have particular consequences for Blacks.

Enough is enough, Black people are in need of leaders who without apology are committed to the very real needs of Black Americans, We urge the leaders who feel trapped by their Blackness to go quickly to the task of providing leadership for all these other groups so that we can get away from their mis-leadership long enough to get out of our current political and economic ditch.

It Is Time To Bring Black Back!

Are you ready to Bring Back Black?
Dec. '06

I KNOW I AM. I AM ready to connect with brothers and sisters who are unwavering and unapologetic when it comes to who they are and what their obligation is to our people. I am ready to stand shoulder to shoulder with Black folks who are unafraid and unflappable when attacked from without and from within. I am ready to work with a new cadre of Black leaders, not new in experience but new as it relates to their current unsung status, their active youth status, and new in respect to what they have done and are doing "under the radar screen" so to speak. There are many "new" leaders out there, and I am ready to follow them as we Bring Back Black.

The book by W.D. Wright, The Crisis of the Black Intellectual, which I highly recommend you read, contains the following passage on page 311. (Get your copy from Third World Press, Chicago, IL)

"Today there is no general Black leadership and the Black political body is fragmented isolated, individualistic, fanciful, delusional, susceptible to posturing, and has no real sense of engaging with Black politics that are designed to help Black people in America, specifically those millions still 'stuck at the bottom.' What could interrupt this situation and force Blacks back to a general leadership and to a consciousness of Black politics would be the emergence of new and differently oriented local Black leaders. This would include some individuals drawn from those 'stuck at the bottom.' There are enough Black local leaders, community organizers, and activists who could initiate this new and different leadership across the country and who could consciously and actively seek to recruit and train individuals 'up from varied misery' for local leadership."

The weekend of December 8, 2006 was the first step on a journey some of us have taken before. It was the weekend when strong, dedicated, determined, and consciously Black brothers and sisters gathered to begin the Bring Back Black movement. We came together because we know W.D. Wright is correct in his assessment of Black leadership. We came together to find one another, to meet one another, to connect with one another, to support one another, and to work with one another.

The Bring Back Black gathering comprised stalwart and resolute Black folks, some of who have been working for decades empowering our people. No need to name them; they are not looking for the spotlight. No need to number them; they are not looking for accolades. This group, as well as those who wanted to be there but could not, simply works to overcome the psychological barriers that now prevent Black people from moving forward together as well as individually.

They do their work quietly and without fanfare, in the same manner that Frederick Douglass described Harriet Tubman and the work she did. They work by building their own businesses, opening their own schools, and being serious about their political involvement. They do their work by meeting payrolls from which their Black employees take care of their families. They do it by standing up and speaking out against injustice and inequity. They do it by sacrificing their time and their resources for the collective cause of Black people. That's why they came to the Bring Back Black gathering, which was held in the city Kwesi Mfume called "ground zero": Cincinnati, Ohio.

I want to publicly state my gratitude to all who came, and those who could not, for your trust and confidence in me. Yes, I made the call, but you came, and it was all of you who made our gathering a milestone in the annals of our history in this country. It was you, all of us, who have etched a new thought into the minds of our people, a thought that if nurtured and promoted, will surely take root and spring up as the movement we have searched for during the past 40 years.

In the 1960's we had the Black Power Movement, in which our songs, our products, our language, our clothing, our hair, our gestures, and our love of self, displayed a new thought, a new resolve, and a new dedication.

What happened to it? Those were the first stages of what could have been a most powerful movement for Black people. The remnants are still with us, but the substance of collective progressiveness and prosperity are far lacking.

Shortly after Martin Luther King's death it seems Black folks were more susceptible to being bought off; they were more pliable and, thus, easy targets for political and social program positions and handouts. During that period, in which strong, fist-in-the-air, Black men and women capitulated to the temptations of betrayal, we heard the death knell of our movement. It was sad to see strong Black voices silenced by the lure of "jobs" "grants" "sponsorships" and appointments to "Advisory Boards." But to many in 1960's, I suppose, it beat the alternative of being ostracized like Tommy Smith and John Carlos were, or even murdered like Fred Hampton was.

So what do we do now? We seek and follow new leadership; we take more control of our children's education; we get serious about politics by playing to win rather than just playing to play; we take better care of our bodies; we use technology and commercial media, to its fullest, to tell our own story; we connect with our brothers and sisters in Africa, in Haiti, Jamaica, and other Caribbean islands, and in Brazil's Bahia, and in London, and throughout the world. And finally, but importantly, we pool some of our money and invest in our own projects.

Those are the things we did at our Bring Back Black meeting. Now, I ask you again: Are you ready to Bring Back Black?   See www.bringbackblack.org for more information

New Year—New Strategy
Dec. '06

FOR THOSE OF US WHO WERE blessed to see it, another year has arrived and brings with it another opportunity to start afresh with new ways to move our people closer to economic empowerment. The New Year brings a clean slate, so to speak, since we like to make resolutions and promises regarding things we would like to change. So what will we write on our 2007 slate? What will be our agenda this year? What strategy will we employ to empower our people? Will we stay on the endless circular path that has led us to where we are today? Will we follow a new path? Will we adopt a new strategy?

Whatever we decide to commit ourselves to will certainly not be new; everything we need to do in 2007 and beyond has already been done by our ancestors who lived and survived in this country for centuries, under the worst treatment human beings could suffer. But 2007 will be new, and it's always good to look at our commitments in a new light, with a new resolve, and out of a renewed strength. Are you ready?

Here we go. Don't fall for the same old tired rhetoric we hear everyday from self-appointed "leaders" who do what James Brown described as "talkin' loud and sayin' nothing." Don't continue following folks that are only sending you deeper into the woods of poverty, while they relax in the lush fields of prosperity.

Don't get hood-winked by pandering politicians and pontificating preachers who are only interested in what they can get for themselves, and how they can use you to get another pair of "gators," a Bentley, a mansion, or elected to public office. Don't be lulled to sleep by intellectual banter that makes you feel good but never tells you how to do good, or do well, for that matter.

Don't succumb to celebrity claptrap, which only excites the *Paparazzi* rather than enlightens our people. Don't get down in the muck with entertainers who denigrate themselves and their own people. And please don't subscribe to the same old "okey-doke" that has literally and figuratively programmed our people to such a degree that some of us are still waiting to be rescued by people who really care very little about us. Please stop the nonsensical behavior in 2007, and let's get down to the business of taking better care of ourselves.

What must we do? First, raise the level of your Black consciousness by reading, by studying, by listening, and by associating with brothers and sisters who are serious about doing the work of liberation and unashamed to proclaim their Blackness. Connect with other individuals and collectively establish economic initiatives that benefit Black people; trust me, there is absolutely nothing wrong with that; other groups do it all the time.

Be prepared to make the small individual sacrifices required to move the masses of Black people forward, both locally and nationally—and then let's move on to the international stage. Always define yourself, and do not accept definitions like "minority" and "person of color." Terms like those really lose something in translation, namely, us.

Stand up against injustice and wrongdoing, no matter who the perpetrator is, white, Black, or any other color. Follow through on your commitments to one another and the commitments to yourself. Get fired up, but stay fired up long enough to get the work done. Teach your children how to navigate through this world; that's right, you teach them. If you don't know what to teach them, get some help for yourself, and then teach them.

Take better care of yourself. Find something physical that you can do and keep doing it for the rest of your life. Yes, it will hurt sometimes, but it's worth it. I ride a bicycle, and I plan to ride as long as I am physically able to pedal and hold the handlebars. Besides that, I love it. Anyone out there want to race? Try not to eat so much of whatever you are eating. Just eat less of everything and get up and do something to burn some calories.

Do kind things for those less fortunate than you. It doesn't always have to be money. It could be an encouraging word, a hug without words, some baked cookies, a small gift just because, or a few hours spent with a child who may not have a father or a mother. You don't need a program to do this; you just need yourself.

Seek out new Black leadership, authentic leadership, or be a leader yourself. There are young folks all across this country waiting to step up to the task of leadership, many of who are leading right now. Find them, especially you old soldiers out there; you can't hang on forever, you know. Teach the young and pass the baton to them, not to someone on the other team.

Start viable businesses, grow those businesses, and create jobs for our people. Build economic enclaves throughout this country, like our relatives did two hundred years ago. Identify industries where we have the competitive advantage because of our consumerism, and build vertically integrated businesses within those industries. James Brown also said, "Let's get together and get some land; raise our food like the man. Save our money like the mob; put up a factory and own the jobs."

Boycott prisons! Stay out of the cells and get into sales, the legal kind. And finally, do all of these things under the Bring Back Black mantra, because the time is long overdue for us to take our rightful place in this country, politically, socially, educationally, and most of all economically. Please have a wonderfully blessed year in 2007, 2008, 2009, 2010, and beyond.

The Culmination of Freedom
June '07

CONSIDERING HOW JUNETEENTH HAS BECOME the celebration of freedom for Black people, our Independence Day, as some call it, we should give some deep thought to what freedom really is all about for our people. Anyone who reads the Emancipation Proclamation can see that it did not free our enslaved ancestors, despite what we were taught. We know the Emancipation called for freedom among those who were not under the jurisdiction of the Union, thus lacking the real power to impose its will on the southern confederacy. It also failed to free those who were under the jurisdiction of the Union, thus, it really freed no one. Then along came General Gordon Granger to Galveston, Texas.

Granger read the General Order freeing the enslaved of Texas on June 19, 1865, which is said to be two years late; but you could say it was six months early because the 13th Amendment, which "freed" Black people once again, was not ratified until December 1865. Texas did not ratify the 13th Amendment until February of 1870! We were "really" free this time. Or were we?

Let's see now; we were freed by the Emancipation, but oops, it really didn't free us. Then came Juneteenth, which freed us either too late or too early, depending on how you look at it. Then came the 13th Amendment which, to this day, says slavery is abolished "except" for those duly convicted of crimes; oops, sorry about that. How many times is that, three? We have been "freed" more than any other people on earth.

Reconstruction followed our new found freedom with the 14th Amendment, ratified in 1868, which was supposed to provide due process and equal treatment for Black people; free again, y'all. Then the 15th Amendment was ratified in 1870, which freed us once again to be able to vote, but old Rutherford B. Hayes would have no part of that. He just withdrew the federal troops and looked the other way as Black people were once again prevented from attaining their freedom by attempting to cast their votes. Foiled again!

The next 100 years saw Black people fighting for public accommodations, education, and yes, voting rights, which were given to us again in 1965, but even today certain aspects of the law must be "reviewed" "extended," or "renewed" every now and then. Freedom? You tell me.

Having fought the battles for civil rights, education, and voting, and after being "freed" so many times it makes my head swim, Black people are still in a battle to attain true freedom. What is true freedom? It is all those things that we were supposed to have been granted after the Civil War, with the ratifying of the 13th 14th and 15th Amendments. But, the culmination of freedom for Black people in America is economic freedom.

It was great to get freed so many times, but freedom in 1865 with no money, no forty acres, and no mules, was not freedom at all. Unlike the Israelites who were instructed by God, Himself, to go back and get reparations from their former captors, we received nothing but more trouble, Thaddeus Stevens' 1867 Reparations Bill notwithstanding.

When we did get some money, it was nice to have the choice of spending it in businesses we did not own, but it was better to support those businesses we did own. It was nice to be able to go to school with white folks who hated us, but better to have our own schools. It was nice to finally have the right to vote without being threatened, but better to have our votes count for something other than condescension and false promises, which would not have been the case if we had maintained our economic base.

That's why I say the culmination of freedom, if we are really free at all, is economic freedom. I don't mean individual economic freedom, although that's great for those brothers and sisters who have attained that status, but rather collective economic freedom. When we reach that status as a group of people in this country we will have completed that long journey that began at the Door of No Return.

How can we do it? Well, we can begin by loving and trusting one another enough to be willing to make an individual sacrifice for the betterment of our group. We will accomplish it when we are able to maintain our own institutions and organizations with our own dollars, rather than having to close them down or downsize because corporate donations dry up. We will do it when we care enough about our children to educate them ourselves, or at least take more control over what they are taught in school.

We will reach the zenith of true freedom when we own and control a proportionate share of this country's assets, when we have more banks, more hotels, more office buildings, more manufacturing, more distribution, more development rights, more equity funds, more investment funds, more real estate investment trusts, more revolving credit associations, more bartering associations, and more collective activity among Black people.

Yes, the culmination of freedom, even after all of the times we have been "freed," is economic freedom. In this capitalistic society where the almighty dollar rules, people are truly free when they are economically free, not just free to eat where they want, free to go to the bathroom when and wherever they happen to be, free to attend public schools with other folks, or free to cast a vote.

The culmination of freedom, economic freedom, for Black people is our last charge in this country, our "final imperative," as George Fraser puts it, the final movement in our Freedom Suite, and the final chapter in our historic and heroic existence in this land of plenty.

Epilogue

Definition: A short section at the end of a book, sometimes dealing with the fate of its characters.

There you have it, brothers and sisters; from the Good Stuff to the Right Stuff, I have shared my love for my people as well as my anger, my attitude, and my indignation not so much at our state, but more at our fate if we fail to chart a new course for the Black Ship of State. Yes, it takes a while to turn a huge ship, but we have the resources, the expertise, and the muscle to do it. The question is: Do we have the will to do it?

The fate of the characters in this book (As Ken Bridges would say, "That be us, y'all,") lies in the work of our own hands. We will not only survive, we will thrive, if we work together to build an economic foundation for Black people.

Our fate can either be bright and glorious, or it can be dismal and hopeless. It's really up to those of us who are willing to contribute to the uplift of our people with whatever gifts we possess, those of us who are conscious, and those of us who are working to raise our consciousness; we are the ones who will make the needed changes. Where do you stand when it comes to the fate of the characters in this book? "That be us, y'all."

I will end with a few thoughts on one particular character that is present throughout this book. This character's fate is certainly worthy of consideration as well, as his work follows in the footsteps of some of our most revered ancestors. Although his words fall on deaf ears sometimes, and even though he does not always share in the rewards of his labor, he continues to "stick with his work," as the plaque on his office wall directs him to do. This is the person I call, "The Tree Shaker."

This Black man has made a career of enthusiastically and forcefully shaking fruit trees for Black people; the results of his continuous shaking have been some of the juiciest plums, the reddest apples, and sweetest cherries ever enjoyed by Black folks. Yes, he is the Tree Shaker all right.

And you know what? He is not like some of those other so-called tree shakers who stand on the ground, shake a branch of the tree, and are the first to reach down and select the best of the fruit before anyone else can get there. No, this Brother climbs up into the tree, way up near the top where the best fruit is, where the sun's life-giving rays are unobstructed by the leaves. He goes where the risk is the greatest, to heights where, if he falls, he would surely suffer considerable physical and psychological damage. Nevertheless, he goes because he loves his people. He loves to see them "do good" and do well. He rejoices in their wellbeing and prosperity, no matter their status, that is, as long as they use the fruit he shakes to ground to "do good" for other Black people.

Despite the risky climb and the selflessness of his mission, he keeps going into the trees, climbing higher and higher, and shaking luscious fruit from their stems and branches, down to the ground below where other brothers and sisters eagerly gather the bounty of the Tree Shaker's work.

Unfortunately, after his work is done and he comes down from the tree, scarred and scratched from its branches, all of the good fruit has been taken and no one is there waiting to share their fruit with him and his family. As a matter of fact, some of the very ones standing under the tree while he was shaking it were not even his friends; but he shook the tree anyway, mainly because he believes in Black folks, gives everyone the benefit of the doubt, preferring to believe they will end up doing the right thing. After all, if it were not for him, The Tree Shaker, their lives would not be as fruitful as they are. "They'll come around; they'll share the bounty," he thought.

As time went by, The Tree Shaker began to question why he kept climbing the trees to shake the fruit to the ground for everyone else, but received so little in return for his tireless efforts. He also felt guilty for taking the risk of climbing the trees and doing so much good for others only to have so little for his family when he returned home. Was it all worth it? Has he been a fool all along? Were the others just using him for their personal gain?

He assumed, and rightly so, that the Black people who benefited from his tree-shaking would at least drop by and offer him some of the fruit. They never came. He knew that those who were eating because of his work, enjoying a better life because of the risks he took, and those who have risen to a higher status should be beating a path to his door, not only to thank him for his work but also to share with him some of their fruit. They did not come.

One day the Tree Shaker got his own wake-up call. He decided it was futile to think that selfish fruit gatherers would change their ways. He came to the full realization that they had, indeed, been using him.

They used his consciousness because they had none; they used his backbone because they were spineless; they used his temerity because they were reticent; they used his hope because they were apathetic; they used his strength because they were weaklings; they used his uprightness because they were only willing to lie down; they used his boisterousness because they would only whisper; they used his anger because they were timid; they used his love because they were haters; they used his guts because they were cowards. They finally used him up.

Now the Tree Shaker looks back on his life and has to admit that he did not do everything he should have for his own immediate family. His work put a huge strain on his "queen," who picked up and carried the load caused by the lack of reciprocity from those who gained so much from the Tree Shaker's work.

Coming home, tired and worn out from a long day of shaking trees but with very little to show for his labor, the Tree Shaker retires to a quiet space and cries in secret. He sheds tears for his family. He cries for his people. He weeps for other Tree Shakers who have died "on their way to freedom." He grieves for the millions of Black children who face a dismal future as they continue to suffer from a lack of education, a lack of economic resources, a lack of political power, and a general lack of fruit as a result of the selfishness of the relative few Black people who have an abundance of fruit but will not share it.

The Tree Shaker prays for his family, for his people, and for himself: "Lord, please help us; help us to see ourselves through Your eyes, the One who made us in His image and likeness; help us to love, trust, respect, and support one another more. Help us, oh Lord, to know that You made each of us for a purpose; help us to find that purpose and execute it. Help us, Heavenly Father, to do what is right in Your eyes. Help us to be better people, better spouses, better parents, and better children. Help us to understand that righteous indignation, when we use it in accordance with Your will, can change our world for the better. Help us find the correct balance, Lord. Help us to heal.

Thank You, Lord, for bestowing Your bountiful blessings on our people. I know sometimes we don't show our appreciation and we fail to bless others with our blessings, but please forgive us and help us do better.

Finally, Lord, may we always realize that all the trees and all the fruit thereon belong to You, and it is here for us to share with one another. Please remove our selfishness. Amen."

For all of you "Tree Shakers" out there, below are the words on that plaque that hangs on my wall. They were written and presented to me by Brother Arnelious Crenshaw, Minister of the Northeast Church of Christ in Oklahoma City, in appreciation of my participation in the church's Black History Month Program in 2005. These words guide me and even keep me sane when things get rough. May they also guide you in your journey and aid you in your quest to help empower our people. Peace.

Being About the Father's Business

Stick with your work. Do not flinch because the lion roars; do not stop to stone the devil's dogs; do not fool away your time chasing the devil's rabbits. **Do your work.** Let liars lie, let sectarians quarrel, let critics malign, let enemies accuse, let the devil do his worst; but see to it that nothing hinders you from fulfilling with joy the work that God has given you to do.

He has not commanded you to be admired or esteemed. He has never bidden you to defend your character. He has not set you at work to contradict falsehood (about yourself) which Satan's or God's servants may start to peddle, or to track down every rumor that threatens your reputation. If you do these things you will do nothing else; you will be at work for yourself and not for the Lord.

Keep at your work. Let your aim be steady as a star. You may be assaulted, wronged, insulted, slandered, wounded, and rejected, misunderstood or assigned impure motives; you may be abused by foes, forsaken by friends, and despised and rejected of men. But see to it with steadfast determination, with unfaltering zeal, that you pursue the great purpose of your life and object of your being until at last you can say,

"I have finished the work which Thou gavest me to do."

More Stuff You Should Know

Here is a very short list of Black owned businesses you should support; add to it, and let's get the word out about Black owned businesses throughout this nation.

Compro Tax—More than 125 offices across the country!
www.comprotax.com

Kemet World—The largest Black Owned Cyber-Mall in the world; an "intentional international community" Sign up!
www.kemetworld.com

Milligan Books—"Literacy is everybody's business."
www.milliganbooks.com

Nia Books—"Lack of knowledge is darker than night." Making sure the knowledge is available.
www.niabooks.com

Third World Press—One of the nation's oldest and independent Black publishers
www.thirdworldpressinc.com

Mattah Network—A People, a Movement, a Business
www.themattahmovement.com

Ice Supreme—"Tastes like ice cream; grab a spoon." No dairy, no soy, no animal products
www.icesupreme.com

Legends to Legacy—Clothing Manufacturers. All kinds of apparel.
www.legendstolegacy.com
The Bedford Group-For over twenty years, The Bedford Group has specialized in revitalizing urban landscapes.
www.thebedfordgroup.com

Dudley Hair Products—One business that needs no introduction
www.dudleycosmetics.com

Black Empowerment with Attitude!

C & C Wellness-A "Christ-centered business" that provides community health education and health promotion.
www.cenellclarkwellness.com

SIS Fitness—Philly's complete fitness center for men and women
www.sisfitness.com

BabyStar Productions-Your "gateway" to exploring the history of African Americans.
www.knowyourhistory.com

Compro Credit-Empowering people through credit education,
www.comprocredit.com

Imani Enterprises—"Transforming teachers to transform students to transform the world." Master Teacher, Chike Akua
www.ImaniEnterprises.org

Getting the Word Out Enterprises-Provides Inspiration, Education, Coaching, and Mentoring on how to profit from your passions
www.ProfitsWithAPassion.com

Black Pages International—Look it up, and hook it up!
www.theblackpagesinternational.com

Black Pages Atlanta—See what's hot in "Hot-Lanta"
www.blackpagesatlanta.com

Ready!!! Or Not!—Designed to Encourage, Empower, and Reveal
www.get-your-mind-ready.com

The Harold Dawson Company-Two generations of commercial and residential real estate expertise, knowledge, and professionalism
www.hadcoinc.com

Port of Harlem Magazine—named after the world's most famous Pan-African Community
www.portofharlem.net

ONLI STUDIOS-Produces the oldest annual Black Age of Comics Convention in Chicago
www.ecbacc.com

Six Acres Bed and Breakfast-Built between 1850 and 1860 this beautiful home has a unique connection to the Underground Railroad. Spend a few nights and "feel" Black History. Look for "Kristen in the Kitchen."
www.sixacresbb.com

Izania-Browse over 2275 Black-owned businesses across the country! Thanks, Roger Madison!
www.izania.com

Emerging Minds-A fresh and progressive approach to news, culture, and business by Saadiq Mance
www.emergingminds.org

Grandma's Chicken and Waffles-This is one restaurant in Baltimore where real GRANDMAS are cooking in the kitchen!!!!!!!
www.grandmassoulfood.com

Body Talk-Low impact workout programs using several types of dance, designed to give you a full body workout.
www.bodytalkllc.com

Araminta Financial Group-A nationwide company committed to excellence in serving the financial and home ownership needs and goals of its clients.
www.aramintafinancialgroup.com

Dancy Communications Network—The Political Agitator, Curmilus Dancy, is definitely "Unbought and Unbossed"
www.thepoliticalagitator.com

Amariah Naturals-*Bringing you skin-friendly body care products created with all of the good things Nature has to offer.*
www.amariahnaturals.com

Poli-tainment-A mixture of politics and entertainment used to educate, with an emphasis on pro-black and progressive thoughts and issues. Brother Opio Sokoni
www.poli-tainment.com

Black Empowerment with Attitude!

Eady Associates—A network and array of expertise and support resources such as marketing, public relations, capital funding, media, architecture, construction, diversity management, and international marketing.
www.kermiteady.com

Farley's Coffee—"The coffee with a classic taste."
www.farleyscoffeeinc.com

Sankofa Book and Video Store—Going back to reclaim our past.
www.sankofastore.com

Sweet Unity Farms Coffee-A co-op of several hundred small scale coffee farmers based in Tanzania, founded by Jackie Robinson's son, David Robinson.
www.sweetunityfarmscoffee.com

Afrikan World Book Store—A leader in Black book distribution.
www.afrikanworldbooks.com

The Majority Press, Inc.—The world's leading site for academic literature on Marcus Garvey.
www.themajoritypress.com

Chris and Lakisha Simmons—Event and family travel service
www.MarriedTravelers.com; www.KingDestinations.com

Black Star Media—Brother Keidi Awadu is always "on the case."
www.LIBRadio.com
www.LIBtv.com
www.BlackMarketSolutions.com

Harambee Radio—Brother Dalani & Junious Ricardo Stanton
www.harambeeradio.com

Blake Radio- Rainbow Soul, Music Massage, and more
www.blakeradio.com

Woodcrafts By O'Banion-The best in high-value, low-priced, culturally-based, handcrafted, wood products for your home and/or office. "I have one of their African Clocks in my home."
www.woodcraftsbyobanion.com

National Black Business Trade Association—Get to know one another's business.
www.nbbta.org

Premier Palette—Manchester, New Hampshire's ONLY restaurant offering Authentic Soul Food. Prepared by a true Southerner.
www.eatwithyourpal.com

D & Q Communications, Inc.-"For your survival and liberation, you gotta know...What the Problem is! This site will bring news, features, and other forms of information in service to the Afrikan Community globally!"
www.whattheproblemis.com

BCE-Corporate Training and Public Speaking-Always "Rising" to the occasion!
www.burnetteclingman.com

Shades Magazine—A self-esteem magazine for black girls.
www.shadesmag.com

Soul Xpress-Soul food on the Go!
www.ilovefoodgroupnetwork.com

JV Cook-Printing and Graphic Design
jvcookinc@sbcglobal.net

World Focus Photography
www.worldfocusphotography.com

Exclusive Staffing—Providing human capital resources in administrative, clerical, financial, operations, legal, and information technology positions.
www.exclusivestaffing.com

Spirit of Beauty Etiquette & Social Development
www.myspiritofbeauty.com

Wu Li Turtle Corp—Keynote presentations, executive and life coaching
www.wuliturtle.com

Black Empowerment with Attitude!

Imorpheus Business Consulting-International experience. www.imorpheus.pageout.net

Advanced Records Technology, Inc-A full service company specializing in Document Imaging and Micrographics, since 1987.
www.artcorpinc.com

R.J. Dale Advertising-Advertising and Public Relations Agency in Chicago
www.rjdale.com

Digital Millennium LLC-Providing world-class technology solutions for corporations, not-for-profit organizations, institutions, and government agencies.
www.digitalmllc.com

GaBelle Designs by G A B Designs-One-of-a-kind and unique apparel for women size 10-32.
www.gabelledesigns.com

Black Restaurant Association of Central Ohio—Raising the profile and awareness of the Black owned restaurants in Central Ohio.
www.bracoonline.com

WURD Radio—Philadelphia's only Black owned and operated radio station. Listen, and support it with your advertising dollars.
www.900amwurd.com

BBH TOURS—Based in Baltimore, Maryland, Black Heritage Tours offers a one-stop shop for all your travel and tourism needs.
www.bbhtours.com

Global Financial Network—Enhance your knowledge of finance
www.globalfinet.com

Ladybug Cuisine—Asheville, North Carolina's finest Caterer!
www.ladybugcuisine.com

Artistic Tees—A fantastic array of T-Shirts! and other items
www.artistictees.com

Say it Loud!—Book promotions and special events. Since 1997, our Readers and Writers Series have provided opportunities in literature for youth in Little Rock, AR.
www.speakloudly.com

EZ Internet Solutions—One of my personal favorites—They designed and host my website, **Blackonomics**
www.enterzone.com

Community Insurance Center, Inc
www.communityins.com

Alter EatGo Restaurants, LLC—Taste the delicious and "healthy meals" prepared by Chef Eric Paul in Chicago. They deliver!
www.altereatgo.com

Le Divas of Chicago Catering—Chi-Town's AmeriCajun Cuisine Catering Services. Hmmm Good!
http://www.ledivas.com

The Matlock Group-For your health, wealth, and travel needs, contact Sister Garnet Hall.
www.myenergycel.com/6134
www.travel.travelreaction.com/5134299

ABOUT THE AUTHOR

James Clingman is an award-winning syndicated newspaper columnist. For more than twenty-five years he has written, given speeches, taught, and advocated for economic empowerment via entrepreneurship. Clingman has written five books on economic empowerment, and his newspaper column has been in circulation for twenty-four years.

He is a true activist and follows his words with action. Clingman founded the Cincinnati Black Chamber of Commerce and played a key role in the development of twelve other Black Chambers around the nation. He started a public Entrepreneurship High School, a national charitable initiative called the Blackonomics Million Dollar Club (BMDC), and a local self-help fund for those in need called O.U.R.S., Organized and United Resources for Self-Sufficiency.

Clingman is nationally and internationally recognized for his down-to-earth writing and speaking style in keeping with his description of his linguistic acumen, "I write to express, not to impress." He is a serious writer who leads by example and puts his personal actions behind the words he writes.

Contact Jim at 513 315 9866 and/or jclingman@blackonomics.com, Facebook, and Twitter. Purchase his other books from his website, www.blackonomics.com

www.ingramcontent.com/pod-product-compliance
Lightning Source LLC
Chambersburg PA
CBHW020727180526
45163CB00001B/138